Feminist Activism
in the 1990s

Edited by

Gabriele Griffin

Taylor & Francis
Publishers since 1798

UK   Taylor & Francis Ltd, 4 John St., London WC1N 2ET
USA   Taylor & Francis Inc., 1900 Frost Road, Suite 101, Bristol, PA 19007

First published 1995

**Library catalogue record for this book is available from the
British Library**

ISBN 0 7484 0289 6
ISBN 0 7484 0290 X

**Library of Congress Cataloging-in-Publication Data are
available on request**

Cover design by Amanda Barragry.

Typeset in Times by Solidus (Bristol) Limited

*Printed in Great Britain by Burgess Science Press, Basingstoke on
paper which has a specified pH value on final paper manufacture of
not less than 7.5 and is therefore 'acid free'.*

Contents

Contents

Acknowledgments

Of all the women who deserve thanks for enabling this volume to happen, the contributors ought to be mentioned first. They worked hard, to sometimes difficult deadlines, whilst still continuing to engage in their many other activisms, some of which are detailed in this book, and despite occasionally taxing personal circumstances. My sincere thanks to them.

I would also like to thank CS for (sometimes inadvertently) jollying me along during the making of this book, Comfort Jegede of Taylor & Francis for being a sympathetic and *sympatica* editor, Jane Marshall from Nene College Library for being the most wonderful faculty librarian I have ever encountered, and the students from the MA in Women's Studies (Erneita Bhebhe, Rose French, Sandra Hodge, Sandra Kirkland, Anne Mitchell, Susan Ottway, Lucy Smith, Linda Taylor, Jane Wren), as well as Jill Radford, in whose presence the idea for this volume was conceived.

Introduction

Gabriele Griffin

Feminist Activism in the 1990s

The good news first: feminist activism is alive and well in the 1990s. By this I mean that vast numbers of women, only a very few of whom could have a voice in a volume of this length, are engaged in organized activities designed to improve the conditions of women's varied existence. Every single chapter in this volume documents this; the struggle for change in women's lives which feminist activism entails, a struggle that has been going on for a very long time and is continuing to do so.[1]

Against this foreground of activity, in the form of the not so good news, runs a current of despair about feminist activism,[2] giving rise to questions such as

> What is the future for feminism — and, more importantly, for women —
>   in the 1980s? (Wilson, 1980: 28)
> What do women want? (Rowbotham, 1985: 49)
> Isn't it time the connection between Women's Studies and the Women's
>   Movement is fully recognised? (Lees, 1991: 91)

These questions tend to be fuelled by three factors: a discontent with the present, and possibly the past; a desire for improvement in the future; and a (self-)questioning in the face of struggle.

It seems that the condition of women's existence is *to be in movement*, to struggle towards transformations never fully realized, always superceded — even as they are attempted — by changes which in themselves demand adjustments of the goals set and of the tools, strategies and organizational structures[3] used in the attempt to reach the desired ends. The recognition that the very interdependence of what women want with the context in which they want results in shifting structures, and that therefore the question 'what do women want?' can never be fully answered (except with the word 'change'), can be a source of frustration and despair to some women. Thus, Frigga Haug (1989) lyrically proclaimed:

1

> We are reluctant to see this general sickness in ourselves, but the evidence is becoming ever more clear. After travelling through fifteen countries, I can no longer shut my eyes to it: like water in a mountain stream, the women's movement is drying up. (p. 111)

Or, to quote Zaidie Parr (Parr and Bodle, 1988):

> On a bad day I can still find it possible to believe that women and men may come to share power equally — but on a bad day I foresee a society not improved by the change. (p. 203)

The women's movement and feminist activism are not synonymous. To say that the former is dying does not mean that the latter does not occur. Not everyone even agrees that the women's movement is dead.[4] In 1988, Penny Holland simply offered the assertion that, notwithstanding all the struggles: 'I am still a feminist, I am still a lesbian, I am still fighting' (p. 138). In 1991, Beatrix Campbell wrote: 'we did not go away, we did not die; ... our politics did not disintegrate and disappear; ... we were not defeated; ... we are here today' (Campbell, 1992: 13). Caught between perceptions of the demise of feminism on the one hand and the evidence of feminist activism on the other, there is a need to take account of that activism, to consider how it contributes to change and to make that the basis from which to negotiate change in and for the future.

Sharing Knowledge

The idea for this volume was born one Tuesday evening in the spring of 1994 when Jill Radford came to give a talk about Rights of Women (RoW) for the MA in Women's Studies students who were on a course run at Nene College, Northampton. The evening was very lively, with much discussion about women's knowledge about feminist activism as it occurs during the 1990s and the work women do now to promote change in their lives. What emerged was how little knowledge the women felt they had about what was going on outside their own particular sphere of activity, with the consequence that they thought 'the movement is dead, or gone, or doesn't exist any more' (Sebestyen, 1988: x).

A similar discussion had occurred in preparation for the 1993 Women's Studies Network (UK) Association Annual Conference. There the view was expressed that women, especially those new to feminism and to Women's Studies, needed to develop a sense and knowledge of their collective feminist history that had enabled the legal, political, social and economic changes from which they were benefitting, or otherwise, in the 1990s. It was thought that women who had long-term involvements in feminist movements took for granted too readily the knowledge they had accumulated of that history, and that this knowledge needed to be shared to enable other women to understand how the present — whatever its shape — had been built from the past. As part of the WSN's attempt to establish a shared sense of feminist history, Jill Radford was invited to give an historicized account of her involvement with feminism (1994: 40–58). A similar project, published as *'68, '78, '88: From Women's Liberation to Feminism*, had been undertaken by Amanda Sebestyen (1988) but the need to document the history of women's movements and of feminist activism was clearly not exhausted by this, in part precisely because it is on-going.

Documenting Feminist History

One of the issues of documenting feminist history[5] is that the very idea points to the past, to something that has been left behind. In an era in which the term 'postfeminism' has become a point of debate, the very existence of this latter phrase seems to suggest that feminist activism is a thing of the past.[6] But, as this volume clearly demonstrates, feminist activism is still very much in evidence and perhaps more diverse, far-reaching and impact-achieving than ever before. However, in contrast to the *idea* (as opposed to the *reality*) of the Women's (Liberation) Movement, which implies mass mobilization and a 'politics of spectacle in the public domain' (Campbell, 1992: 14) in the form of large-scale rallies and demonstrations for example, feminist activism has taken on a multiplicity of forms. This volume seeks to document some of the forms that current feminist activism takes, both as regards the issues it addresses and in terms of the organizational bases from which it works. It is intended to counteract the notion that feminist activism is a thing of the past, enabling women new to feminism to realize the diversity and possibilities of feminist activism and to celebrate — by way of documenting it — that activism.

The Issue of Fragmentation

The fact that many people, even women active in some capacity or other to promote change for women, do not know about the range of feminist activism going on today is indicative of how that activism has changed over time. Central to this is the idea that the women's movement is fragmented and has, in fact, shattered as a result of this fragmentation. Where unity was once proclaimed, diversity now rules. Some would say that in the debates about 'equality of the sexes *versus* difference or otherness' (Haug, 1989: 113) difference has won: women, mindful of the specificity of their selves and situations, now divide into identity and issue groups beyond which they do not engage because they have made their identity or issue the be-all and end-all of their analysis and activism. Again, the evidence of this volume would belie this. It is the case that many women's groups give themselves titles which specify certain identities. Many organizations, such as Lesbians Organizing Together (LOT), Southall Black Sisters (SBS), Women in Accountancy (WIA) or Women Against Fundamentalism (WAF), work from the basis of a specific identification whether this is in terms of sexual, geographical, ethnic, professional or an issue-based identity. The assumption is that women will unite to work for change because they have a particular investment in a certain issue on the basis of a specific identification. This identification provides the impetus for their activism. On one level, feminist activism based on identity politics leads to the fragmentation which many feminists regard as typical for the current political climate and which is supposed to be in direct contrast to the homogeneity, common purpose and mass mobilization of the Women's (Liberation) Movement, all with capital letters. The latter seems to me to be a myth, a nostalgic retrospective view of some golden age of feminism that probably never was.[7] Single issue or single identity feminist organizations such as are common in the 1990s may have the drawback of overly localized politics but their very specificity can also be a guarantee for expertise and impact, for maximum, clearly defined effort within a specific arena.

It is also the case that organizations that establish themselves on the basis of a particular identity may work on a multiplicity of issues, as do Southall Black Sisters, for example, because they consider inequality to be fundamental to a range of interconnected problems. In order to alleviate inequality and power imbalances beyond the specific individual instance, they consider it paramount that diverse causes are simultaneously addressed so that the desired impact is more sustained and more wide-spread.

Many women are active in more than one organization or grouping, working under separate banners for different but related causes. The surface fragmentation of feminist activism into lots of discreet entities may thus be belied by the membership of those groups, with much more exchange and joint action occurring than is imagined. Simultaneously, there have been increasing calls for and attempts at coalition-building among diverse feminist organizations to maximize their strategic impact, raise their profiles and exert greater pressure to promote change.

Finally, in very practical terms, one person or group or organization cannot do everything; having diverse groups or individuals take on different issues may thus be a way of maximizing interventions.

In the big 'single-issue versus global concerns' debate, different feminist organizations take diverse positions with some regarding the local issue as the platform from which to address and understand global problems while others take up a single issue that needs specific interventions for change to happen. Justice for Women, for example, focuses exclusively on women who kill violent men in self-defence. Their effectiveness relies on using the individual case to make general points about women's position in and *vis-à-vis* the law. This does not necessarily imply that they lack an analysis which looks beyond the local issue.

Institutionalization and Professionalization

From the early 1980s, in particular during Margaret Thatcher's time as Prime Minister, feminist activism was increasingly characterized by *institutionalization* and *professionalization*, both of which have worked to the benefit *and* to the detriment of women. Benefits include the possibility of impacting directly at sites where change is needed such as the law, education, or the labour market. To the extent that feminists have an organized voice either within decision-making establishments or can address these, they have the opportunity of intervening for the benefit of women. The changes women have managed to effect in this way, changes in the law and in education, for example, are all too often too readily dismissed.

Detriments include the vexed question of compromise and 'selling-out', frequently directed at those who work from within institutions to effect change. The question that always needs to be asked is, when does being strategic result in having one's political tooth pulled? The absorption into institutions and the establishment of specific organizations can mean that feminist activism is ingested into social and political structures to such an extent that its radical potential is masked or even eliminated. But it can also become the virus in the system which then acts as an agent for changing the whole.

The institutionalization of feminist activism is perhaps most obviously visible in the widespread establishment, especially during the 1980s and 1990s, of Women's Studies as a discipline in higher education. Alex Warwick and Rosemary Auchmuty discuss some of the issues arising out of that move in this volume. They highlight that many women teaching and studying Women's Studies are feminist activists beyond their studies, working in a variety of contexts designed to facilitate change for women. It is clear from their chapter that to see Women's Studies as separate from or inferior to other forms of feminist activism is misleading and undermining; partly because it ignores the multi-faceted nature of women's activism; partly because it constructs hierarchies of 'worthy' women/causes/activisms which, oppressive in their own right, also ignore the reality that many women participate in much and diverse activist work; and partly because it assumes that what pertains to Women's Studies does not apply elsewhere. However, the way in which feminist activism has developed during the last 15 years shows that that is not the case.

Histories of Feminist Activism

Current feminist activism has a history. Each chapter in this volume maps something of that history. Those histories have certain similarities. They move from informal expressions among women of the need to change (typically indicated in the formation of Lesbians Organizing Together, for example) a particular situation which is affecting women adversely to setting up organizations designed to work for change. On a very basic level, women — whatever their identity or concerns — still need to put themselves on to public agendas if they want to be heard and if they want change. This is particularly evident in the area of women's mental and physical health as chapters by Tamsin Wilton and Nicki Hastie, Sarah Porch and Lou Brown make clear. These chapters point out that women's activism is about identifying the issues that concern us and then establishing procedures for creating change. They highlight the continued marginalization of women within governmental policies, and demonstrate the ongoing need for women to work towards changing political agendas.

The depressing aspect of the histories of diverse feminist activisms is that many of the issues that were addressed by feminists 10, 20 or even 30 years ago are still with us, albeit in changed form — in other words, what women have fought for over the last few decades has not resulted in lasting positive changes. This is apparent in Anja Hohmeyer's chapter on the National Abortion Campaign which focuses on one of the concerns that has been prominently with women since 'second wave feminism' first came into being and beyond. Hohmeyer makes it plain that, though the emphasis of some of the National Abortion Campaign's work has shifted, we are far from having achieved the demand for free abortion on demand for all women. This point is reinforced in the chapters by Irish contributors, such as Ailbhe Smyth's, which point out the plight of Irish women seeking abortion. However, against the recognition that women's situation has only partially changed for the better — there are now numerous feminist organizations that work on specific issues on behalf of women — the fact that, far from being defeated, feminists have simply organized more and more diversely has to be set. Struggle is definitely still the name of the game.

Towards an Understanding of the Diversity of Feminist Activism

Most of the feminist activism addressed in this volume is concerned with the work of organized groups either inside or outside institutions. Debi Morgan's chapter differs in this respect in that she discusses the activism of individual young women and their marginalization within the women's movement and in feminist writing as a whole. One could point to many more omissions or marginalizations, both within this volume and within feminism, such as activism going on among older women or women with disabilities. It would, of course, be a hopeless undertaking to try and cover everything that is happening in the 1990s by way of feminist activism, and that assertion in itself is a cause for celebration.

One area of feminist activism that has received relatively little attention outside its own parameters is activism in the context of women and work/training/business. One major reason for this neglect may be the association of that world with Conservative politics, with Thatcherism and with women's move into and their assumed submission to the ethos (or absence thereof) which informs the business world and which is aligned with everything that feminism has always tended to offer resistance to, in particular patriarchy and capitalism. Many women are still wary of the traditional 'male' sphere of business, technology and science. And with good reason. However, it is also the case that women increasingly participate in these worlds. There are growing numbers of women-centred initiatives such as 'Springboard' designed by women for women to empower women to effect changes. Frances Moss's chapter on Women in Accountancy provides an insight into one such initiative and offers some reasons why women should take an interest in this sphere such as access to resources. This last point is of major importance for all women because, without access to appropriate resources, sustained effective political interventions are difficult to achieve.

Funding Feminist Activism

One of the major changes in feminist activism during the 1980s — with a knock-on effect in the 1990s — was the way in which funding was sought by women's organizations and provided by diverse fiscal bodies. The core funding (i.e. funding that allowed workers for particular organizations/projects to be waged, offices to be maintained, etc., thus enabling continuity of provision) for many women's organizations came from' local government or European funding bodies or, sometimes, through the effective independent fund-raising of the women concerned. The relevant funding policies of government and European funding bodies were not, however, driven by a feminist agenda but by the recognition that there was an economic need for women to be involved in the labour market, that the decentralization of funding for all kinds of social provision and the 'care in the community' plans which went with it needed the support of those communities who could provide those services of which the government was divesting itself. One might argue, cynically, that Conservative politics enabled certain kinds of feminist activism and, indeed, the professionalization of feminist activism by providing the wages necessary for that endeavour. As Hannana Siddiqui of Southall Black Sisters said to me:

> Ironically, we had increases under the Conservatives . . . I think there were a number of reasons why the Tories supported us; it partly had to do with the fact that we are a service and we supported Social Services through our work. It also had to do with the fact that we were known, we had a public face . . . Maybe they also didn't feel too threatened by us because we deal with domestic violence, particularly in Asian communities.

One very specific problem that can occur, and which frequently causes concern in women's organizations that have some core funding, is the relationship between women of different status within organizations. Thus tensions can arise between volunteers, who come in for maybe only a few hours every week, but who work from the basis of a particular ideological commitment, and paid workers, who are present all the time but for whom the work is also, and sometimes foremost, a 'job' rather than regarding it as political work which is done for ideological reasons.

Organizing for Change

One of the issues addressed by a number of chapters in this volume is the actual organization of women's groups seeking to promote change. As feminists, or women aware of the problems that arise in hierarchical formations, most of the organizations whose structures are discussed here, as in Maria Power's chapter on Lesbians Organizing Together (LOT) or Frances Moss's on Women in Accountancy (WIA), document the struggle they have in trying to balance the need of the organization to work in an effective, open and accountable manner with seeking to promote equality and democracy within the organization. Getting the balance right between allowing everyone to speak and/or sharing the work equitably on the one hand, and being able to function effectively for the empowerment of women on the other, requires much skill, patience and dedication as well as the repeated willingness of all participants to review procedures. Despite the fact that discussions about how to organize can use up much time and energy, the critical questioning of how work is shared out and done has, as one of its major benefits, the fact that in organizations trying to work collectively, all participants get to do most of the jobs at some point and thus acquire skills and knowledge not readily available to them elsewhere. Feminist activism thus offers significant secondary benefits to its participants.

Service Provision or Campaigning Work?

Hannana Siddiqui made the point to me that public funding for feminist activism was particularly fostered in arenas of service provision — women would get money to enable other women through a service which either had not existed before or which the Social Services or the Health Service, for example, were supposed to provide, or should provide but could not or would not. Apart from the fact that service provision serves the state, it also focuses on individual women who need specific and immediate help. The difficulty here is that women working in service-providing organizations can find all their energies being drawn into service provision which then leaves little or no space for the campaigning work (for which, in any event, it is difficult to get funding other than through fund-raising) which is essential to create change on a wider scale through influencing legislative bodies, for example.

This dilemma, being caught between service provision and campaigning work, is one that many feminist activists face in their daily work. It is one which can lead to conflict among women because the need for services and for the alleviation of specific women's individual needs is recognized by all women as vital; yet there is also the sometimes less immediately tangible need to promote change on a larger scale, which involves time and energy, too. If all one's energies are absorbed in service provision, political energies may be dissipated and result in acquiescent organizations which have no time to do political work. Thus service provision can become a way of containing women, utilizing their energies and services to help the state deal with its responsibilities towards women while avoiding the need to address the political and social issues underlying the conditions that necessitate the service in the first place.

Feminist Activism and Communities

Feminist activists are frequently confronted with hostility from the communities within which they work. This is particularly evident in the contributions from the Irish women (Ailbhe Smyth, Maria Power, Rosemary Gibney, Patricia Carey, Izzy Kamikaze and Kate Frances) and in those from Asian and Black women (Hannana Siddiqui, Anjona Roy, Debjani Chatterjee, Debbie Weekes). The attempt to undermine these women's work by portraying them as unrepresentative of their communities, trying to sideline them in policy-making processes that affect them directly as well as indirectly, silencing them or intimidating them can be read as a reaction to the effectiveness of these women's activism. But it is also energy- and time-consuming, having to resist it, having to insist on being heard, having to argue for one's space.

Moving On

The 1990s have seen much discussion of women as agents for political change.[8] That agentic sense of self is strongly present in the contributions to this volume and informs how women go about trying to achieve change in those areas that are vital for the improvement of women's situation. These include:

- women's representation in and through the law/the state;
- women's position and role in public institutions and private enterprise;
- women's health and welfare;
- mobilizing for change among diverse groups of women with sometimes conflicting agendas;
- the relationship between local and global issues;
- access to resources;
- concerns about coalition-building (with whom and for what).

As we move into the twenty-first century, we need to continue to ask ourselves what women want, not in order to bemoan the past but so as to move on in the present and the future.

Notes

1   See Sheila Rowbotham's (1992) *Women in Movement*.
2   This despair, just like feminist activism, has a long history (see Wilson, 1980; Haug, 1989) associated both with women's (self-)critical stance being part of their political practice and with the specificity of British feminists' engagement with socialism.
3   In 'Beyond the Ghetto' (1980) Elizabeth Wilson raised questions about the ways in which feminists organize or think they ought to, suggesting that feminists had been overly influenced by the Left in their ideas of which structures to use to effect change for women.
4   See 'Strategies and Visions for a Women's Movement' by the Spare Rib Collective (1990).
5   In 'Beyond the Ghetto' (1980) Elizabeth Wilson makes the point that in British feminism there has been a tendency to 'subordinate feminism to socialism' (p. 31) and not to think enough about feminism as discrete from socialism and left-wing party politics.
6   However, I take 'postfeminism' as a suggestion to be part of what Susan Faludi (1992) and others have aptly described as 'the backlash'.
7   See Sebestyen (1988) for some very diverse accounts of women's experiences of the

period 1968–1988.
8   See Chantal Mouffe's *The Return of the Political* (1993) and Judith Butler and Joan W. Scott's *Feminists Theorize the Poliical* (1992).

References

Butler, J. and Scott, J.W. (Eds) (1992) *Feminists Theorize the Political*, London: Routledge.

Campbell, B. (1992) 'Feminist Politics After Thatcher', in Hinds, H. *et al.* (Eds) *Working Out: New Directions for Women's Studies*, London: Taylor & Francis, pp. 13–17.

Faludi, S. (1992) *Backlash: The Undeclared War Against Women*, London: Chatto and Windus.

Harne, L. (1988) 'From 1971: Reinventing the Wheel', in Sebestyen, A. (Ed.) *'68, '78, '88: From Women's Liberation to Feminism*, Bridport: Prism Press, pp. 63–71.

Haug, F. (1989) 'Lessons from the Women's Movement in Europe', *Feminist Review*, **31**, Spring, pp. 107–16.

Holland, P. (1988) 'Still Revolting', in Sebestyen, A. (Ed.) *'68, '78, '88: From Women's Liberation to Feminism*, Bridport: Prism Press, pp. 134–42.

Lees, S. (1991) 'Feminist Politics and Women's Studies: Struggle, Not Incorporation', in Aaron, J. and Walby, S. (Eds) *Out of the Margins: Women's Studies in the Nineties*, London: Falmer Press, pp. 90–104.

Mouffe, C. (1993) *The Return of the Political*, London: Verso.

Parr, Z. and Bodle, R. (1988) '20 Years in the Lives of Zaidie and Rachel', in Sebestyen, A. (Ed.) *'68, '78, '88: From Women's Liberation to Feminism*, Bridport: Prism Press, pp. 193–203.

Radford, J. (1994) 'History of Women's Liberation Movements in Britain: A Reflective Personal History', in Griffin, G., Hester, M., Rai, S. and Roseneil, S. (Eds) *Stirring it: Challenges for Feminism*, London: Taylor & Francis, pp. 40–58.

Rowbotham, S. (1985) 'What Do Women Want? Woman-Centred Values and the World As It Is', *Feminist Review*, **20**, Summer, pp. 49–69.

Rowbotham, S. (1992) *Women in Movement*, London: Routledge.

Sebestyen, A. (Ed.) (1988) *'68, '78, '88: From Women's Liberation to Feminism*, Bridport: Prism Press.

Spare Rib Collective (1990) 'Strategies and Visions for a Women's Movement', in Scanlan, J. (Ed.) *Surviving the Blues: Growing Up in the Thatcher Decade*, London: Virago, pp. 184–91.

Wilson, E. (1980) 'Beyond the Ghetto: Thoughts on "Beyond the Fragments — Feminism and the Making of Socialism"', *Feminist Review*, **4**, pp. 28–44.

Part I
Fighting for Women's Health

Chapter 1

Doing It Ourselves: Promoting Women's Health as Feminist Action

Nicki Hastie, Sarah Porch and Lou Brown

In this chapter, we explore the possibilities for feminist action within agencies working in the field of health promotion. Health promotion work around women's health faces considerable challenges in the 1990s following the publication of Government targets for disease prevention (*The Health of the Nation* White Paper, 1992) and recent reforms and structural changes within the National Health Service (NHS) (Troop and Killoran, 1990; Ham, 1991). We demonstrate how conventional medical practice and Government bodies have consistently ignored the debates and research around women's health needs which grew out of the Women's Liberation Movement, and consider, in particular, how *The Health of the Nation* has impacted on activities and strategies for women's health. We argue that, at a time when the health of women as a group is considered to be low priority,[1] the commitment of strong and wide-ranging feminist-based activities and campaigns in the community keep alive the politics in health promotion for women.

As part of this study we conducted a postal survey of Health Authority Health Promotion Departments throughout England. Our questionnaire aimed to examine existing practice in women's health within these departments, and to gather opinions on *The Health of the Nation* as it affects women's health. Our emphasis on England, at the expense of Scotland, Wales and Northern Ireland, deserves some explanation. *The Health of the Nation* is the strategy document relating to the health of people in England alone. Wales, Scotland and Northern Ireland are covered by their own specific documents and in many respects demand to be treated separately.[2] Time factors and the potential size of the survey if extended to the whole of Great Britain influenced our decision to focus on the situation in England. Additionally, England has by far the largest number of Health Promotion Departments in the British Isles, allowing us to review a wide range of activities and projects.[3] However, information we have gained through correspondence with health promotion workers in Wales suggests that the climate is similar to that in England, allowing certain analogies to be drawn.

Feminist Activism and the Women's Health Movement

In conducting our research, we have been reminded of hostilities toward feminism and the fear of activities which carry the label 'feminist'. One respondent to the survey commented: 'I think it is unfortunate that you are going to use an outdated concept like "feminist" to describe women's activism in health promotion.' Her statement may imply either that feminism is a thing of the past, or a sense of distrust of feminism as a divisive strategy which irritates and alienates some/many individuals. In any event, she did not offer an alternative to 'feminist'. This individual's view, although isolated amongst the responses, is significant because it underlines that we need to be clear about what we understand by 'feminist activism' throughout this chapter.

We investigate these concerns within the history and context of the women's health movement, which has analysed and campaigned around the role that women play in health and healing systems, both as recipients and as providers of health care. The women's health movement is linked to the re-emergence of feminism in the 1960s/1970s. As feminists began to question the level of women's health status and the quality of care received within conventional health services, the rallying cry of the women's health movement encouraged women to 'take control of our bodies and our care'. One of the earliest books supporting this position was *Our Bodies Ourselves* (originally produced by the Boston Women's Health Collective; British edition by Phillips and Rakusen, 1978), shortly followed by specific volumes focusing on self-help therapies (e.g. McKeith, 1978; Ernst and Goodison, 1981) which took a woman's right to choice and control in her own health as their central philosophy.

Feminist interventions into health and health care have contributed valuable definitions to the concept of 'being healthy'. These are important correctives to the traditional medicalized models which understand health through the parameters of sickness and disease. From the beginning, the emphasis of the women's health movement was on the promotion of preventive rather than curative medicine, and on meeting the needs of the 'whole woman' (Doyal, 1983; Orr, 1987). Feminists redefined women's health through a holistic model which acknowledged the personal experiences of women and the social, historical, political, cultural, economic, emotional, as well as physical determinants of health. This social perspective on health argues that women's health needs and concerns are entirely incompatible with the conventional medical model, which ignores widespread inequalities in society and depends simplistically on morbidity and mortality statistics.

'Women's health' is defined in this chapter in relation to this holistic model, and in choosing our 'feminist' perspective, we are in agreement that 'to promote women's health is to facilitate choice' (Pattenson and Burns, 1990: 40). Although women may share certain health concerns, it is also important to challenge approaches to women's health which consider women as an homogenous group. A woman's age, her social class, ethnic background, sexual identity, religion, and level of education and experience all affect how appropriate certain definitions of 'health' may be to her, and how possible it is to incorporate certain health strategies into her way of life. It is necessary to 'empower *all* women to understand their own bodies and for them to have access to appropriate (language reading level, relevant to own issues) information for the "choices" they face' (Worcester and Whatley, 1992: 23).

Theories of Health Promotion and Parallels with Feminist Activism

In 1981, P. Reagan made explicit the connections between the actions of the women's health movement and good practice in health promotion:

> When one reads of preventive health concepts, self-awareness or personal control, the likelihood is that one would think these to be definitions of health education. Interestingly, these terms also describe the rebirth of another important program, the women's health movement. The rejuvenation of the women's health movement and the growing credibility of the self-care movement deserve to be viewed for what they are — important, although neglected, parts of health education ... above all, health education can do for women what it does best for all. It can help people feel good about their ability to be themselves, ... to have a sense of self that allows for positive decision-making and self-actualised behaviour.
>
> (Quoted in Pattenson and Burns, 1990: 39–40).

Reagan refers to health education here because she is writing before the aims of 'health education' and 'health promotion' became distinct. 'Health promotion' as a specific practice received definition in the early 1980s with the growing recognition that determinants of ill health are often found in social, economic and environmental conditions such as poor housing, unemployment, poverty and disadvantage. Health education, while an integral part of health promotion, has been found to be largely ineffective on its own. The action and aims of the women's health movement clearly have much in common with the philosophy of health promotion. Health promotion is defined by the World Health Organization (1984) as 'the process of enabling people to increase control over, and to improve, their health'. Ewles and Simnett (1992) understand health promotion as an umbrella term which includes health education programmes, preventive health services, economic and regulatory activities, environmental health measures, organizational development, healthy public policies and community-based work. Health promotion can ideally operate on many levels, empowering individuals and communities to clarify and meet their own health needs, including emotional issues and interpersonal relationships (Evans *et al.*, 1994).

Health promotion can be divided into policy development and health education. Three techniques of health education are **information giving**, **self-empowerment**, and **collective action** (French and Adams, 1986); but these are not adequate on their own. The role of health promotion in policy development emphasizes how it is necessary to alter environmental, economic and social structures in order to promote health, a view supported by Townsend and Davidson's (1982) research into inequalities in health.

The **information giving** approach has developed in relation to psychological models which explain and predict behaviour. Most important is the Health Belief Model (French and Adams, 1986) which states that for behaviour change to occur, individuals must have sufficient concern about health issues and believe that (1) they are susceptible; (2) behaviour change can remove the threat of illness; and (3) behaviour can be changed at an acceptable cost.

The **self-empowerment** approach is described as 'a process by which one increasingly takes greater charge of oneself and one's life' (Hopson and Scally, 1981). Self-empowerment aims to encourage considered decisions about health according to the priorities and interests of the individual. This often involves training in life skills to equip the individual with the information, opportunity and skills to make appropriate decisions. It therefore involves participatory methods of learning, and aims not only to raise levels of awareness but also to enable the mobilization of such knowledge through assertiveness training.

The **collective action** approach aims to enact a change in external environments, not through policy development within existing structures but through change emerging from grass-roots activity. This can be brought about by community groups or individuals acting in their own interests. Collective action seeks to mobilize people against stigmatization and misinformation. Here, the physical, social and political environment is seen as the key determinant of health.

Self-empowerment and collective action approaches are appropriate models for feminist health activists because they can be viewed as stages toward a fourth social transformatory model of health education. Interaction with community groups, where individuals are involved as active participants rather than passive receptors of information, reflects a move towards a more sophisticated appreciation of the social factors affecting health, and insight into the ways in which concepts of 'health' and 'well-being' are socially constructed. In 1990, the Health Education Authority (HEA) published its rationale for the use of assertiveness training in promoting women's health (Pattenson and Burns, 1990). This presented a strong argument for an ongoing and wide-ranging campaign around women's health which could feed into all health promotion programmes and settings.[4] The 1990 rationale also interpreted health promotion for women within the history of the women's health movement. Pattenson and Burns list four levels which build upon each other and combine to improve women's right to choice and control over their own health:

1. to be aware of choice and information about options available;
2. to have the decision-making skills required to set goals and ascertain appropriate courses of action to achieve them;
3. to have the self-confidence and self-esteem to believe one has the right to make such choices;
4. to have the ability to carry out these choices, which usually involves making them known to, understood and respected by and adhered to by others (p. 40).

We take these points as a model for feminist activism within health promotion work with women, but also recognize that change cannot be facilitated simply through individual self-empowerment. It is important to acknowledge that individual 'choices' about health may not be choices at all, influenced as they are by wider social and material contexts and interactions with one's peers.

Unfortunately, the UK Government has mainly backed the information-giving model, where health educators decide what it is that people need to know (usually without consultation) and make information available through the media. Information is delivered to the public on particular diseases, how to avoid them, and how to get well. Conventional health education is therefore firmly set within the medical model founded on the principles of behaviourism and individualism. The emphasis here is on individual behaviour change, with little acknowledgement of the structural constraints which limit people's power and ability to effect change and to make 'healthy' choices. Similarly, when initiatives such as breast and cervical screening are evaluated, there is a tendency to concentrate on individuals' attitudes and behaviours and to neglect social or collective responses.

Public health policy and reforms developed in the 1990s have given greater emphasis to health promotion and the need for preventative health care (*Health of the Nation*, 1992). However, the Government has not released any additional funds to help facilitate such efforts, and also continues to prioritize specific diseases and medical conditions, thus ignoring wider social contexts and inequalities. This has significant implications for future health promotion activities around the health of women. We consider below some of the effects of *Health of the Nation* from a feminist perspective, before examining a number of community-focused health promotion initiatives with women which, in spite of the current climate, adopt self-empowerment and collective action models as positive steps toward social transformation.

Women's Health After *The Health of the Nation*

In June 1991, the Government published its Green Paper *The Health of the Nation: A Consultative Document for Health in England*, outlining a strategy for health promotion and disease prevention. As its title suggests, this was a preliminary document inviting comment and debate from relevant individuals and organizations which could feed into the production of a more central strategy: the White Paper on the nation's health, which was to be published one year later (July 1992). The White Paper plays a fundamental role in defining (and limiting) health and health-promotion activity for the 1990s because it sets out targets for disease and risk prevention which are to be achieved, in many cases, by the year 2000. The challenge for feminist health activists in the 1990s is to once again redefine 'women's health', through and against *The Health of the Nation* (hereafter referred to as *HoN*) in order to address the shortcomings of this document and to establish innovative projects out of the wishes and needs of specific communities of women.

The shortcomings of the Green Paper were soon noted, both within health journals and the popular media. Criticisms were often levelled at the Paper's exclusions: 'Perhaps the most important word in the whole document is the one it goes to great pains to leave out — poverty' (Moore, 1991); 'Perhaps the most glaring omission in the document is the failure to address inequalities in health' (Radical Statistics Health Group, 1991). These omissions reflect a complete denial of the social and holistic model of health advanced by the women's health movement. Further responses criticized the Government's individualistic philosophy (Jacobson, 1991), due to the Paper's emphasis on individual lifestyles and the need to modify these through education, advice and information, despite evidence that without wider legislative and policy controls these tend to be ineffective (e.g. Townsend and Davidson, 1982). This is highlighted through the example of targets for the reduction of smoking and smoking-related diseases, at a time when the Government was actively opposing the EC directive to ban tobacco advertising. Unfortunately, this emphasis on individual lifestyles and personal responsibility for one's level of health reveals how the medical establishment can co-opt the language and philosophies of the feminist-supported self-care movement, turning pro-active campaigns for choice, control and equity into a process of victim-blaming. Women are often doubly implicated in this process of victim-blaming, responsible not only for our own health, but for the health of our partners and families when placed in the conventional role of carer and nurturer.

A striking feature of the White Paper is that it seems to have learnt little from the consultation process. The five key areas identified for action are: coronary heart disease and stroke; cancers; mental illness; HIV/AIDS and sexual health; and accidents. Poverty and inequalities are merely paid lip service in the 'Introduction'. The White Paper is also indicative of the Government's agenda on morality. It is worth asking how far the sexual health targets relating to the prevention of teenage pregnancy are really about the health of young women, or whether they are principally concerned with saving costs and the moral issue of 'family values'. There is more need than ever to redefine women's health away from conventional models and to take into account the contradictions in women's lived experiences; for example, a limited view of teenage pregnancy which constructs these pregnancies as 'unwanted', 'inconvenient', or 'inappropriate', or which simplistically views young women choosing pregnancy in return for social security benefits, fails to acknowledge the complex reality of these women's situation.

The White Paper does acknowledge that people in specific groups have particular health needs and concerns, and includes women as one of these groups. But the Paper's understanding of women's health is severely limited by its emphasis on disease and illness. Women's specific health needs are reduced to pregnancy and childbirth; cancer of the cervix, womb and breasts; premenstrual and menopausal problems; and specific conditions such as osteoporosis and cystitis. Throughout the five key area targets, women's health needs feature in terms of reducing obesity; unhealthy diet; smoking; alcohol consumption; cancer prevention; accident prevention; HIV/AIDS and sexual health; and mental illness. But there is little acknowledgement of the external influences and pressures which impinge on women's empowerment and ability to effect appropriate changes.

The Paper asserts that 'women's health has been a priority in recent years'

(Appendix F) and lists Government initiatives aimed at improving the health of women. These include research into the benefits of hormone replacement therapy (HRT) and techniques for osteoporosis screening. Worcester and Whatley report that where until quite recently, many women had never heard of osteoporosis, this condition, along with HRT, has now become a household term. They admit that this change has occurred chiefly due to the responses of the medical establishment. Why then, they ask, should feminist activists remain dissatisfied with the medical profession's response to the health of women? (p. 1).

Reasons for dissatisfaction are clear if we take as examples just a few of the areas relating to the health of women in *HoN*, and consider women's responses. *HoN* proudly states that the UK was the first country in the European Community to launch a nationwide breast cancer screening programme. These programmes have received priority funding within the NHS in recent years, and specific targets for the reduction of breast and cervical cancers comprise the major part of the *HoN* strategy for improving women's health. This has prompted angry comments from survey respondents who object to women's health being reduced to 'breasts and cervix ... pipes and plumbing'.[5] Screening programmes are useful for the traditional medical establishment because they provide quantifiable data and produce target statistics which suggest that much is being achieved within the disease and illness model of health. But women have begun to question whether breast screening programmes are in the best interests of women (Roberts, 1989; Whittaker, 1990). Shortly before her death from breast cancer, Dr Maureen Roberts[6] demanded research into the psychological effects on women of breast screening. The implications of the fear and anxiety experienced by many women when attending for screening and waiting for results are currently obscured. 'Future governments ... should back up commitment to the breast screening programme and women's health with adequate resources', allowing women of all ages access to appropriate women-centred counselling facilities (Whittaker, 1990: 13).

Initiatives for osteoporosis prevention also induce fear in women. 'The marketing of hormone products to menopausal and postmenopausal women is particularly cruel in the way that it plays on the fears of specific disabling or life-threatening conditions and also, very purposefully, on women's fear of ageing' (Worcester and Whatley, 1992: 3). Osteoporosis is falsely constructed as a symptom of the menopause, and one which only hormones can control. There is still inadequate information addressed to women which considers the potential risks to health of hormone replacement therapies. 'In weighing up the risks of breast cancer versus the possibility that ORT or HRT can prevent osteoporosis or heart disease, women essentially need to decide which disease they fear the most' (Worcester and Whatley, 1992: 21). What are the costs to women's mental health?

Diet and nutrition feature prominently in *HoN*, particularly in relation to obesity and fats consumption within targets for the prevention of coronary heart disease. Health promotion strategies around eating habits have tended to be directed toward women because of the traditional perception of women as purchasers and preparers of food. Yet there is no acknowledgement in *HoN* of psychological responses to food and its consumption, nor of the powerful relationship between food and body image for women. These are central elements in feminist analyses of nutrition issues (Thorogood and Coulter, 1992; Mckie, Wood and Gregory, 1993).

> [G]ender, health and food are bound together in a complex relationship which reflects consumption in society in its broadest sense. Health education programmes which aim to reduce fats intake must be based upon understanding of personal health belief systems and the related socio-economic systems which are fundamental determinants of health status. (Mckie *et al.*, 1993: 36, 39–40)

Suggested action for the achievement of obesity targets emphasizes education and information provision to encourage healthy eating and the uptake of physical activity, without recognition of the impact of issues such as poverty, psychological health, time restraints and access to safe environments in which to carry out physical activity.

Survey Responses to *HoN*

The significance of *HoN* for future work in women's health, even though the strategy does not present a policy or position on women's health, supports Moore's contention that what is most important about *HoN* is what is missing from it. Certainly, what is most important about the health of women is missing from the Paper. From a feminist perspective, the issues which should be prioritized are those which specific groups of women identify for themselves. In answer to the question, 'How far do you feel *The Health of the Nation* White Paper has shown a commitment to women's health issues, or has made a positive move to encourage health promotion work for/with women?', 69 per cent of our survey respondents put forward criticisms of the Paper, with a further 17 per cent indicating their ambivalence and 4 per cent offering no comment.[7] Many of these responses identified how the emphasis on disease and illness in *HoN* was proving detrimental to work around women's health.

> By the very nature of *HoN* it doesn't deal with women holistically . . . It falls short on acknowledging community-led work and allowing people/women to express their own health needs which are often outside the remit of *HoN*. A review of what has been achieved to promote women's health is needed to highlight remaining barriers and lack of provision.

> Because of *HoN* in particular, I feel it is becoming more difficult to prioritise this very important area of health promotion work.

> By not specifically addressing inequalities in health, the *HoN* does not recognise the specific problems faced by women when *accessing* services and the specific health issues affecting black, working-class and lesbian

women. Therefore any real commitment to fundamental change or supporting positive health initiatives for women is being lost in the drive to achieve
the specific targets.

In some ways it could be said that *HoN* has restricted the flexibility of health
promotion departments to appoint women's health posts.

As 51 (50 per cent) of all 102 responding Departments report that they have never
had, or are not aware of having a worker with a specific remit for women's health,
it is clear that women's health issues within Health Promotion Departments have
received inadequate resourcing for some time. But it is significant that of the
Departments who have at one time employed a women's health officer, 28 per cent
have now lost this worker, and others report further losses to follow shortly. The
majority of these respondents blame *HoN* targets and/or NHS reforms and
restructuring.

Yet, among the criticisms, there is some recognition of how *HoN* may be used
positively and constructively by feminists to highlight the gaps and inconsistencies
in current health provisions for women.

The positive side of *HoN* is that it has made us focus on the 'gaps' in health
promotion work for and with women. The challenge is to demonstrate good
practice particularly in relation to involving/consulting women re. their
needs, and then planning appropriate health promotion initiatives which
will contribute to the targets being achieved locally.

Local Health Plans and Needs

The *HoN*'s directive to local Health Authorities that they produce their own local
strategic plan based on local needs suggests a context in which there may be
increased opportunities for the consideration of women's health needs. But again,
because women's health issues are not prioritized within *HoN*, there is no guarantee
that local health plans will address women's concerns. How much consultation is
carried out within the community and who, in the end, is responsible for setting local
targets can significantly affect the content of such a document. Also, local health
policy practitioners are still required to follow the framework of *HoN* fairly rigidly.
Guidance on setting local targets stresses that these 'should, where possible, be
regional versions of the twenty-seven national targets in the five key areas' (*Local
Target Setting*, 1993). Additional local targets have to be 'framed in the same terms
as national targets', or 'capable of being related either to the primary targets or to
any national progress targets'. These guidelines are to enable monitoring and review
processes; but if local health needs include health issues difficult to quantify in terms
of statistical targets, how easy will it be to commit resources to these areas of work?
Mental illness targets in *HoN* concentrate on suicide rates and specific mental
illnesses, ignoring mental health and well-being in its broadest sense. How do you
quantify the mental health of women?

There remains very little emphasis in these targets on collecting information from local communities about health needs, although recent surveys (both formal and informal) have attempted to identify women's specific health needs. One example is the *Women With a View* (1994) survey, carried out in Leicester. Nine groups of women were consulted, chosen to reflect a range of ages, ethnic backgrounds, educational opportunities and locations. This survey provides a useful illustration of women's needs nationally because consultation with local women was based on information gained via other surveys from around the country (e.g. West Yorkshire Health Authority, 1991; Huddersfield Health, 1992), and *Women With a View* demonstrates how views expressed by Leicester women frequently reinforced national concerns. Women consistently identified the following areas of concern: social pressures, such as the media; stress; fear of stigma; and they made a particular plea for health workers to avoid assuming women's needs and to provide appropriate information for particular groups of women, as well as being culturally sensitive to different women's requirements.

Perhaps the best indicator of women's health needs is illustrated by locally-based projects which are the result of groups of women participating in action to meet their own health needs.

Feminist Projects

In this section, we focus on feminist health promotion projects which are situated in local communities. The projects we feature are local to Leicester, but similar projects are underway throughout the UK. In many cases, the existence of such projects is dependent upon the organization and support of the women who run them, often, to begin with, relying on the dedication and vision of individual women. These are innovative projects which combine elements of self-empowerment and collective action, and which develop the four principles highlighted by Pattenson and Burns within the context of peer-led education.

Community outreach work has proved to be a successful way of contacting hard-to-reach individuals and groups who are not effectively served by existing health care provision or by traditional health education services. However, many individuals remain 'hidden' and are not contacted by outreach work. Community peer-support initiatives not only respond to recognized needs but actively involve those individuals and groups who have made their needs known so that deeper inroads are made into the community and health promotion work can continue beyond a project's limited funding. Peer-education projects acknowledge that the pressures on individuals to comply with the values of peer-group norms can be used to exert a positive influence on health-related beliefs and behaviours. Peer health-education projects operate through consultation with a particular community, targeting interested individuals who then become educators of others who share similar social situations and experiences.

Rhodes (1994) demonstrates how this approach can lead to collective change as well as individual self-empowerment. By influencing the wider social everyday context, thus recognizing the importance of socio-political change, peer endorsement of behaviour changes has proven to be one of the most significant factors in determining whether change is attempted, sustained and achieved. Peer health-education projects assert the right of marginalized communities to collective control and ownership of what is 'healthy' and 'unhealthy'.

The Leicester-based **WHIP (Women's Health In Prostitution)** project recognizes that women sex workers can be marginalized by existing health services. WHIP was initiated in October 1990 by a student on placement with the Leicestershire AIDS Support Services (LASS). The project began by providing information, advice and support to prostitutes on issues relating to HIV and sexually transmitted infections. Early aims also included the encouragement of self-esteem, mutual support and peer education amongst women sex workers. Since the appointment of a Project Co-ordinator in 1993, the project has developed further in these areas. WHIP has an ethos of empowering women sex workers to look after themselves. WHIP's non-judgemental and democratic philosophy encourages women's active involvement, and motivates and educates women toward achieving 'ownership' of their own health agenda. A firm commitment to social and holistic models of health means that the project is not limited to issues around safer sex, but also addresses the wider health implications of women working as prostitutes, including safety, and relations with the police and other groups in the local community. WHIP has worked to include women in negotiations and meetings with other members of the community, and has responded to areas of need identified by the women themselves, particularly self defence and assertiveness training. WHIP also has direct access to refuge provision for working women and their children.

The continued growth of the project based on enthusiasm among the women themselves is indicated by the fact that there are currently (September 1994) 270 women sex workers involved. The number of volunteers taking on outreach work has doubled within six months (currently 40). It is important to note that although WHIP is part of an independent voluntary organization and therefore depends on the support of volunteer workers, this type of health-promotion activity should not be seen as a 'cheap' option (Hanslope, 1994). Projects will not succeed unless it is clearly demonstrable to the women involved that their lives, experiences and contributions are valued. This underlines the importance of adequate resourcing, as well as a need for cooperation from project funders to enable women to take control and ownership of their own health care. Leicestershire Health Authority, a major funder of WHIP, recognizes the positive impact of the project and allows it the autonomy to develop according to the needs of women. It is because of the efforts of women in local settings, who remain committed to self-help techniques, that projects such as WHIP have grown in stature and provide models of good practice for collaborative health promotion activities nationwide. WHIP is not alone in offering this kind of service. WHIP belongs to a Forum which meets bi-monthly, representing similar projects throughout the Midlands area. WHIP also has much in common with the documented work around drugs/HIV peer education among Birkenhead women sex workers (Hanslope, 1994).

Another peer-led project in Leicestershire is the **Peer Health Education**

Project based within Leicestershire Health Promotion Centre. In 1994, a worker was appointed for one year to set up a peer education project with young people in Leicestershire around the issue of sexual health. It is significant to note that peer education approaches can offer project workers greater freedom to interpret 'health' in its broadest sense and to introduce effective initiatives in women's health. There was no specific remit to carry out this peer-led sexual health project with young homeless women, but the project worker was given sufficient choice of target group to enable this focus. She responded to the lack of support and action around young women with experiences of homelessness, a group of women who have been identified through fieldwork and research as being 'at risk'. The project officer trains and supports a group of young women who will be able to positively influence others to develop the social skills needed to negotiate and practise safer sex. Such projects not only provide women with knowledge and skills so that they may educate and support their peers, but they have also been linked with increased feelings of personal worth and a greater sense of achievement which offers women the self-confidence to act as a group and to initiate community and collective change (Clements and Buckzkiewicz, 1993).

Conclusion

While our analysis of *HoN* suggests that it has become harder to focus on women's health concerns within existing Health Authority Health Promotion Departments, our survey identified positive projects and multi-agency work addressing women's health in its broadest sense. Many respondents reacted enthusiastically to our request for information, valuing the opportunity to share experiences, and reinforcing our belief that feminist-oriented perspectives and action around the control of women's bodies and health are crucial responses in health promotion work for the 1990s (see also *Health of Half the Nation*, 1992). There was also a demand for a collective and supportive network approach to women's health issues in health promotion, which could connect women on a national scale, for the purpose of sharing information and devising policy and good practice.

Such action has been restricted recently due to the continued focus on disease and illness, which has limited the funding available for local and national initiatives focusing on wider health issues. It is worth noting that the Leicestershire Peer Health Education Project was funded for one year only. We request a commitment from funding bodies to community-based action, for without continued funding for such initiatives, how can *HoN* targets be achieved? By beginning work in local communities of women and addressing women's immediate concerns and needs first, the target areas highlighted for women in *HoN* will be better addressed, once women are more empowered in their own lives and locations.

> Women living in situations of disadvantage need programmes tailored to their needs; poverty, housing, childcare, employment are more immediate issues of concern. An approach that builds on women's self-confidence and

self-esteem will eventually lead to topic areas being addressed when women are ready to address them.

There is a further factor to be considered that clearly demonstrates the shortcomings of Government initiatives for improving health. The Department of Health may have identified precise targets and action, yet how realistic can these be when Government departments continue to work in isolation? The Department of Education has recently produced guidelines on sex education in schools that restrict opportunities for sexual health promotion work, despite targets set out in *HoN* to reduce 'unwanted' pregnancies and sexually transmitted infections.

The projects we have outlined offer hope for women's health promotion in that they involve women at a community level and take account of women's actual needs. It is heartening that in spite of considerable constraints, community-appropriate, accessible and political health promotion work around women's health continues to develop through the actions of women who mobilize for themselves. The commitment of women as initiators and participants in community-led projects shows a way forward for collective activism and change. We present our analysis as supporting evidence in efforts to campaign for improved funding for community-based and collective action in health promotion.

Acknowledgments

We wish to express our grateful thanks to all those who took the time to complete and return our postal questionnaire, especially those who provided examples of resources, contact names and other useful reference points. Thanks also to Maz Soar, Project Co-ordinator with WHIP, to Ann Britton, Project Officer for the sexual health and young homeless women peer health education project, and to Helen Webb, at Leicester City Council Women's Equality Unit, for information on surveys around women's health needs.

Notes

1   That is, by those in Government and senior management positions with a responsibility for health. We provide support for this view throughout the chapter. Significantly, the most recent report from the Chief Medical Officer of the Department of Health (*On the State of the Public Health*, 1994) considers the health of *men* to be a priority: 'Although many of the major causes of death and illness are similar in men and women alike, men have specific health and health care needs which should be recognised' (p. 9). There is no mention of the specific health and health care needs of women. Unless women happen to be adolescents, mothers, or above pensionable age, their health needs are ignored within the Chief Medical Officer's report.

2   The strategy for health in Wales is presented in *Health For All In Wales* (1990); Scotland's targets for health are set out in *Health For All by the Year 2000: Targets for Scotland* (1989); and Northern Ireland is covered by *A Regional Strategy for the*

Northern Ireland Health and Personal Social Services 1992–97 (1992).

3   We distributed 182 questionnaires and received 102 returns (a 56 per cent response rate). However, because of recent restructurings in the NHS at a regional level, this number does not represent the current number of Health Authority Health Promotion Departments in England. The August 1994 edition of *Health Education Units Addresses* (London: Health Education Authority) lists 194 Health Promotion Departments in England. We completed our survey in May–June 1994, before this list became available. Wales is currently listed as having 10 departments; Scotland 16; and Northern Ireland 5.

4   However, this rationale has now largely been forgotten by those in positions to influence public health policy. The HEA, reflecting the Government's voice on health education and health promotion in England, has removed all traces of women's health needs and issues of self-confidence/self-esteem in its strategy for 1993–1998 (1993).

5   Any unreferenced quotes are taken from survey responses. Respondents' rights to personal and/or institutional anonymity have been respected.

6   Former clinical director of the Edinburgh Breast Screening Project.

7   A full report of survey findings can be obtained from the authors, c/o Leicestershire Health Promotion Centre, Enkalon House, 92 Regent Road, Leicester LE1 7PE.

References

CLEMENTS, IAN and BUCZKIEWICZ, MARTIN (1993) *Approaches to Peer-Led Health Education: A Guide for Youth Workers*, London: Health Education Authority.

DOYAL, LESLEY (1983) 'Women, Health and the Sexual Division of Labour: A Case Study of the Women's Health Movement in Britain', *Critical Social Policy*, 7, pp. 21–33.

ERNST, S. and GOODISON, L. (1981) *In Our Own Hands: A Book of Self-Help Therapy*, London: Women's Press.

EVANS, D., HEAD, M. and SPELLER, V. (1994) *Assuring Quality in Health Promotion: How to Develop Standards of Good Practice*, London: Health Education Authority.

EWLES, L. and SIMNETT, I. (1992) *Promoting Health: A Practical Guide*, 2nd edn, London: Scutari Press.

FRENCH, J. and ADAMS, L. (1986) 'From Analysis to Synthesis: Theories of Health Education', *Health Education Journal*, **45**, p. 74.

HAM, CHRIS (1991) *The New National Health Service: Organisation and Management*, Oxford: Radcliffe Medical Press.

HANSLOPE, JANET (1994) 'Healthy Women', *Druglink*, March–April, pp. 16–17.

Health For All by the Year 2000: Targets for Scotland (1989), Edinburgh: Information and Statistics Division.

Health For All in Wales (1990) (a series of documents under this strategic title), Cardiff: Health Promotion Authority for Wales.

Health of Half the Nation (1992), London: Royal College of Nursing.

The Health of the Nation: A Consultative Document for Health in England (Green Paper) (1991), London: HMSO.

The Health of the Nation: A Strategy for Health in England (White Paper) (1992), London: HMSO.

HOPSON, B. and SCALLY, M. (1981) *Lifeskills Teaching*, London: McGraw-Hill.

HUDDERSFIELD HEALTH (1992) *Report on Discussion Groups on Women's Health Issues*, Huddersfield: Huddersfield Health.

JACOBSON, BOBBIE (1991) 'The Gaps in the Strategy', *Health Service Journal*, 20 June, p. 8.

Local Target Setting: A Discussion Paper (1993), London: NHS Management Executive.

MCKEITH, N. (1978) *The New Women's Health Handbook*, London: Virago.

MCKIE, L.J., WOOD, R.C. and GREGORY, S. (1993) 'Women Defining Health: Food, Diet and Body Image', *Health Education Research: Theory and Practice*, **8**, 1, pp. 35–41.

MOORE, WENDY (1991) 'A Notional Health Service', *Health Service Journal*, 13 June, p. 19.

On the State of the Public Health: The Annual Report of the Chief Medical Officer of the Department of Health for the Year 1993 (1994), London: HMSO.

ORR, JEAN (Ed.) (1987) *Women's Health in the Community*, Chichester: John Wiley & Sons.

PATTENSON, LESLEY and BURNS, IAN (1990) *Women, Assertiveness and Health: A Rationale for the Use of Assertiveness Training in Promoting Women's Health*, London: Health Education Authority.

PHILLIPS, ANGELA and RAKUSEN, JILL (1978) *Our Bodies Ourselves: A Health Book By and For Women* (British edn), Harmondsworth: Penguin.

RADICAL STATISTICS HEALTH GROUP (1991) 'Ignoring Inequality', *Health Matters*, **8**, p. 7.

A Regional Strategy for the Northern Ireland Health and Personal Social Services 1992–97 (1992), Belfast: Department of Health and Social Services in Northern Ireland.

RHODES, TIM (1994) 'HIV Outreach, Peer Education and Community Change: Developments and Dilemmas', *Health Education Journal*, **53**, pp. 92–9.

ROBERTS, MAUREEN (1989) 'Breast Screening: Time for a Re-think?', *British Medical Journal*, **289**, pp. 1153–55.

THOROGOOD, MARGARET and COULTER, ANGELA (1992) 'Food for Thought: Women and Nutrition', in ROBERTS, HELEN (Ed.) *Women's Health Matters*, London: Routledge, pp. 47–62.

TOWNSEND, PETER and DAVIDSON, NICK (Eds) (1982) *Inequalities in Health: The Black Report* (DHSS, 1980), Harmondsworth: Penguin.

TROOP, PAT and KILLORAN, AMANDA (1990) *Health Promotion and Implementation of the NHS White Paper: Report of a Joint Cambridge Health Authority/Health Education Authority Workshop on 2 May 1990*, London: Health Education Authority.

WEST YORKSHIRE HEALTH AUTHORITY (1991) *Report of Women's Health Forums*, Bradford: West Yorkshire Health Authority.

WHITTAKER, DAWN (1990) 'The Best We Can Offer?', *Health Matters*, **5**, pp. 12–13.

Women With a View: Leicester Women's Health (1994), Leicester: Leicester City Council Health Promotion Unit.

WORCESTER, NANCY and WHATLEY, MARIANNE, H. (1992) 'The Selling of HRT: Playing on the Fear Factor', *Feminist Review*, **41**, pp. 1–26.

WORLD HEALTH ORGANIZATION (1984) *Health Promotion: A WHO Document on the Concepts and Principles*, Geneva: World Health Organization.

Further Reading

PLEANER, MELANIE, CURRAN, MARY, BENNET, CHRIS and BLACK, JANE (1990) *Health Education for Women: A Report and Evaluation of Work in the WEA North Western District*, Manchester: WEA North Western District and Amazon Press.

WILKINSON, SUE and KITZINGER, CELIA (Eds) (1994) *Women and Health: Feminist Perspectives*, London: Taylor & Francis.

Chapter 2

Madness and Feminism: Bristol Crisis Service for Women[1]

Tamsin Wilton

> We now deny moral, personal, political and social controversies by
> pretending that they are psychiatric problems; in short, by playing the
> medical game.
>
> (Thomas Szasz, 1961: 189)

> The dissenters profit from the rhetoric ... but ... their pronouncements ...
> have a hollow ring in the ... lonely, desperate isolation of the world of many
> who feel mad and who want this recognised.
>
> (Jane Ussher, 1991: 221)

In my experience, coming out as a lesbian, although never easy, tends to be less
problematic than coming out as someone once diagnosed 'mentally ill'. I discuss
why this might be so below, but I want to start by making clear my own involvement
in the issues that I write about in this chapter.

Although I am an academic and a radical feminist, with a theoretical and
political perspective on women's 'mental health', I am *not* a detached commentator.
I have twice been diagnosed as 'clinically depressed'; have taken prescribed
psychotropic drugs; and have had to resist (medical) pressure to enter a psychiatric
unit. For six painful years, I was the lover of a woman who had a history of
(unwilling) psychiatric incarceration, who self-injured and struggled unsuccessfully
with alcoholism and eating disorders, and some of my close women friends self-
injure or have attempted suicide (one successfully).

Bristol Crisis Service for Women (BCSW) is also personally significant to me,
in that I was active in setting up and running the helpline from 1987 to 1989. I joined
BCSW while recovering from 'cracking up'[2], and it was immensely powerful to
work with other women survivors of the mental health system. The group gave me
a new and coherent conceptual framework for experiences that had been secret and
shameful, offering a *political* language for talking about madness. This was
empowering and therapeutic.

The Ravings of a Lunatic: Stigma and Silencing

I am far from unusual in having 'cracked up'. 'Mental illness' is extremely common, especially among women: in Britain one in nine men and one in six women will spend part of their lives in a psychiatric institution (Bristol Women's Studies Group, 1979: 94), and some British surveys have shown that 'about 70% of women and 50% of men will at some time in their lives consult their general practitioner about a mental health problem' (Hair, 1994). What is unusual is choosing to report this in a public arena. 'Mental illness', despite its re-write in politically correct terminology (Ussher, 1991), remains highly stigmatizing. People diagnosed as mentally ill suffer a profound and subtle loss of status not comparable to anything else. On diagnosis we lose our full humanity; our judgement, maturity, capacity for logical thought and trustworthiness are all called into question and we take our place in that imaginary Bedlam, which still signifies 'insanity' to the majority who consider themselves 'sane'. 'Madness is shut away from sight, shamed, brutalized, denied and feared' (Chessler, 1972, cited in Humm, 1992: 229).

This oppression is far from merely symbolic. People diagnosed 'mentally ill' may lose the right to vote, to serve on juries, or (often of immediate significance) to decide for themselves what medical treatments they are given (Faulder, 1985). They may lose their job, their liberty, or be denied certain kinds of insurance. All this indicates that madness is a civil rights/human rights issue, but why should it concern feminists?

Why Lunacy is a Feminist Issue

Madness is not a modern phenomenon. What *is* historically recent is the co-option of madness by the medical industry as part of a more general process, the 'medicalization' of life:

> The term medicalization refers to two interrelated processes. First, certain behaviours or conditions are given medical meaning — that is, defined in terms of health and illness. Second, medical practice becomes a vehicle for eliminating or controlling problematic experiences that are defined as deviant, for the purposes of securing adherence to social norms.
>
> (Kohler Reissman, 1992: 124)

Writers such as Thomas Szasz (1961, 1970) and Michel Foucault (1979) have made clear that science, and especially medical science, historically displaced religion as the dominant discourse in Western culture from the time of the Enlightenment. Madness, once the province of priests and exorcists, was re-presented in medical terms, as a disease (Szasz, 1961).

The shifting of dominance among discourses is of more than theoretical interest, since social practices, institutions and policies develop in relation to discursive activity. The medical profession has enormous social and political power:

The medical mode of response to deviance is thus being applied to more and more behaviour in our society ... In our day, what has been called crime, lunacy, degeneracy, sin and even poverty in the past is now being called illness, and social policy has been moving towards adopting a perspective appropriate to the imputation of illness.

(Freidson, 1975, cited in Miles, 1991: 184)

The social control function of any institution tends to maintain existing power relations. 'The political dimension inherent in medicalization is underscored when we note that structurally dependent populations — like children, old people, racial minorities and women — are subject disproportionately to medical labelling' (Kohler Reissman, 1992: 126).

The social control of women by medicine has been widely documented (e.g. Doyal with Pennell, 1979; Showalter, 1985), and madness is especially significant in this context. Deviant behaviour in men tends to be interpreted within a *legal* paradigm as criminal, while similar behaviour in women is more often interpreted within a *medical* paradigm as symptomatic of mental illness (Ussher, 1991). It has been suggested that the construct of madness, very like the archaic construct of 'witch', functions to police women's acquiescence to their gender role (Szasz, 1961; Ehrenreich and English, 1979; Ussher, 1991). Ironically, this very insight has resulted in feminists failing to pay adequate attention to the needs of women who experience madness.

This is one reason why madness is a feminist issue — the patriarchal social construct of 'madness' is instrumental in women's subordination. Other reasons include the sheer numbers of women diagnosed as 'mentally ill', and the different strategies open to men and women to relieve emotional pain. The statistics, although inadequate, are telling:

In most informal and formal interactions with women or women's groups aimed at discussing their health, emotional and mental health problems are identified as being a primary concern ... [In one Glasgow community study] ... 70% of women placed 'improving emotional and mental health' as their first priority when asked to rank five women's health issues, with 91% placing it as either their first or second priority.

(Hair, 1994: 30)

Although women are *not* over-represented among those diagnosed with the so-called psychoses (the 'major mental illnesses' such as schizophrenia), they far outstrip men in rates of diagnosis for the 'affective disorders', principally depression and anxiety (Lewis, 1981; Weissman and Klerman 1981). Women themselves define 'mental health' as central to their well-being, and are more likely than men to seek medical help for 'mental health' problems. They receive less specialist treatment than men, and are usually treated by GPs rather than referred to psychiatric specialists (Smyke, 1991; Doyal, 1995).

Feminists have two kinds of explanation for the apparent prevalence of 'mental illness' among women. The first is that women's lives make them mad (e.g. Ussher, 1991); the second is that the social construction of mental illness is itself gendered, and interacts with the social construction of women as unstable and neurotic, so that women's behaviour and symptoms are more often seen as indicative of mental illness than those of men. There is ample evidence to support both propositions.

Brown and Harris's classic study of depression is among many that suggest that being a housewife and mother makes women more vulnerable to depression and anxiety (Brown and Harris, 1978). As Miles suggests, 'there is much support for the influence of social factors in the causation of anxiety disorders and depression and it can be argued that the reason for women having higher rates of these conditions lies in their unsatisfactory lives' (Miles, 1991: 187). For many women homophobia, disablism, poverty, ageism and racism are additional stressors. There is, for example, evidence that lesbians are especially prone to alcohol dependency (Nicoloff and Stiglitz, 1987; Deevey and Wall, 1992; Hall, 1992).

There is also evidence to suggest that the meanings of gender and 'mental illness' within the dominant psychiatric paradigm result in over-diagnosis of mental illness in women. A study by Broverman *et al.* (1970) demonstrated that medical professionals' definition of a mentally healthy adult closely matched their definition of masculinity, while their definition of femininity incorporated elements suggestive of mental/emotional instability. Thus, within the medical paradigm, mental *health* is itself *gendered masculine*; femaleness is intrinsically pathological. Bernstein and Kane demonstrated that patients presenting identical symptoms will get different treatment from medical staff depending on their gender: 'When doctors are confronted with similar "cases" they are more likely to attribute symptoms in women to psychological causes and those in men to physical problems' (1981, summarized in Doyal, 1995). As Agnes Miles suggests:

> anxiety and depression in women are essentially social phenomena, rooted in the social structure that shapes their lives, and ... the ways in which women become defined as psychiatric patients are also social in nature and are linked to the power of psychiatry and the powerlessness of women.
>
> (Miles, 1991: 190)

It is also the case that different coping strategies are available to women and to men, and that differential access to such strategies is an intrinsic part of the policing of gender roles. Men's access to the labour market, the public sphere and material wealth is greater than that of women. Consequently women tend to have fewer material resources at their disposal, and are more likely — especially when caring for young children or other dependents — to be largely confined to the home. Other factors such as cultural/religious expectations, lack of leisure facilities for women, sexual harassment and the threat of male violence combine to reinforce this. The strategies for dealing with emotional pain in western society are largely chemical, what Doyal calls the 'drugs of solace': tobacco, alcohol, street drugs and prescribed psychotropic drugs. Access to these drugs is controlled by material and social factors — to get drunk on a regular basis requires considerable expenditure and the ability to purchase alcohol from public outlets, while tranquilliser use may be more 'respectable' for women, and is cheaper. Small wonder that, while men's major drug ab/use problems coalesce around alcohol, women are more likely to resort to prescription drugs or to abuse food (Doyal, 1995).

It is against this background that women's consumption of prescribed psycho-tropic drugs must be seen. With restricted access to non-chemical resources[3] (work, money, leisure pursuits, religion, community support) and other 'drugs of solace', women have few alternatives. Increasing disquiet about the over-prescription of such drugs to women, coming not least from women's health groups, has resulted in a massive decrease in their use. Ironically, this has meant that many women now find it very difficult to obtain prescriptions for tranquillisers or sleeping pills, and there is some evidence that a correlative increase in nicotine consumption has resulted. To refuse prescription drugs without tackling the structural inequalities that make them necessary may result in other chemical dependencies and health problems.

For all these reasons, then, madness is a feminist issue. Women's oppression makes them 'mad'; within medical discourse women are, in any case, discursively constituted as mad and madness as feminine; women remain the chief users of psychotropic drugs; and the social construction of 'mental illness' polices deviance, including deviant gender behaviour. So how has feminism dealt with madness?

Invisible, Unheard: Mad Women in Feminism

There has been a politics of madness at least since the 1960s, when R.D. Laing, Thomas Szasz and others in the anti-psychiatry movement identified 'mental illness' as a social/political construct, instrumental in the policing of conformity. The anti-psychiatry movement was dominated by men and little informed by sexual politics; although Laing did protest the construction of the 'schizophrenogenic mother', observing that mothers 'are always the first to get the blame for everything' (Laing, 1967: 93) and Szasz, discussing the parallels between psychiatry and witch-hunting, drew attention to the role of both in the social control of women (Szasz, 1961). Anti-psychiatric discourse took the then revolutionary step of validating the experiences of the mad, and this was doubtless instrumental in the development of the policy of speaking out among survivors of the psychiatric system which is such a feature of current mental health activism.

However, there has been no sustained feminist critique of the mental health system. Most histories of the second wave of the women's liberation movement do not mention madness or 'mental health' as areas of theoretical, political or practical intervention (e.g. Bassnett, 1986; Sebestyen, 1988; Neustatter, 1989; Ryan, 1992), nor do most introductory texts for women's studies courses (e.g. Humm, 1992; Jackson *et al.*, 1993). The handful of important feminist texts on madness (Chessler, 1972; Showalter, 1987; Ussher, 1991) have not catalysed debate in the way that, for example, key texts on sexuality or representation have. Although autobiographical accounts constitute privileged truth-telling within both feminism and the psychiatric resistance movement, women's autobiographical accounts of madness tend to be located primarily within the 'mental health' arena rather than within feminism unless they come under the heading of 'literature' (e.g. Plath, 1963; Perkins Gilman, 1973; Frame, 1984). Notable in this context is the lack of feminist response to Kate Millett's autobiographical account *The Loony Bin Trip* (1990). As one of the key figures in US feminism, Millett's account of psychiatric oppression might have been expected to prompt a vigorous feminist challenge to the psychiatric system and mental health discourse. This did not happen.

Instead, feminists have engaged in a highly theoretical debate with psychoanalytic theory (Nancy Chodorow and Juliet Mitchell are among the names that spring to mind), focusing on questions of sexual difference, penis envy, the Oedipal complex and issues of psychoanalytic essentialism. The central focus has been on whether or not psychoanalysis is useful for understanding gender rather than on its role in the medical model of mental health or on its usefulness or otherwise for women experiencing madness.

Women within the mental health professions in Britain have become organized — the first Women and Psychiatry group was formed in the early 1970s, and the journal *Feminism and Psychology* began publication in 1992 — but the issue of madness has never been seen with the urgency of, say, abortion or male violence. Despite this, a small number of community and self-help groups for women have been established, including Edinburgh's 'Women Talking to Women', Hackney's 'Women's Action for Mental Health' and the Islington Women and Mental Health Project (Phillips and Rakusen, 1989).

There has also been a woman-centred therapy movement, whose central figures in Britain have been Luise Eichenbaum and Susie Orbach (see Orbach, 1979; Eichenbaum and Orbach, 1982, 1983) who together set up the Women's Therapy Centre in London. However, woman-centred therapy has been vocally challenged by those women who see all forms of psychotherapy as individualistic and anti-political. Women users of 'talking cures' have been obliged to defend themselves against the accusation that they are *damaging feminism* by doing so:

> I have had to try and explain how psychotherapy, which has helped me enormously, can be justified as an option for women within a feminist perspective. This has meant ... dealing with the anti-psychiatry arguments of feminists, radical psychiatrists and the friends who have helped me write this.
>
> (Seton, 1976)

Revolutionary feminist Sheila Jeffreys claims that 'The upturn in therapy in the women's liberation movement means the liberalisation and defusing of the movement ... The implicit assumption behind the flowering of therapy is that the women's liberation movement has already failed' (Jeffreys, 1977: 145). There are good reasons for feminist's suspicion of psychotherapy. Sophie Laws writes:

> Feminists have always understood that there is a close connection between women's individual mental suffering and women's oppression ... For many

of us, feminism has been therapeutic. For some of us this led to a position against therapy, seeing it as being about adjusting the woman to the situation rather than about changing the world.

(Laws, 1991: 20)

It is this interpretation of therapy as a patriarchal strategy for reconciling women to their lot that led Mary Daly to call it 'mind rape' (Daly, 1979: 287). This emotive association of therapy with male sexual violence automatically renders 'feminist therapy' oxymoronic and feminist therapists mere dupes of (and collaborators with) patriarchy.

The anti-therapy position within feminism asserts moreover that therapy somehow dilutes and privatizes the pain and anger that patriarchy engenders in women and that *should*, according to anti-therapists, be used to fuel feminist revolution:

Another danger is the actual deflection of revolutionary anger. That which is being thrashed out on a cushion is not being channelled against the oppressor. Those qualities which make us revolutionaries, anger, hate and fear, are our strengths not our weaknesses.

(Jeffreys, 1977: 144–145)

This argument has been taken up recently by Perkins and Kitzinger (1993) who are not the first to recognize how fatuous (and ignorant) a claim it is. 'Psychiatric illness is usually a sign of powerlessness, rather than revolutionary strength and energy' (Cook, 1985, cited in Kitzinger and Perkins 1993: 164). However, although they support a woman's right to use drugs, insisting that to regard drugs as 'evil per se' is 'an able-minded perspective that actively oppresses those of us who gain benefit from medication' (p. 183), their entire book rests on the argument that therapy is bad for lesbians. Because they do not bother to explain why this is *not* an able-minded perspective that actively oppresses those of us who benefit from therapy,[4] their anti-therapy position becomes simply another 'expert' prescription, further disempowering already powerless women.

What does the feminist critique of therapy offer women who are suffering? It is not enough to suggest, as Kitzinger and Perkins do, that a mythical community of women should rally round. This not only ignores important class issues (professional, childless women may be able to take time off domestic and paid work to support a friend through weeks or months of madness, how many working-class women and mothers can do so?), but also underestimates the pressure that may be involved when a woman is trying to stay out of the psychiatric system and is forced to depend on the scarce resources available to her elsewhere:

The community around her may try to support her, but they will still have only their own resources to draw on, and the strain on others can be devastating. Few private therapists will even see someone who carries a label from the psychiatric system — but someone who is too distressed to hold down a job would be unlikely to be able to pay for psychotherapy in any case.

(Laws, 1991: 8–9)

Which begs the question, would it not be more productive to ensure that all women have access to therapy if they want it? It is in this gap between theoretical challenge and service provision that the anti-therapist argument fails. Feminists must remain wary of the abuses of psychotherapy. But recognizing that therapy may be politically/personally problematic should not mean charging women users of therapy with treason against feminism. I believe that this (extreme and callous) position says much about the continuing fear and ignorance among feminists about madness.

I would not deny that much (not all) women's madness is a result of our oppression. So are the broken bones of a woman whose male partner beats her. But it would be unacceptable to insist that battered women refuse medical treatment on the grounds that medicine is a patriarchal institution or that medical treatment privatizes women's suffering and prevents them using the pain of sickness and injury as revolutionary weapons. It would be absurd not to recognize that healing must take place before revolutionary activity is possible, or that revolutionary activity may have to be undertaken *by others on her behalf* when a woman is sick or injured.

This is *not* to replace madness within the medical model. It is to insist that madness is *not* the same as revolutionary anger, that it may be as incapacitating as broken bones, that when we are mad we do not need to be told that our struggle to survive is distracting us from the 'real' fight. What we do need is for feminists to recognize that our struggle *is itself* an important part of the feminist struggle. We need women to join in and fight *on our behalf*, as they would were we incapacitated through domestic violence, for services which *we* decide we need. The significance of this cannot be overstated. In every other arena the guiding feminist principle is that women be heard, that their judgements about their needs be respected. That mad women are — with such rudeness — *not* listened to by CAM[5] women leads me to suspect that the silencing and disenfranchizing of the insane, which is such a powerful instrument of psychiatric oppression, is reproduced within feminism.

Activism in Bristol

In 1986, three lesbians in a locked ward of a Bristol mental hospital began devising woman-centred alternatives to the 'mental health' services. From this developed the Bristol Women and Mental Health Network, which gave rise to a unique range of services: Missing Link, which provides housing and counselling to homeless women who are or have been users of psychiatric services; Womankind, which is a networking/facilitating service for self-help groups focusing on depression; and Bristol Crisis Service for Women (BCSW), a telephone helpline set up in January 1988 for women in crisis, focusing particularly on self-injury. It is BCSW that I concentrate on here.

The helpline, staffed by trained volunteers, was set up in 1988 and has been running for two nights a week ever since. Small self-adhesive stickers bearing the helpline number and basic information are regularly put up in women's toilets locally, and there is an occasional public service advertisement on local television explaining the group's work. Articles about BCSW, particularly its work in the area of self-injury, have been published from time to time in the national press, and this always results in a flood of calls from outside the local area.

BCSW has all the problems of a woman's voluntary organization. Too much energy must go into the interminable task of endless fund-raising. Bristol City Council Women's Committee offered limited financial support before its own demise, and funding has subsequently come from a variety of agencies (The Mental Health Foundation, the Mental Health Task Force, and Opportunities for Volunteers), private sector businesses, foundations and trusts. Such grants are generally to fund specific time-limited pieces of work, such as evaluating the service or researching self-injury. Few are interested in paying running costs. As I write, the coordinator, whose job was recently 'rescued' by a grant from an anonymous Foundation after three months of redundancy, faces redundancy once more in six months' time. The continued existence of the line is always in doubt.

Volunteers come and go, sometimes being overwhelmed by the distressing nature of the work, sometimes leaving without warning, necessitating frequent training and changes to support systems. New issues (like HIV/AIDS) demand new information and yet more training. Such difficulties are common among women's groups, but BCSW has additional problems directly related to its work.

Self-injury: An Invisible Political Issue

Self-injury — deliberately cutting, burning, or bruising one's own body or causing pain and injury in other ways — is poorly understood and largely hidden. It is far more common among women than among men (BCSW, 1994a) and is almost entirely absent from feminist literature on women's health. Some see it as part of a continuum of self-destructive coping strategies ranging from overwork and over-eating to alcohol and other substance misuse (BCSW, 1994a), but there is no doubt that the act of doing immediate violence to one's own body provokes reactions of fear and disgust that set self-injury apart from more socially acceptable forms of self-harm.

Because of the conspiracy of silence surrounding self-injury, women may believe themselves to be alone in this behaviour. When their injuries are bad enough to require medical attention, they commonly meet with hostility or sadistic treatment from ill-informed medical staff (Jeffery 1984; BCSW, 1994a). Partners, friends and family (when self-injury is not kept secret from them) may be distressed, self-blaming or hostile. As with other self-destructive coping strategies, self-injury can become a way of manipulating others and can wreak havoc with intimate relationships, sometimes stretching much needed support systems to breaking point.

The Mental Health Foundation has funded BCSW to employ a temporary worker to carry out a two-year self-injury research, information and training project.

What is starting to emerge from this research is a link between self-injury and childhood physical or sexual abuse (BCSW, 1994a). Women who self-injure also seem to come from families where communication was poor and they were not listened to. Above all, their self-esteem is generally low (BCSW, 1994b). Clearly all these factors — child sexual abuse, refusal to validate girl children's feelings and need to speak, the chronic damage to women's self-esteem in a patriarchal and androcentric culture — mark women's self-injury as a political issue. Yet it is generally ignored in feminist theory and campaigning. BCSW's work in this area marks an important step forward, particularly because the participation of women who self-injure is an integral and valued element.

Putting the Politics Back In?

The lack of research or training around self-injury means that BCSW risks being drawn more and more into offering a (cheap) professionalized service; providing training in self-injury for other voluntary organizations, mental health and social services professionals. This risks drawing energy away from direct provision of support and counselling. Both kinds of work are desperately needed. Over 50 per cent of calls to the line in 1993–1994 were about self-injury, and women call from all over Britain. But it is also crucial that the majority of self-injuring women, whom BCSW cannot directly help, get appropriate and supportive treatment from health and social services professionals.

BCSW supports *FACES* (For Acceptance and Care to Express Self-harm), a local self-help group which publishes a newsletter *SHOUT* (Self-Harm Overcome by Understanding and Tolerance). In *FACES* and *SHOUT*, women themselves take responsibility for setting the agenda around self-injury, speak out in resistance to their silencing and misrepresentation, and devise the kinds of support strategies that they want and that they find effective. In this, feminist principles are put into practice in a very direct and productive way. Yet, still, self-injury and madness remain largely absent from feminist texts.

There is a tendency for feminists to assume that activism has become institutionalized and that feminist theory has gained a secure place in the academy. In the case of madness, this is certainly far from the truth. Although they are central to women's oppression, madness and psychiatric praxis have not yet been either adequately critiqued within feminist theory or subject to feminist political activism. We need a national programme to set up refuges and crisis counselling for women in extreme distress, to monitor and evaluate the effectiveness of various helping/survival strategies and to challenge the discursive gendering of notions of sanity and insanity. We need to interrogate the medical model of 'mental illness' and to challenge the incorporation of women's depression, anxiety, etc. into both the psychiatric paradigm and the revolutionary feminist agenda. BCSW, and groups like it, represent feminist activism on the front line. It is high time that this was recognized.

Acknowledgments

I would like to thank Hilary Lindsay and Lois Arnold of BCSW for their help in writing this piece, and Lesley Doyal for her thoughtful and insightful criticism. I would also like to dedicate this chapter to the memory of Maggie Ross, with love. We miss you, Maggie.

Notes

1   'Mental health' and 'mental illness' are clinical terms and refer to the contested notion that something called 'the mind' can become 'ill'. This disease model can become a way of invalidating pain, anger or grief by dismissing it as irrational and pathological. At the other extreme, to call such experiences 'unhappiness' or 'emotional distress' implies that there is no difference between feeling desperately miserable and feeling mad. Believe me, there is. In this chapter I have chosen, as some other writers have (e.g. Showalter, 1987; Ussher, 1991) to use the word 'madness', but this is a personal decision and should not be taken as licence to label women who choose other ways to describe their experiences.

 Bristol Crisis Service for Women may be contacted at PO Box 654, Bristol BS99 1XH. Helpline Fri/Sat evenings 9pm–12.30am. SHOUT and FACE may be contacted c/o BCSW at the above address. Any donations you can afford to help the work of BCSW or FACE would also be very welcome.

2   Again, 'cracking up' is a phrase that I chose because it adequately describes my experience. It is not one which other women would necessarily claim.

3   There is some evidence to suggest that, in Britain at least, Black women have access to more non-chemical resources than non-Black women (Doyal, 1995) and are less likely to seek medical help for 'mental illness'. To this I would want to add that the well-documented racism of the psychiatric system is probably an additional factor preventing Black women seeking medical help.

4   Therapy is more likely to benefit feminists on a material level: mental health workers whose practice is guided by feminist insights are more likely to be therapists and counsellors than directors of pharmaceutical companies.

5   CAM is my acronym; currently able-minded. It is inspired by the disability rights movement's TAB (temporarily able-bodied) and is a parallel attempt to destabilize the (illusory) boundary between normality and deviance. A useful feature of Kitzinger and Perkins' book, is their development of a disability model for 'mental illness', although the model is weakened by their lack of clarity in distinguishing between 'psychosis' and 'affective disorder', and by their use of 'we' to indicate lesbians who find *other lesbians'* behaviour (not 'our own') distressing (see Kitzinger and Perkins, 1993: 156). For me, insisting on qualifying 'able-minded' with 'currently' flags up a *shared* vulnerability that is important.

References

BASNETT, SUSAN (1986) *Feminist Experiences: The Women's Movement in Four Cultures*, London: Allen & Unwin.

BRISTOL CRISIS SERVICE FOR WOMEN (1993) *Annual Report*, Bristol: BCSW.

BRISTOL CRISIS SERVICE FOR WOMEN (1994a) *Understanding Self-Injury*, Bristol: BCSW.

BRISTOL CRISIS SERVICE FOR WOMEN (1994b) *For Friends and Family: A Guide for Supporters of Women and Girls Who Self-injure*, Bristol: BCSW.

BRISTOL WOMEN'S STUDIES GROUP (1979) *Half the Sky: An Introduction to Women's Studies*, London: Virago.

BROVERMAN, K., BROVERMAN, P., CLARKSON, F., ROSENKRANTZ, P. and VOGEL, S. (1970) 'Sex Role Stereotypes and Clinical Judgements of Mental Health', *Journal of Consulting and Clinical Psychology*, **34**, 1, pp. 1–7.

BROWN, G. and HARRIS, T. (1978) *Social Origins of Depression*, London: Tavistock.

CHESSLER, PHYLLIS (1972) *Women and Madness*, New York: Doubleday.

DALY, MARY (1979) Gyn/Ecology: *The Metaethics of Radical Feminism*, London: Women's Press.

DEEVEY, SHARON and WALL, LANA (1992) 'How do Lesbian Women Develop Serenity?', in NOREAGER STERN, PHYLLIS (Ed.) *Lesbian Health: What are The Issues?*, London: Taylor & Francis.

DOYAL, LESLEY (1995) *What Makes Women Sick? Feminism and the Political Economy of Health*, London: Macmillan.

DOYAL, LESLEY and PENNELL, IMOGEN (1979) *The Political Economy of Health*, London: Pluto.

EHRENREICH, BARBARA and ENGLISH, DEIRDRE (1979) *For Her Own Good: 150 Years of the Experts' Advice to Women*, London: Pluto.

EICHENBAUM, LUISE and ORBACH, SUSIE (1982) *Outside In, Inside Out: Women's Psychology: A Feminist Approach*, Harmondsworth: Penguin.

EICHENBAUM, LUISE and ORBACH, SUSIE (1983) *What do Women Want*, London: Fontana.

FAULDER, CAROLYN (1985) *Whose Body is It? The Troubling Issue of Informed Consent*, London: Virago.

FOUCAULT, MICHEL (1976) *The History of Sexuality Vol. 1, An Introduction*, London: Allen Lane.

FRAME, JANET (1984) *An Angel at My Table*, London: Women's Press.

HAIR, SIOBHAN (Ed.) (1994) *Glasgow's Health: Women Count*, Glasgow: Glasgow Healthy City Project.

HALL, JOANNE (1992) 'An Exploration of Lesbians' Images of Recovery from Alcohol Problems', in NOREAGER STERN, PHYLLIS (Ed.) *Lesbian Health: What Are the Issues?*, London: Taylor & Francis.

HUMM, MAGGIE (Ed.) (1992) *Feminisms: A Reader*, London: Harvester Wheatsheaf.

JACKSON, STEVI *et al.* (1993) *Women Studies: A Reader*, London: Harvester Wheatsheaf.

JEFFERY, ROGER (1984) 'Normal Rubbish: Deviant Patients in Casualty Departments', in BLACK, NICK, BOSWELL, DAVID, GRAY, ALASTAIR, MURPHY, SEAN and POPAY, JENNIE (Eds) *Health and Disease: A Reader*, Milton Keynes: Open University Press.

JEFFREYS, SHEILA (1977) 'Against Therapy', in O'SULLIVAN, SUE (Ed.) (1990) *Women's Health, A Spare Rib Reader*, London: Pandora.

Kitzinger, Celia and Perkins, Rachel (1993) *Changing Our Minds*, London: Onlywomen Press.

Kohler Reissman, Catherine (1992) 'Women and Medicalization: A New Perspective', in Kirkup, Gille and Smith Keller, Laurie (Eds) *Inventing Women: Science, Technology and Gender*, Milton Keynes: Open University Press.

Laing, R.D. (1967) *The Politics of Experience and the Bird of Paradise*, Harmondsworth: Penguin.

Laws, Sophie (1991) 'Women on the Verge', *Trouble and Strife*, 20, Spring.

Lewis, Helen (1981) 'Madness in Women', in Howell, Elizabeth and Bayes, Marjorie (Eds) *Women and Mental Health*, New York: Basic Books.

Miles, Agnes (1991) *Women, Health and Medicine*, Milton Keynes: Open University Press.

Millett, Kate (1990) *The Loony Bin Trip*, London: Virago.

Neustatter, Angela (1989) *Hyenas in Petticoats: A Look at Twenty Years of Feminism*, London: Harrap.

Nicoloff, Lee and Stiglitz, Eloise (1987) 'Lesbian Alcoholism: Etiology, Treatment and Recovery', in The Boston Lesbian Psychologies Collective (Eds) *Lesbian Psychologies: Explorations and Challenges*, Chicago: Unversity of Illinois Press.

Ordach, Susie (1979) *Fat is a Feminist Issue*, London: Hamlyn.

Psychologies Collective (Eds) *Lesbian Psychologies: Explorations and Challenges*, Chicago: University of Illinois Press.

Perkins Gilman, Charlotte (1973) *The Yellow Wallpaper*, New York: The Feminist Press.

Phillips, Angela and Rakusen, Jill (1989) *The New Our Bodies Ourselves*, Harmondsworth: Penguin.

Plath, Sylvia (1963)*The Bell Jar*, London: Faber & Faber.

Ryan, Barbara (1992) *Feminism and the Women's Movement*, New York: Routledge.

Sebestyen, Amanda (1988) *'68, '78, '88: From Women's Liberation Movement to Feminism*, Bridport: Prism Press.

Seton, Frances (1976) 'Opening Myself to Change', *Spare Rib*, 44, March.

Showalter, Elaine (1985) *The Female Malady: Women, Madness and English Culture 1830–1980*, London: Virago.

Smyke, Patricia (1991) *Women and Health*, London: Zed Books.

Szasz, Thomas (1961) *The Myth of Mental Illness*, London: Secker & Warburg.

Szasz, Thomas (1970) *Ideology and Insanity*, Harmondsworth: Penguin.

Ussher, Jane (1991) *Women's Madness: Misogyny or Mental Illness?*, London: Harvester Wheatsheaf.

Weissman, Myrna and Klerman, Gerald (1981)'Sex Differences and the Epidemiology of Depression', in Howell, Elizabeth and Bayes, Marjorie (Eds) *Women and Mental Health*, New York: Basic Books.

Chapter 3

The National Abortion Campaign — Changing the Law and Fighting for a Real Choice

Anja Hohmeyer

Introduction

Although the National Abortion Campaign (NAC) is commonly identified as 'the streetfighter's end of the pro-choice movement', its membership of over 800 organizations and individuals undoubtedly makes it Britain's largest and most successful pro-choice campaign. Since its inception in 1975, NAC has predominantly campaigned on a grass-roots level, and has successfully raised, as well as influenced, public awareness and opinion. Although the aims and strategies of the organization have been very political and although the bulk of its support in terms of money and membership has historically come from the Left, it has never been party political.

As abortion is a feminist issue, NAC sees itself as part of the Women's Movement and is, therefore, strongly committed to making NAC a feminist organization. Although men can join NAC as members and volunteers, the Management Committee is open to women only and there is a policy of employing only a *woman* worker.

Over the past ten years, NAC has been regularly associated with defending the 1967 Act. The 1967 Act is a bill that was presented by Liberal MP David Steel in 1967 to legalize abortion in this country. It became law on 27 October by 167 votes to 83 after being given extra time by the Labour Government. In this context, the latter part of the 1980s is worth mentioning because there was a resurgence of attacks on the existing abortion legislation. In 1988, David Alton's private member's bill, for example, proposed to reduce the time limit for abortion (generally taken at 28 weeks) to 18 weeks. In response, NAC launched the 'Fight Alton's Bill' (FAB) campaign and David Alton was successfully defeated.

Shortly after this victory, in the autumn of 1989, the Government introduced the 'Human Fertilization and Embryology Bill' (a bill which covered all aspects of the 'new reproductive technology'), and agreed simultaneously to allow a vote on abortion time limits. This was the first time, since the Labour Government had given extra time for David Steel's bill in 1967, that Government time had been allowed for the issue to be discussed. It was a quite different situation from that facing a private member's bill, where lack of time is the biggest enemy. NAC set up the 'Stop the Amendment Campaign' (STAC) and although the general time limit for abortions was changed to 24 weeks, Parliament agreed that in certain cases the Infant Life Preservation Act no longer applied to abortion. This means that a doctor who performs a late abortion cannot be prosecuted. Whilst this was a huge success for NAC and STAC, the anti-abortionists were somewhat amazed at the result; for years they had been blaming their failures in Parliament on the fact that MPs had never had a proper chance to vote on this issue. The bill finally became law in 1990 and the present legislation is outlined below.

Both of these campaigns were not only vital for the pro-choice movement, they were also crucial for NAC's public profile. The FAB and STAC campaigns trebled NAC's membership and made the media acknowledge NAC's critical role in keeping abortion safe and legal. As a result, since the late 1980s, NAC has been extensively consulted by the press, radio and television whenever an issue surrounding abortion made headlines on the news.

However, because the tide of unrest around abortion has subsided over the past four years, the public has been led to believe that NAC has worked itself out of existence, and many wonder why the National Abortion Campaign still remains. The problem lies in the assumption that an organization such as NAC plays a predominantly reactive role and only gains in momentum when the abortion legislation is threatened. This attitude ignores the fact that NAC's reactive stance during the 1980s originated from the necessity of defending the 1967 Act and that the political climate of the 1990s is very different. Thanks to the successful campaigns of the last decade, NAC envisages a more pro-active role for itself in the 1990s and aims to draw attention to the limitations of the current abortion law and the effects of NHS cuts on women's access to abortion. NAC's strategy for the 1990s is, thus, to campaign actively for what has always been its aim: a change in the abortion law enabling women to decide for themselves whether or not they want to continue with a pregnancy.

The Climate of the 1990s

Over three million British women have had legal abortions since 1968. Although the majority received prompt medical help when they needed it, the experience of a large number of women who struggled for many traumatic weeks before finally finding help or else giving up proves that the view that abortion is readily available on request in this country is far from true. The 1967 Abortion Act allows abortion only if two doctors certify that the pregnancy is not beyond 24 weeks and that there is a risk to:

1. the woman's physical and mental health greater than if her pregnancy was

terminated, or
2.   to the health of her existing children, or
3.   that the child is likely to be seriously disabled.

Doctors are able to take into account a woman's 'reasonably foreseeable environment' so that social factors can be included when making the medical decision. Abortions after 24 weeks are permissible where the woman's health is seriously at risk, or where there is a definite risk of the expected baby having a bad disability. In some parts of the country, however, it is almost impossible to find an NHS doctor willing to approve an abortion and many hospitals set their own time limit of 12 weeks.

As a result the horror stories of backstreet abortions (which were common before abortion became legal) have been replaced by horror stories of women struggling for weeks within the NHS system and only finding help much later than necessary. The true scale of the problem is unknown because quantitative evidence of delays or refusals is difficult to collect. Charitable pregnancy advisory services estimate that 25–30 per cent of pregnant women who come to them have faced delay or refusal, or else expected their own doctors to be unhelpful. The British Pregnancy Advisory Service (BPAS) and the Pregnancy Advisory Service (PAS) in London often see women who have been misdiagnosed, held up or turned away by their doctors, even though they had legal grounds for an abortion. Brook Advisory Centres and family planning clinics are often asked to help women who have been unable to gain access to abortion services through their own GP.

An example of this dilemma is the story of 18-year-old Mary, unmarried but living with the father of her twins, who went to her GP when eight weeks pregnant. The GP promised to arrange for her to see a local consultant and told her to return in a week for the details. When she went back, the GP said he had forgotten but did eventually make an appointment. When Mary arrived at the hospital the consultant told her he had just finished his shift and she would have to make another appointment. She finally saw him when 14 weeks pregnant and was told it was too late for an NHS abortion. She went to BPAS at 18 weeks (Pro-Choice Alliance, 1991: 3).

Mary's case is certainly not an isolated one. Other studies have also shown evidence of delay:

•   In 1981, a Policy Studies Institute report sponsored by the Department of Health concluded that there was a need to arrange quicker referral procedures for abortion (Pro-Choice Alliance, 1991: 4).
•   In a comprehensive study of late abortions, the Royal College of Obstetricians and Gynaecologists reported in 1984 'that some unnecessary delays were caused by inefficiencies in the administration of abortion services' (Pro-Choice Alliance, 1991).

Thus the problems women face under the current abortion law are manifold: in 1992 only 49.56 per cent of all abortions for women from England and Wales were funded by the NHS, although it is estimated that only 10 per cent of the population normally choose to pay for medical treatment (Lloyd, 1994: 13). Several health authorities who are unable or unwilling to provide an abortion service for more than a very small number of women now have agency arrangements with local charitable or private clinics. Although this is an encouraging improvement, only about 5 per cent of all abortions are paid for by the NHS in this way (Lloyd, 1994: 13). As NHS finances are severely restricted, anti-abortion prejudice or opposition to so-called 'social' abortions by some GPs, consultant gynaecologists and health authority administrators play a great part in deciding the number of NHS abortions provided in many districts. As a result too many women are delayed or refused and as a last resort, end up paying for abortions themselves.

Abortion has to be acknowledged as a fact of life. A Harris Research Centre poll, carried out in 1991, showed that 81 per cent of the adult population agreed that women should make their own decision on abortion (Lloyd, 1994: 13). Instead of denying this reality, it would be more appropriate to campaign for early abortion on request. In 1992, 89 per cent of abortions in this country were performed before 13 weeks (Lloyd, 1994: 12) and this percentage could be increased by making it easier for women to obtain help during that time span, thus reducing the number of late abortions and the physical and emotional stress that they may cause.

No woman asks for an abortion without having considered carefully the possibility of carrying on with the pregnancy and the effects this would have on her life. Under the present law, choice for women is considerably reduced because abortion is still illegal unless two doctors give their consent. The evidence above shows that allowing doctors to accept or refuse a woman's request for abortion gives them the power to make decisions that are not based on medical or scientific facts but on their own moral judgements. In this country, doctors who oppose abortion are under no obligation to declare their conscientious objection although they have the legal right to refuse to take part in abortions. A woman should have the right to be promptly referred to another source of help should her doctor object to abortion. Forcing a woman to go ahead with an unwanted pregnancy is punitive. It is of no benefit to the woman, her family and, least of all, to the resented child.

NAC's Strategy for the 1990s

Despite the facts that abortion is widely supported by the general public and constitutes a reality which is confronted by thousands of women every year, access to abortion in Britain is still controlled by health authorities and individual doctors. Consequently, women are treated as a disenfranchised group and are not perceived as being able to make their own decisions. As a result, access to abortion in Britain is not a right but depends on the financial situation of the individual woman, i.e. on whether she can afford a private abortion or whether she is forced to endure the delays of the NHS.

On the basis of the political climate of the 1990s and the limitations that the 1967 Abortion Act currently imposes on women, NAC has identified for itself a particular role in the pro-choice movement and is now exclusively campaigning 'to ensure that *all* women (irrespective of their social, economic and cultural background) have equal access to safe, free abortion on request' (The National Abortion Campaign Strategy Statement, October 1994). In order to secure this goal NAC has to focus its attention on three different areas:

1. public awareness;
2. internal organizational structures;
3 the quality of abortion experiences.

Public Awareness

NAC has always operated from a grass-roots level, public support is crucial for its existence. It is, therefore, most important that not only our members but also the general public agree that the current law is inadequate and in need of change. On the one hand, a high public profile and the commitment of trade unions, women's groups, ethnic minorities and political organizations have an important role to play in informing non-members that safe, equal access to abortion as a legal right is vital for all women's autonomy and equality. On the other hand, NAC's educational work, which involves responding to hundreds of requests from students, journalists, trade unionists, MPs, and people from all over the world, is the most effective way of reaching the public. Information is usually given over the phone, sent through the post, or imparted in personal interviews in the office.

NAC is also aware that every year a large number of women, who are not resident in England and Wales, have their abortion experience here. In 1992, for example, 11568 women came from outside of England and Wales in order to have an abortion (Lloyd, 1994: 21). Of these 11568, nearly 2000 came from Northern Ireland (Lloyd, 1994: 21), where the 1967 Act does not apply and women can only get an abortion under very difficult circumstances. Additionally, every year thousands of women travel to England from the Irish Republic, where abortion is completely illegal. In 1992, over 4000 women were officially registered as having come for terminations (Lloyd, 1994: 21), but as with Northern Ireland the numbers are believed to be much higher because many women give the address of an English friend or relative. In addition to the women from the British Isles, over 3600 women from the rest of Europe and 784 women from the rest of the world travelled to England and Wales in order to have an abortion (Lloyd, 1994).

The fact that so many women find it impossible to obtain an abortion in their own countries cannot be ignored. For the last few years, NAC has been working closely with international pro-choice organizations abroad and has, in the past, organized many pickets and rallies at their request. NAC's latest picket was organized in July 1994 when NAC members demonstrated in front of the Irish embassy in London in order to express their solidarity with Irish women and to call upon the Irish government to introduce abortion legislation immediately. Additionally, in 1991 NAC helped to set up a European Network called ENWRAC (European

Network for Women's Right to Abortion and Contraception) whose secretariat has since been based in the NAC office. With its international solidarity work NAC aims to increase the recognition that a woman's equality and autonomy worldwide involves her right to exercise control over her own fertility and to make her own decision about abortion. Although NAC's campaigning work focuses upon the single issue of abortion, it is committed to reproductive rights and accepts that a woman's autonomy does not only presuppose her right to safe and legal abortion, but also her right to choose to have children whether planned or unplanned.

Internal Organizational Structures

The second area of concern (which is vital to the success of the campaign) is NAC's own organizational structure. Due to its overtly political agenda, NAC cannot be a charity and thus needs to generate most of its income from donations and affiliations. This means that NAC's political objectives have to be coupled with the need to sustain the campaign financially. Although the selling of merchandise and literature and the holding of benefits have proved to be vital sources of additional income in the past, they did not prevent the campaign from plummetting into a serious financial crisis during late-1993.

At that point, NAC acknowledged that, in order to campaign for a change in the law to allow free abortion on request, it not only had to operate a financially secure organization, but also needed a committed and diverse membership. Over the past year, therefore, NAC has tried to ensure the active commitment of its membership and volunteers by introducing a democratic organization with an accountable management committee, answerable to its membership. The diversification of NAC's membership is another priority, because ethnic minority women and women from outside London were under-represented in NAC's previous structural organization. In order to redress this situation NAC has committed itself to becoming a more pro-active campaign which reflects the interests of ethnic minority women and addresses the needs of a geographically and culturally diverse membership.

The Quality of Abortion Experiences

The last area of concern focuses on the issue of the abortion experience itself. There is probably no way in which an unwanted pregnancy can be completely satisfactorily resolved. Undoubtedly, physical side effects such as infection, excessive bleeding and perforation, as well as psychological effects like depression and guilt, can occur. But these cases are exceptional. In 1991, the rate of complications for abortions under 13 weeks was 2.95 per cent per 1000 people (Lloyd, 1994: 36). There have been literally hundreds of pieces of research looking at the effects of abortion, some in the short term, others following women over many years. They show that for the majority of women who have abortions, the most common feeling afterwards is relief and that for most of them, this feeling persists for many years later (Lloyd, 1994: 36).

However, to ensure that women receive the best care possible they need to be kept informed of all the abortion and counselling services available to them. Based on accurate information and with the advice of a counsellor, a woman can work out how an unplanned pregnancy would affect her. Every day NAC receives phone calls from women who do not know anything about time limits and abortion procedures. Many young women who call are afraid to consult their family doctor in case he informs the parents, and they simply want to be advised where to go. The needs of these women make it necessary for all pro-choice organizations to cooperate in working to campaign for the continuance, extension and improvement of the quality of care provided by abortion and contraception services.

The attitudes of abortion providers affect women's experience of abortion. In the case of women from different social, cultural and ethnic minority backgrounds, the biased approaches of GPs and consultants often lead to unjust treatment. There is evidence, for example, that Black women and women of colour are pressured into having abortions. One Black woman told the Abortion Rights Tribunal in 1977: 'I managed to get an NHS abortion after the usual palavers but I was disturbed by what I learned subsequently. My GP is more liberal in referring Black women because he feels they "breed too much". He does not refer white women for abortions nor does he prescribe the pill for them'. Black and working-class women are also more likely to be expected to accept sterilization at the same time as abortion. This is a combination that increases the risk of both. The combined procedure is far more common on the NHS than in the private sector (Phillips, 1989: 223).

Although there is evidence of unjust treatment, official statistics on instances of discrimination do not exist. NAC has made it one of its priorities to research and publicize cases of unjust treatment of women who seek an abortion and who, by virtue of their background, are particularly vulnerable to unequal care within the health service.

Conclusion

Although the current political climate allows NAC to play a more pro-active role in the pro-choice movement, further attacks on abortion rights, both inside and outside Parliament, can be expected. After their defeat in Parliament in 1990, anti-abortionists such as LIFE and SPUC (The Society for the Protection of the Unborn Child) responded by stepping up their campaigning outside Parliament. They have been concentrating on propaganda emphasizing the harm that they claim abortion does to women. Both LIFE and SPUC have set up groups of women who say they have been harmed because of having an abortion.

Additionally, since the early 1990s, an anti-abortion group which originated in America has become active in this country. The American group is called 'Operation Rescue' and it has sent its members to Britain and other countries in Europe to set up similar groups. The British group calls itself 'Rescue UK'. In April 1993, these militant anti-abortionists from North America joined their British counterparts to attempt blockades of clinics. Operation Rescue is known for its rallies, where members try to persuade women not to go into clinics for abortions. Whilst they claim to use non-violent methods, such as hymn-singing, prayer, shouting slogans, waving placards and distributing leaflets, in practice their tactics include intimidation and assault of clinic clients and staff. An 'Operation Rescue' member was responsible for killing a Florida abortion clinic doctor in the spring of 1993.

On 4 September 1993, in response to 'Rescue's' announced attack on British abortion clinics, NAC organized a public meeting at London's South Bank University Student Union where women of all ages and backgrounds, including some well-known women, spoke openly of their abortion experiences. Events like this always draw the public's attention to NAC's work. As a result of the 'Speak Out' NAC's membership soared again and the increased interest in the campaign led to a record number of TV and radio appearances. It is without doubt that as long as anti-abortionists insist on trying to impose their views on others, not by means of reasoned debate and argument, but via the force of law and through the violence of direct actions outside clinics, NAC will need to exist. However, it is also imperative that we go beyond defending the law and work towards a change of the 1967 Abortion Act.

References

HIMMELWEIT, SUSAN (1988) 'More than "A Woman's Right to Choose"', *Feminist Review*, 29.

LLOYD, LEONORA (1994) *Abortion – Facts and Figures*, London: Unison Press.

NATIONAL ABORTION CAMPAIGN (1991) *All about NAC*, London: National Abortion Campaign.

NATIONAL ABORTION CAMPAIGN (1992) *A Celebration of 25 Years of Safe Legal Abortion*, London: National Abortion Campaign.

PHILLIPS, ANGELA (1989) *The New Our Bodies, Ourselves*, London: Penguin.

PRO CHOICE ALLIANCE (1991) *Abortion — Who Decides?* London: Pro Choice Alliance.

Part II
Women's Rights

Chapter 4

Rights of Women — Twenty Years of Feminist Activism

Jill Radford

Introduction

The year 1995 marks the twentieth anniversary of Rights of Women (ROW), a feminist legal project based in London, England. This chapter celebrates its history. It begins with ROW's summary of the organization as it is today, and then looks back to our beginnings, re-viewing some of the changes and continuities in the work and structure of the organization. There is no conclusion, as ROW's work is far from concluded. Instead the chapter ends by focusing on one aspect of our work, lesbian parenting, to illustrate in more detail some of the many forms and levels of feminist activist ways of working on women's relationship to law.

This account is based on conversations with women involved at different stages in ROW's history, ROW's fragmented archives, published accounts and my own experience as a paid worker who joined ROW in 1986.

ROW Today

The contemporary work and structure of ROW is documented in our current information leaflet 'What is ROW?' which states:

> Founded in 1975, Rights of Women is a feminist organisation which informs women of their rights and promotes the interests of women in relation to the law. Our recommendations have been presented to governments, lawyers, other voluntary sector organisations, the media, women's groups. We also provide free, sympathetic, quality legal advice on a range of issues including relationship breakdown, sexual and domestic violence and employment rights.
>
> Rights of Women has been a part of several successful policy initiatives including defending child benefits, and existing rights on abortion, promoting progressive amendments to the Sex Discrimination Act, and the

criminalization of rape in marriage. We have consistently worked to oppose discrimination against lesbians, particularly as parents.

Both our management committee and our collective consists of black and white, lesbian and heterosexual women of different class backgrounds and ages. We are committed, where possible, to make our services accessible to all women.

Our Expertise

While ROW attempts to give advice and information on a wide range of legal issues, we have over the years developed more in depth knowledge in specific areas. These include: relationship breakdown and child-care issues; lesbian parenting; domestic violence; sexual violence and harassment; and employment rights.

Advice Work

The legal advice service is primarily on the telephone. It is staffed by daytime workers, and a team of volunteer advisers in the evenings . . .

Publications

Rights of Women produces a variety of publications relating to women's legal rights, from policy documents to critical commentary in the ROW Bulletin, to leaflets giving information on specific areas of the law . . .

Out of Office Services

Rights of Women is pleased to make our staff available for talks, conferences, training and information giving. Fees are negotiable and may be waived on occasion . . . In line with our equal opportunities commitment, we are particularly keen to make our services available to black/minority ethnic women, lesbians and women with disabilities.

ROW Membership

Becoming a member of ROW is a very positive and inexpensive way to show your support for the work we do. Rights of Women is grateful for the funding received from the London Boroughs Grants Scheme.

ROW's Early History, 1974–1981

Rights of Women was born of and in the Women's Liberation Movement. It was established in response to the fifth of the seven demands of the Women's Liberation Movement: the demand for legal and financial independence for women.[1] From its inception, ROW was committed to a feminism that recognized the power structures of patriarchy, as embodied in white man-made law. An early newsheet (1980) describes how 'a group of legal workers met together to discuss their own experiences of working in that white, bourgeois, male heartland ... the law' (Ginsberg, 1980). Marguerite Russell, a lesbian feminist activist and barrister involved at the time explained:

> The early meetings were a sort of consciousness raising group for women lawyers. Solicitors working for a firm in Hackney, feminists in the Law Centre movement and lawyers active within Women's Aid came together to discuss some of the contradictions we faced as women in a male dominated profession and as feminist lawyers within Women's Liberation — other feminists valued our skills in drawing up constitutions, and in obtaining injunctions, but were suspicious, probably rightly so, of the middle-class nature of our profession. After a few meetings, we grew from a consciousness raising into an activist group. We managed to get premises and a small grant for a part-time worker and set up the legal advice line for women. There were Law Centres in existence by then, but they did not work on specifically women's issues or operate within a feminist perspective. This was a wonderful time, women had the energy to set up groups: Women's Aid was set up in 1974, ROW in 1975 and the first Rape Crisis Centre in 1976.
>
> (Russell, personal communication, October 1994)

Established in the autonomous Women's Liberation Movement (WLM), ROW was committed to feminism, anti-racism, challenging class oppression and heterosexism from the outset. ROW strove to work within the woman-centred, non-hierarchal, collective processes that characterized the WLM more widely. While based in London, ROW, as the only feminist legal project in the UK, networked with feminist and women's organizations both nationally and internationally. Early campaigns that ROW supported included the 'YBA wife' and the 'Don't Do It, Di' campaigns of the late 1970s and the 'Rape in Marriage' campaign of the early 1980s involved networking with feminists across the UK.[2] Lawyers associated with ROW, together with 2000 women from 40 countries including Argentina, Australia, Canada, Chile, India, Iran, Israel, Japan, Korea, Lebanon, Mozambique, Soviet Union, Vietnam, Puerto Rico, as well as Europe and the USA, participated in the International Tribunal on Crimes Against Women in Brussels, 4–8 March 1976, ending on International Women's Day. Simone de Beauvoir, an internationally known French feminist and philosopher, sent a message to this global speak out:

> Dear Sisters, I am deeply sorry that circumstances do not allow me to be among you today, but I am present in my heart. I hold this meeting to be a great historic event ... you are gathered here to denounce the oppression to which women are subjected in this society.
>
> To fight this oppression, for a long time now women have been gathering together in many countries, but these various groups were more or less ignorant of one another. For the first time they will join together, and women coming from all over the world will be conscious of the scandal of their condition ...

> I salute this Tribunal as being the start of a radical decolonization of women.
>
> (Simone de Beauvoir, 4 March 1976, cited in Russell and Van de Ven, 1976: xiii)

Since its beginning, ROW has defined itself in relation to the law and legal processes. Our commitment to feminism has shaped our practice and processes as well as our policies and critiques of the existing law. ROW has sustained a broad approach to feminism and never aligned itself to any single feminist perspective. The name 'Rights of Women', echoing Mary Wollstonecraft (1792), might characterize ROW as a liberal feminist project, and, indeed, some of our work focuses on securing formal rights for women in public spheres, e.g. our support for progressive amendments to sex and race discrimination laws. However, ROW never held the view that formal equality in law alone could end the racism, classism, sexism and heterosexism that permeates both the law and the society in which it is grounded.

Our work around employment and state benefits might characterize ROW as socialist feminist, and it is the case that ROW has networked with trade unions and the labour movement in struggles to improve employment opportunities and conditions for women. ROW's work against sexual and racist harassment at work connects to another key area of our work and links to what tends to be seen as radical feminist concerns, i.e. struggles to end, and provide protection and redress against, domestic and sexual violence. ROW critiques marriage and institutionalized heterosexuality as oppressive institutions underpinning male control of women and children within patriarchy.

Lesbian feminism is well represented within ROW as the presence of the Lesbian Custody Project indicates. Our active anti-racist perspective is influenced by black feminism and shapes our advice and policy work. Specifically it informs ROW's work, in alliance with other feminist and community women's groups, to end the racist immigration laws and practices, particularly those which impact on women directly, e.g. the primary purpose[3] and 12-months[4] rules, which trap migrant women in violent relationships by the threat of deportation.

A commitment to global feminism has been present since the early days. Although constrained by our limited finances, ROW has attempted to link into global feminist struggles in relation to the law, a theme emphasized by Ratna Kapur, a Delhi legal advocate and feminist activist, in a keynote speech at the opening of the 1994 Rights of Women 'Women and the Law' conference. Referring to ROW's participation in a 1994 'Woman and the Law' workshop in Bangalore, India,[5] she said:

> Their presence and participation at this workshop was of enormous help to some of us who are struggling in India to develop feminist approaches to women's rights, law reform and litigation . . .
>
> I believe very strongly in establishing global links. And I am convinced that such linkages can be formed if we are willing to complicate our analysis of experience, and understand the diversity of our struggles

between and within our respective worlds. We must not just share common understandings but also the tensions that exist between us and between our existing worlds. Some of this is already being done, and I am hopeful that during this conference, we will be able to raise and understand our differences without getting paralysed in debates on identity and who can speak. We need to recognise the partiality of our experience and knowledge, without romanticising that partiality. We need to know that women experience a simultaneity of oppression and privilege and that under-standing the complexity of this experience is the only basis on which global linkages can be built. It is a difficult alliance, but one that I feel will help us in developing more meaningful and useful links between our worlds and within our worlds.

(Ratna Kapur, 26 March 1994, ROW, 'Women and the Law' conference, London)

While at times ROW's broad-based feminism has produced tensions, its strength lies in recognizing the connectedness of these issues within women's lives.

1980s: Transformations — From Autonomy and Women's Liberation to Voluntary Sector Feminism

While our location within feminism and struggles around the law and legal process have made for important continuities in ROW, there have been significant changes in the structure of the organization, as ROW has had to accommodate itself to the changed political contexts of the 1980s and 1990s.

In 1981, there was a major change as ROW, along with some, but by no means all, existing women's liberation groups and organizations, accepted substantial funding from local government.[6] During the 1980s we struggled to transform ourselves from an autonomous Women's Liberation group into a voluntary sector feminist organization. This involved developing new structures of accountability as ROW began to employ paid workers.[7] We established a voluntary policy group, with a subgroup to deal with managerial matters. Working groups and projects have been instituted in the primary areas of our work: family law, employment law, sexual violence and lesbian parenting. A rota of volunteer legal advisers has been established to staff the evening advice line. In addition, ROW has a membership, presently numbering about 500 women, including solicitors, barristers, academics, students, activists and feminist groups, concerned about women's relationship to the law.

Funding changed the organization and relations within it. It presented new opportunities, new challenges and new constraints. It injected a lot of energy into ROW, enabling more outreach work; the advice line expanded; our publicity increased and we published several full-length books,[8] upgraded the ROW Bulletin, produced briefing papers and guides for taking legal action on a range of issues.[9] Our submissions to the Law Commission and other government bodies were given attention and at times were not without influence. We were able to do more networking with other feminist groups, community groups and students; facilitate more workshops, working groups and trainings; respond to media requests for press statements and interviews, requests to facilitate trainings, workshops and talks at Conferences; and even organized conferences ourselves.[10]

Funding presented its own difficulties. Accountability to funders is necessary, but has generated considerable bureaucracy. Working out relationships between paid workers, volunteers, the various working groups, policy and management groups, and individual women who constitute our membership has required constant review and re-negotiation. Not engaging in 'party politics' has been a condition of funding and we have been required to give undertakings that 'we do not promote homosexuality', following Clause 28, subsequently S 2A of the Local Government Act 1988.

ROW's ways of working on issues relating to women and the law are quite complex and many-levelled, ranging from advice and support to individual women in their encounters with the law; facilitating discussion and working groups; preparation of policy documents and submissions to government bodies, law commissions, Royal Commissions; to promoting our policies politically through networking with community groups, law reform groups and women's organizations, the media and parliamentary politics, often in alliances and coalitions with other feminists and feminist organizations.

One of the highest profile areas of recent work has been our participation, together with Southall Black Sisters and Justice for Women, in the struggle to free women imprisoned for killing men who had subjected them to continuing violence. The development and promotion of 'self preservation' as a proposed new defence to the charge of murder, structured around the experiences and circumstances of women facing continuing violence, has generated interest from the international feminist community, parliamentary and political bodies as well as from feminists in the UK.[11]

This short overview of ROW is intended as illustrative, rather than as a comprehensive review of our work. The chapter concludes by looking more closely at one aspect of our work to focus more sharply on the many-levelled nature of feminist activism around the law and the close interconnections between advice and support work, research, and policy development in the struggle to secure progressive change for women in relation to the law.

Lesbian Parenting

The Lesbian Custody Project (LCP) has had a continuing and active presence in ROW since 1982. ROW was successfully lobbied by autonomous activist groups of lesbian parents, which had formed in London and around the country, to provide support for lesbians who had had children in former heterosexual relationships. Many lesbian mothers found themselves facing protracted and difficult legal struggles to live with their children outside of male control. Through the 1970s, lesbian mothers, if caught in a legal dispute with the child's father over who should bring up the child and/or what contact the absent parent should have with the child, faced widespread hostility and discrimination from the courts, judges, legal professionals, psychiatrists, psychologists and welfare officers. This anti-lesbian hostility was compounded by racism if the mother was black or from a minority ethnic group; by class discrimination if she was working class; and by assumptions that the ideal mother be fully able-bodied and law abiding. In custody disputes, a lesbian mother's parenting abilities, material circumstances and the child(ren)'s wishes were all deemed secondary to a perceived need to investigate her personal relationships, politics and sexuality. In court, lesbian mothers were frequently subjected to personal abuse or insult from Court Welfare Officers, the child(ren)'s father, his lawyers and even the Judge. The prevalence of heterosexism in the legal system was such that the courts effectively put 'Lesbian Mothers on Trial'.[12]

ROW allocated one of its substantive posts to lesbian custody when funding was first secured. Whether held by one woman, or job shared, to date all incumbents of this post have been lesbian mothers. To ensure wider accountability and to provide support for the worker, the Lesbian Custody Project was established, made up of lesbian mothers and legal workers.

The early work of LCP included providing legal advice and support to individual lesbian mothers; networking with local lesbian mothers groups; and facilitating lesbian mothers conferences. LCP also engaged in research work, analysing legal judgements and conducting a survey of lesbian mothers' experiences of the legal system. The study of Appeal Court cases demonstrated that the guiding principles for resolving child custody disputes were overturned when lesbianism was raised.[13] Instead, 'lesbianism has been focused on as the dominating factor as to why the mother should not have custody, rather than an examination of the quality and care of the parental relationships ...' (ROW, 1984: 14–15).

Our survey of the experiences of 36 lesbian mothers and their 64 children produced similarly depressing evidence of discrimination against lesbians between 1974 and 1984. Over half the mothers who were in dispute over custody avoided court proceedings because they believed or had been legally advised that they had little chance of winning. 'The results of this survey show discrimination against lesbian mothers at all institutional levels, including the courts, welfare officers, and the legal profession as well as teachers, social services and the medical profession' (ROW, 1984: 34–35).

Challenging and overturning this level of discrimination presented a daunting task for LCP. Working around lesbian custody issues raised particular considerations. Campaigns of support for individual women could not be pursued through the type of street protests and court pickets that had had some success on other issues. In part this was a consequence of the extent of anti-lesbianism which meant that we could not rely on the widespread support needed to generate popular campaigns. More significant was the sensitive nature of every individual case when a mother was at risk of losing her children. Rather than use sensationalism and confrontational tactics, LCP chose to struggle through law. A *Lesbian Mothers' Legal Handbook* (Lesbian Custody Group, ROW, 1986) was compiled, which included a critique of the law and strategic advice for dealing with lawyers and court welfare officers, drawn from shared experiences through the survey and subsequent networking. Training programmes for feminist lawyers were produced and delivered to create a national pool of solicitors and barristers sufficiently skilled and experienced to be entrusted to act in lesbian custody cases. Heterosexism awareness training was developed and used in outreach work with social services, probation officers and students. We also made use of the media to promote positive images of lesbian parenting and cooperated with the making of 'Breaking the Silence: Lesbian Mothers Speak Out', shown on the opening night of Channel 4 television, and with other television and radio programmes, including Woman's Hour and the Channel 4 'Out' series as well as some dire daytime TV discussion programmes.

Another strand of LCP's work was to identify and encourage psychological research which challenges assumptions that lesbians are immature and/or sick, and so by definition unfit to parent, the starting point of much psycho babble. It is also assumed that our children will become lesbian or gay, and that this is a problem, and further that they will be unable to deal with being teased or stigmatized because of their mother's sexuality. Given the significance placed on court reports from these experts, we welcomed and have been able to draw on the study by Susan Golombok's *et al.* (1983) which concluded:

> The findings of this study ... show no difference in children brought up by a single heterosexual parent, with respect of gender identity, sex role behaviour or sexual orientation. The lack of difference seems to negate the hypothesis that children brought up by actively lesbian mothers are likely to show psychological abnormalities.
>
> (ROW, 1984: 20)

In the mid-1980s, as a consequence of this extensive groundwork, lesbian mothers contacting the project were better prepared, better advised and better represented than previously. Although levels of prejudice experienced in courts were still unacceptable, and custody disputes remained highly stressful, increasingly cases were being quietly won.

The Backlash Begins: Clause 28

However, just as it might have seemed as if we were making some impact in our struggle to create a situation in which lesbian mothers were closer to being treated by the courts in the same way as heterosexual mothers, i.e. on the basis of parenting skills and capacities rather than solely in relation to sexuality, we were faced with 'the claws' — Section 28 — now S 2a of the Local Government Act 1988. 'Clause 28' represented a fundamental attack on the human rights of lesbians and gay men and impacted quite specifically on lesbian mothers and our children, labelling us 'pretending families'.[14] Shifting into public protest, lesbians involved in LCP played an active role in the wider campaign against the Clause, speaking at too many meetings to count; participating in TV discussion programmes, briefing Lords and Ladies, giving press interviews. Wearing our 'we are not pretending' badges, we marched in London and travelled, with our pretending children, on the pink train, with pink champagne to the Manchester march.

Our engagement in mixed lesbian and gay politics was indeed a mixed experience. On some occasions campaigning was fun, and at times some of us almost thought that the Clause had done more for lesbian strength than anything else in the last 50 years. But despite our not inconsiderable efforts, the impact of the clause on lesbian mothers and our children never caught the same attention as the more male-dominated arts lobby. Events in the campaign moved so quickly that there was never enough time for reflection or political discussion within the newly emerging lesbian and gay lobbies to fully address some of the contradictions we experienced as lesbian feminists working in alliance with gay groups. Because there were unresolved issues, on more than one occasion we sat in embarrassed silence rather than raise dissent in public forums, given the weight of the wider political stakes.

The Clause, however, did not impact directly on lesbian custody cases, being about local authority spending not family law. But it did change the political climate in which they were heard. It marked the beginning of a backlash against lesbian mothers which moved swiftly to include all single mothers, mothers threatening the roots of patriarchy by bringing up children outside of male control. Our experience has shown us that whenever lesbians are targeted for attack, it is never long before it is extended more widely to all women who challenge patriarchal power.

Sisters are Doing it for Ourselves

The attack on lesbian parenting did not stop with Section 28. It surfaced again in debates around the Human Embryology and Fertilization Bill in 1989–90. The first evidence that something nasty was afoot was the appearance of a pernicious and unambiguous Early Day Motion.

> That this House notes with profound concern the recent revelation that 55 lesbian couples and eight single lesbians have been impregnated by one sperm bank alone during the last three years; expresses its dismay at the ease with which these and two thousand other unmarried women who are not infertile were able to gain access to such facilities; believes that such practices undermine the status of marriage, corrupt the family unit, and leave the ensuing children at grave risk of emotional harm; and calls upon the Secretary of State to review his policy on such matters and to bring forward legislation before the House which will enable it to come to a decision as to whether or not such practices should be allowed.
>
> (Early Day Motion, no 1324, Hansard Order Paper no. 165)

The Human Embryology and Fertilization Bill 1989 proved opportune for the supporters of the motion. Although primarily concerned with new reproductive technologies, it was hijacked by those wishing to deny lesbians and single women access to a much older technology — donor insemination. In contrast with Clause 28, struggle against this attack on women's rights to have children did not mobilize much support from gay or feminist communities. LCP played a strategic role in founding a campaigning group CADI, Campaign for Access to Donor Insemination, which organized a campaign of parliamentary lobbying and a rally. It won support from the National Abortion Campaign. LCP monitored the committee stage of the bill, working actively with MPs against these measures preparing briefing papers, sometimes overnight, to keep up with new amendments. All explicitly discriminatory amendments were rejected in committee, presumably as too crude and obvious an attempt by the state to control women's fertility. Virginia Bottomley, representing the government's position, argued that any concerns about 'the family' (Radford, 1992) were already met by the welfare principle. On its final reading in the full House, a further attempt to restrict fertility services by amending the welfare principle was accepted. It now reads:

> a woman shall not be provided with treatment services unless account has been taken of the welfare of any child who may be born as a result of the treatment, and of any other child who may be affected by the birth, including the need of that child for a father.
>
> (S 13/5, Human Embryology and Fertilization Act, 1990)

While no-one would argue with the principle of prioritizing a child's welfare, in practice the principle gives absolute power to the patriarchal state — the judiciary and welfare professionals decide what is in a child's best interests (Harne and Radford, 1994). This means that certain women will be deemed 'good enough to mother' and others will not. Clinics providing donor insemination are required to evaluate not a woman's actual parenting abilities, but her potential abilities and to consider not the welfare of an actual child, but the potential welfare of a potential child. It is unclear what if any criteria might be appropriate! In the absence of clear criteria, presumably any such judgements rest on the idealized white, heterosexual, able-bodied, middle-class family norm, and discriminate against women living otherwise. The wording of the amendment is perhaps not as tight as its promoters hoped. The reference to the 'needs of "that" child' particularizes, and does not assert that all children need fathers — a loophole big enough for sperm to slip through when clinics are willing (Radford, 1991).

While the practical consequences of the new law may be small, given that assisted pregnancy services are accorded low priority in our over-stretched NHS and that private treatments are expensive, its ideological significance is immense. A state that attempts to legislate which women are allowed to bear children and which are not, based on criteria informed by racism, heterosexism and class values, is a state shifting into fascism. The interconnectedness of attacks on lesbians and single women becomes increasingly clear as the moral panic gathers pace in the 1990s.

The ink was barely dry on the Human Embryology and Fertilization Act when lesbian parenting was once again the subject of hysterical attention and moral panic.

This time the context was lesbians as foster and adoptive parents. LCP knows of many lesbians who have been successful foster and adoptive parents over the years. In 1991, a storm of controversy was orchestrated by the local press when Newcastle City Council placed a boy with disabilities with lesbian adoptive parents. Space does not permit a full discussion of the struggles around the eligibility of lesbians and gay men to be considered as potential foster and adoptive parents. They were largely played out through the consultation process of the Review of Adoption Law. At the time of writing (autumn 1994), this slow process remains incomplete, but fierce resistance from lesbian and gay organizations has prevented the inclusion of the explicitly discriminatory recommendations of early proposals from the Ministry of Health and the Welsh Office.

Lesbian parenting continues to be a high profile and controversial issue in 1994. The year started well as the courts began to recognize and accord legitimacy to lesbian co-parents by awarding 'contact orders' and residence orders carrying 'parental responsibility' to lesbian co-parents under the provisions of the Children Act 1989.[15] The first few cases were not reported, so this good news spread quietly around the lesbian community. The first case to catch media attention occurred in July 1994. Heard in the High Court, it involved two lesbians, one of whom became pregnant through self-insemination. In granting the order, the judge stated that his 'first and paramount consideration was the welfare of the child'. The Official Solicitor, representing the child, supported the order. The granting of these orders gives legal recognition to lesbian co-parents for the first time. This decision was followed, in September, by further good news from the Appeal Court. In awarding a residence order to a lesbian mother, Lord Justice Neill and Lord Justice Saville, relying on earlier similar judgements in the early 1990s, categorically stated that lesbianism *per se* did not make a woman an unfit mother. In comparison with the judgements between 1974 and 1984, the Appeal Court has come a long way in the last ten years.

Rarely, as lesbians or as feminists, are we allowed to celebrate small victories for very long. The media coverage was predictably patronizing in the quality press and fully offensive in the tabloids — the *Daily Mail* suggested that 'Britain was floundering in moral vacuum'. Media anti-lesbianism had become dangerous by 1994. One Hackney lesbian headmistress was vilified and forced into hiding, with her partner and children. We are hearing about more street attacks on lesbians, and lesbians being thrown out of restaurants in London. At the time of writing, October 1994, Sandi Toksvig has just received an apology from 'Save the Children' who dropped her from their 75th anniversary celebrations after she came out as a lesbian mother.

In contrast, The Children's Society has still to withdraw its ban on considering lesbians as prospective foster or adoption parents. LCP has played a strategic networking role in resistance struggles. But neither LCP nor ROW can do enough without the support of a visible, including, explicitly anti-racist, anti-heterosexist feminist movement, which acknowledges the connections and commonalities in women's experiences while recognizing and finding ways of working in alliance and collaboration across the power relations and differences, acting locally, thinking globally.

Notes

1   Seven Demands of the Women's Liberation Movement. The women's liberation movement asserts a woman's right to define her own sexuality and demands:
    1.   Equal pay for equal work;
    2.   Equal education and job opportunities;
    3.   Free contraception and abortion on demand;
    4.   Free 24-hour community controlled child care;
    5.   Legal and financial independence for women;
    6.   An end to discrimination against lesbians;
    7.   Freedom for all women from intimidation by the threat or use of male violence. An end to the laws, assumptions and institutions that perpetuate male dominance and men's aggression towards women.
    Demands 1–4 were agreed at the 1970 National Women's Liberation conference, 5 and 6 were added in 1975 and the declaration as cited above was agreed at the National Women's Liberation Conference in Birmingham, 1978.

2   The 'YBA wife' campaign was an autonomous and nationwide campaign aimed at rising awareness about discrimination against married women in law. It was based on the 5th demand of the Women's Liberation Movement and promoted 'a woman's right to control her own sexuality'. In the late 1970s, married women were discriminated against in tax law and were unable to claim social security benefits; rape in marriage was not outlawed until 1993.
    The 'Don't Do it, Di' campaign also emphasized feminist critiques of marriage and institutionalized heterosexuality, and was part of the wider feminist response to the media hype surrounding the wedding of Lady Diana and Prince Charles in 1979.

3   The primary purpose rule (HC 251, para 50) impinges on the right to family unity and life of certain groups of people. Immigration officials view marriages within minority ethnic communities as problematic, particularly when they are contracted differently. The assumption is that marriage where one partner is not settled here, is entered into for 'the primary purpose' of living in this country (see Southall Black Sisters, undated).

4   The 12-months rule (HC 251, para 51, 131, 132) requires that the applicant, having been given initial leave to enter or remain in the UK on the basis of marriage, must remain within that marriage for 12 months, before she or he is given indefinite leave to remain. This rule effectively prevents groups of women from seeking protection and safety from violence and abuse. It represents a gross violation of human rights. For discussion of the impact of this rule see Southall Black Sisters, undated.

5   Indo-British Workshop on Women and Law, with reference to sexual assault, indecent representation and prostitution. Discussions aimed at perfecting three draft bills on the subjects of prostitution, rape and indecent representation of women. Organized by the National Law School of India University, Bangalore, British High Commission, British Council Division in association with the National Commission for Women, 3–5 January 1994 in Bangalore, 7–8 January in New Delhi.

6   Initially, funding was granted by the Greater London Council; subsequent to its abolition in March 1986, funding has been from the London Boroughs Grants Committee.

7   For most of the period between 1981 and 1995, ROW had 3.2 full-time posts, job-shared in different ways by between 5 and 6 workers.

8   See ROW publications in the bibliography.

9   These include the 'Guide for Taking Legal Action on Domestic Violence', 'Guide for

Taking Legal Action on Sexual Assault', 'Guide for Taking Legal Action on Sexual Harassment at Work', 'Guide for Taking Legal Action on Divorce' and 'Injunctions: A Do-It-Yourself Guide'. Additionally, we have produced five leaflets on 'Women's Employment Rights: How to Make the Most of Them':

1. Dismissal and Redundancy
2. Pregnancy and Maternity Rights
3. Racial Discrimination
4. Sex Discrimination and Equal Pay
5. Part-Time Workers' Rights

All are available, for a small charge, from Rights of Women, 52–54 Featherstone St, London EC1Y 8RT.

10 For example, two 'Lesbian Mothers and The New Laws' conferences in the early 1990s, the 'Immigration and Family Law' conference (October 1994), in conjunction with Southall Black Sisters, and the 'Joint Council for the Welfare of Immigrants' (October 1994); and Rights of Women, 'Women and the Law' conference (March 1994).

11 'Self-preservation' was considered by the House of Commons Home Affairs Committee in their report on domestic violence, and was supported by delegates at the 1994 Labour Party Conference. For more information see Rights of Women Bulletins from 1991 to 1994; Julie Bindel, Kate Cook, Liz Kelly, Chapter 5; Lorraine Radford (1993); Jennifer Nadel (1993); Liz Kelly and Jill Radford (1994).

12 Rights of Women, 1984.

13 These principles:
- that the welfare of the child is the first and paramount consideration;
- that young children are better cared for by their mothers;
- maintaining a stable environment for the child by not disturbing the *status quo* without good reason;
- not separating sisters and brothers;
- giving regard to the wishes of the children.

have subsequently been encoded in the check-list in the Children Act 1989, which came into force in October 1991 (see ROW, 1992).

14 Section A of the Local Government Act of 1988 reads:
(1) A local authority shall not:
(a) intentionally promote homosexuality or publish material with the intention of promoting homosexuality;
(b) promote the teaching in any maintained school of the acceptability as a pretended family relationship. (Colvin and Hawksley, 1989)

15 'Parental responsibility' is defined in the Children Act 1989 as 'all the rights, duties, responsibilities and authority which by law a parent of a child has in relation to a child and his property' (Rights of Women, 1992: 3).

Acknowledgements

I would like to thank present and former workers and Policy Group members of Rights of Women for their help and support with this article, specifically Gill Butler, Elaine Ginsberg, Lynne Harne, Elizabeth Woodcraft and Marguerite Russell for sharing their memories of the early days of ROW. However I take responsibility if there are any mistakes.

Jill Radford

References

COLVIN, MADELAINE and HAWKSLEY, JANE (1989) *Section 28: A Practical Guide to the Law and Its Implications*, London: Liberty.
Early Day Motion no. 1324 (25 October 1989) 'Impregnation of Lesbian Women', Hansard Order Paper no. 165, 1 November, no. 6211 Ref.H 5309.
GINSBERG, ELAINE (1981) 'ROW: The First Five Years', Rights of Women Leaflet, London: ROW Archives.
GINSBERG, ELAINE and LERNER, SARA (1989) *Sexual Violence Against Women*, London: ROW.
HARNE, LYNNE and RADFORD, JILL (1994) 'Reinstating Patriarchy: The Politics of the Family and the New Legislation', in MULLENDER, A. and MORLEY, REBECCA (Eds) *Children Living with Domestic Violence: Putting Men's Abuse of Women on the Child Care Agenda*, London: Whiting and Birch.
KELLY, LIZ and RADFORD, JILL (1995) 'Self Preservation: Feminist Activism and Feminist Jurisprudence', paper delivered at the Annual Women's Studies (UK) Network Conference, forthcoming in MAYNARD, M. and PURVIS, J. (Eds) (1995), London: Taylor & Francis.
LESBIAN CUSTODY GROUP, RIGHTS OF WOMEN (1986) *Lesbian Mothers Legal Handbook*, London: Women's Press.
NADEL, JENNIFER (1993) *Sara Thornton: The Story of a Woman Who Killed*, London: Victor Gollancz.
RADFORD, JILL (1991) 'Immaculate Conceptions: Why the Fuss about Virgin Births?', *Trouble and Strife*, **21**, Summer, pp. 8–12.
RADFORD, JILL (1992) 'Backlash Against Lesbian Parenting: First it was Clause 28 and Then . . .', *Health Care for Women International*, **3**, 2 (April–June), pp. 229–236.
RADFORD, JILL (1994) 'Histories of Women's Liberation Movements in Britain: A Reflective Personal History', in GRIFFIN, GABRIELE, HESTER, MARIANNE, RAI and ROSENEIL, SASHA (Eds) *Stirring It: Challenges for Feminism*, pp. 40–58, London: Taylor & Francis.
RADFORD, LORRAINE (1993) 'Pleading for Time: Justice for Battered Women Who Kill', in BIRCH, H. (Ed.) *Moving Targets: Women, Murder and Representation*, London: Virago.
RIGHTS OF WOMEN (1984) *Lesbian Mothers on Trial: A Report on Lesbian Mothers and Child Custody*, London: ROW.
RIGHTS OF WOMEN (1992) *A Guide to the Children Act 1989*, London: ROW.
RIGHTS OF WOMEN (1991) Rights of Women Bulletin, Winter, London: ROW.
RIGHTS OF WOMEN (1992) Rights of Women Bulletin, Summer, London: ROW.
RIGHTS OF WOMEN (1993) Rights of Women Bulletin, Spring, London: ROW.
RIGHTS OF WOMEN (1993) Rights of Women Bulletin, Winter, London: ROW.
RIGHTS OF WOMEN (1994) Rights of Women Bulletin, Spring, London: ROW.
RIGHTS OF WOMEN (1994) Rights of Women Bulletin, Winter, London: ROW.
RUSSELL, DIANA E.H. and VAN DE VEN, NICOLA (Eds) (1976) *Crimes Against Women: Proceedings of the International Tribunal*, Millbrae, California: Les Femmes.
RUSSELL, MARGUERITE (1994) personal communication.
SOUTHALL BLACK SISTERS (undated–1994) 'Domestic Violence and Asian Women: A Collection of Reports and Briefings', available from 52 Norwood Rd, Southall, Middx, UK.
WOLLSTONECRAFT, M. (1792) *A Vindication of the Rights of Women*, Harmondsworth: Penguin.

64

Chapter 5

Trials and Tribulations — *Justice for Women*: A Campaign for the 1990s

Julie Bindel, Kate Cook and Liz Kelly

Violence against women is one of the issues around which feminist activism has been most evident. In the 1970s, women organized refuges, rape crisis lines and Women Against Violence Against Women groups. Campaigns took place at local, national and international levels. In Britain, activism has included: Reclaim the Night marches; local and national demonstrations about domestic violence, rape and child sexual assault; the Rape in Marriage campaign; actions against sex shops and other anti-pornography protests; publicizing the names and actions of particular abusers; 'zap' actions;[1] campaigns for safe transport; graffiti and poster campaigns. Feminists have also challenged agency and institutional practice — especially that of the police and the courts.

Violence against women could be said to be an area of feminist 'success' in that the issue is now one of intense public concern, and many of our particular criticisms have been accepted as valid. For example: it is now widely understood that it is ludicrous to suggest that a woman has 'asked for' a rape by her choice of clothing. Feminist activism has resulted in changes — albeit limited ones — in legislation, agency policy and practice. Nevertheless, there is still plenty of scope for improvements. This will be discussed further below.

I'm Not a Feminist But ...

The 1980s were a period of uncertainty and loss of faith within feminist activism. The impact of simplistic identity politics fuelled divisions among women, and created tension and mistrust. At the same time the economic and broad political climates were changing, which meant that many women's services were threatened with loss of funding. This context limited what it was possible for feminists to do together. One impact was that groups which had previously been involved in campaigning and direct support work, were now under far greater pressure simply to provide a support service.

Ironically, an increased public awareness of issues around male violence also meant that in some women's services the women doing the work changed. During the 1970s, refuges and rape crisis groups were usually set up by women involved in the Women's Liberation Movement (WLM), and the work was regarded as fundamentally political. Now, it is viewed by some as an alternative to social services, not as part of feminism. In these circumstances, campaigning work is no longer seen as part of the function of the group.

In the mid-1980s the emergence of libertarian and anti/post-feminist positions, together with a politics of pleasure and style, further undermined confidence and participation in activism. One element in this changing representation of feminism has been the suggestion by a number of academic and popularist writers in the 1990s that radical feminism has constructed women as victims (see, for example, Paglia, 1993; Wolf, 1993; Roiphe, 1994). The reality of women who kill their abusers highlights the problems with this concept of 'victimhood' feminism, because, whilst undoubtedly victimized, these women have fought back in the most direct way. However, to represent them as strong survivors, 'warriors against the patriarchy', does a different disservice to their experience (Kelly *et al.*, 1996, forthcoming).

Despite the shifts in feminist activity and theory, male violence continues to be an issue around which women organize locally, nationally and internationally. A recent example of international campaigning is the linking at the Vienna United Nations conference in 1994 of feminist coalitions from every continent to get 'gender violence' included in the UN Declaration of Human Rights.

The Background

The particular focus of Justice for Women has been domestic/intimate homicide. During the 1970s and 1980s, there were individual campaigns in support of the Maw sisters, Noreen Winchester and June Greig.[2] Revolutionary feminists in Leeds (and later Women Against Violence Against Women) were involved in these campaigns and consistently drew attention to the ways in which legal practice meant that men were able to 'get away with murder' when the victim was a female current or ex partner. In the second half of the 1980s, a group in Leeds (the Repeated Attacks and Murder of Women Group) began documenting case histories of individual violent men who either attacked the same woman several times or attacked more than one woman (the case of Keith Ward being a major focus).

In other countries, especially the US, more concerted attention was paid to women who kill abusive men. Several studies were published (Jones, 1980; Browne, 1987) and new legal approaches and reforms developed in some US states, as were campaigns for amnesties for groups of women previously convicted (see Gillespie, 1987).

Formation of Justice for Women

Kiranjit Ahluwalia was married to Deepak for 10 years. His violence towards her was severe and began on day three of their marriage. She tried to leave him on several occasions but was threatened by him and told by her family to go back. On the 8 May 1989, after being threatened and burnt by a hot iron, Kiranjit threw petrol over Deepak's feet and lit it as he was sleeping. He died some days later in hospital. Kiranjit was arrested for murder and sent for trial. Crawley Women's Aid and Southall Black Sisters, on becoming aware of the case, began to build a support campaign. Justice for Women was formed in Leeds in 1990 in response to Kiranjit's case and inspired by the campaign for her.

Southall Black Sisters (SBS) began to organize, anticipating Kiranjit's conviction for murder. SBS and Crawley Women's Aid arranged a public meeting in Kiranjit's home town, immediately after the trial at which she was found guilty. At this meeting speakers included Kiranjit's relatives and women from sections of the WLM. Activity then focused on developing grounds for Kiranjit's appeal whilst maintaining her campaign.

Meanwhile, in early 1991, a member of Leeds Justice for Women contacted another feminist activist in London and asked her to organize a demonstration outside the Court of Appeal on behalf of another woman. This was Sara Thornton, with whom the Leeds group had already been in contact following a letter written by Sara which was published in *The Independent*.[3]

In this letter Sara details the circumstances that had resulted in her conviction for murder:

> My husband drank heavily and repeatedly attacked me. Although the police were summoned on many occasions he would only be verbally warned.
>
> After a particularly vicious assault, which resulted in me being treated in hospital, I insisted that charges be pressed. My husband was arrested, charged and then released; he came home again.
>
> A quiet two-week period then erupted in a weekend of violence. As a result I stabbed my husband once; he later died.

Sara's case was featured in a film by Gita Saghal, *The Provoked Wife* (Dispatches, Channel 4, 22 February 1991).

The Court of Appeal demonstration was pulled together by an *ad hoc* group of radical feminists who used skills and media contacts developed during previous campaigning work. Over 100 women took part and press coverage followed.[4] Sara lost her appeal and two days later in Birmingham, a man walked free, after trial for the murder of his 'nagging' wife: Joseph McGrail was given two-years probation. Justice Popplewell commented during sentencing that 'this lady would have tried the patience of a saint'.

London Justice for Women was formed and protested in order to draw attention to the differential way in which violent men and abused women are treated by the criminal justice system.[5] This contrast became a focus for intense press coverage of a kind not previously given to feminist campaigns. Realising the potential of massive media coverage for individual women, Justice for Women decided to cultivate it, and this has become a very effective campaigning tool. On occasion, actions have been created specifically to get news coverage, despite there being no 'news' in women's cases. Justice for Women has also continued to use traditional feminist methods: picketing the Home Office; leafleting; and demonstrating outside Holloway prison. The media continued to cover the actions and this coverage ensured that the Government has not been able to ignore the issues: domestic violence and women who kill. Indeed, sources close to the Government have admitted that it was the demonstrations outside the Home Office that kept domestic violence on the political agenda. Judges are also aware of the campaign, giving the cases a high profile.

The Growth of the Campaign

As public knowledge of Justice for Women grew, so did numbers of requests for support from women in prison, or facing charges. Not all of the women fell within the remit of women who had killed violent men and in these cases referrals were made to other organizations. Different levels of support and publicity work, however, were undertaken in relation to women who did fall within Justice's remit.

During 1991, shortly after its formation, London Justice for Women worked within November Women's Action to organize a national demonstration to commemorate International Day to End Violence Against Women, 25 November. Three thousand women participated in the event which focused on freeing Sara Thornton, Kiranjit Ahluwalia and Amelia Rossiter.[6] Many of the women were workers and residents in refuges throughout Britain and Ireland. For many women the most powerful part of the event was the minute's silence in remembrance of women who had died as a result of male violence which was immediately followed by dancing to the song 'I will Survive' in Trafalgar Square.[7]

Until the end of 1991, Leeds and London remained as the only two Justice for Women groups. As a response to Marie's case (a woman who had killed her violent partner and was awaiting trial) a group formed in York. Their campaign ended when Marie was given a non-custodial sentence for manslaughter in 1994. Groups have now formed in Norwich and Manchester, which were originally set up to support the existing campaigns. Norwich have subsequently taken up a campaign for Josephine Smith. Other women whom Justice for Women have supported are: Emma Humphreys; Carol Peters; Janet Gardner; Diane Deeming; Diane Jones and two other women who cannot be named for legal reasons. Justice for Women's input has been effective in a number of women's trials, and by the beginning of 1995 four women have been freed through the appeal process (notably Kiranjit's release in September 1992). Campaigns continue for Sara Thornton, Emma Humphreys and Josephine Smith.

Ways of Working

Although some groups are open to any woman to join, London Justice for Women is not. Experiences in the early stages of the campaign to free Sara Thornton convinced the London group that some kind of screening of potential new members was a necessary safeguard. Groups such as Militant (in guise of the Campaign Against Domestic Violence) and Wages for Housework had put out their own publicity for both the November Women's Action March and Sara Thornton's campaign. They claimed to be the instigators of these feminist activities and collected donations on this basis. This 'bandwagonning', using the energy created by feminist activism for other ends, has a long history, and invariably resulted in the issues and analysis being changed, and in the division and demoralization within the original feminist campaign. London Justice were determined not to allow this history to repeat itself.

Despite these difficulties, one of Justice for Women's successes has been in giving women — not previously involved — a way into campaigning feminism, at a time when feminism is (allegedly) either dead or inaccessible/academic. One of the key differences between Justice for Women and previous feminist campaigns is that the campaign self-consciously works with individual women, and their cases/stories are a central focus. Rather than the previous reluctance to use women's stories to prompt public response, it is the injustices within each woman's story which form a basic element of each campaign.

However, the women themselves have to want/choose/ask for this. Where women have already been convicted, a version of their story is public knowledge and they are already involved in a process which makes drama out of their lived experience. The task for Justice for Women has been to change the ways in which women's lives and situations are interpreted and understood, both in the media and in the courts. For other women who have not yet had their cases come to trial, legal restrictions limit what it is possible to say publicly. In yet other cases, where the women have not wanted any additional publicity, Justice for Women have provided support.

In all the well-publicized campaigns, Justice groups have worked very closely with the woman herself. One aspect of this has been explaining that Justice for Women is a feminist campaign with a wider agenda than each individual case. This has enabled the women to have access to feminist ideas and activism. Once a woman has chosen to embark on a public campaign with Justice she is fully involved, not merely consulted. To give just one example: Emma Humphreys was involved in discussing the agenda for her public meeting held in February 1995. Obviously she could not attend the meeting but a video of her speaking was shown and the event itself was videoed in order that she could see it later, in prison. Where appropriate, Justice for Women also works with supportive family members and friends. Additionally the work has involved trying to protect the women from the unwanted attentions of men, attracted by the lurid aspects of the media reporting. For instance, after Emma Humphreys's photograph appeared in newspapers and on television and she was described as 'a prostitute', countless men contacted her making it clear that they would wish to have a sexual relationship with her.

Campaigns with and on behalf of individual women inevitably involve some degree of personal support. This has ranged from finding crystal earrings and thermos flasks to take to women in prison, to informal and formal counselling. For some women this has been the first time that they have been able to tell all of their story, an important step both for the women themselves, and for their campaigns. There are, however, sometimes tensions between the campaigning and supporting aspects of the work, a dilemma shared with many other women's groups.

Justice for Women — A National Network

During the late 1993/early 1994, discussions took place at national meetings attended by all of the Justice for Women groups about whether to form some type of network/federation. As a consequence of these discussions a network has been set up with agreed Aims and Objectives, common to all of the existing groups. These make explicit a feminist perspective. The groups hope that, where women want to start Justice for Women groups in other towns or cities, these Aims and Objectives will be used as a basis for their work.

The statement of aims is fairly broad, whilst maintaining the emphasis on work with women who have killed violent men. Thus, there is the possibility of groups existing within the network and having a slightly different focus. For example, the women in the Manchester group are interested in being involved in educational work and, as yet, are not working specifically for any individual woman/women.

Legal Reform

Campaigning for women very quickly revealed problems with existing defences for women who kill violent men. Early in Kiranjit's campaign, SBS organized a meeting with lawyers, feminist academics and activists to explore grounds on which her appeal could be fought. This meeting was the first of many discussions where the tensions between finding something which might work now and inherent difficulties in the law were debated, and until substantial legal reform is achieved this conflict remains.

There is one full defence to murder — self defence, and two partial defences (where intention is established) — diminished responsibility and provocation — which reduce the charge to manslaughter. Any conviction for murder carries a mandatory life sentence, whereas for manslaughter convictions, sentencing is entirely at the judge's discretion and may not even involve a custodial sentence.

Diminished Responsibility

In order to plead diminished responsibility women have to prove an 'abnormality of mind' at the time of the event. This always relies upon expert testimony, usually from psychiatrists, defining women as 'mad' rather than 'bad'. It focuses on her mind rather than on his actions, thus removing responsibility from the violent man. A potential consequence of this medicalizing of women is that even if she is found not guilty of murder she can be 'sentenced' to psychiatric treatment either inside or outside the prison system.

In the USA, this defence has been developed through the use of Battered Women's Syndrome (BWS) (Walker, 1984). The syndrome relies on an expert witness description of the characteristics of battered women, and in particular the development over time of 'learned helplessness'. It thus creates a model into which women have to fit. Justice for Women's concerns about this, which are shared by many American feminists, include:

- it medicalizes a social and political issue;
- it labels women's understandable responses to abuse as a syndrome with the implied need for treatment and cure;
- it requires a uniform response to violence, thereby excluding those women who react differently (this is particularly worrying as women who continue to refuse male control are excluded, and evidence from the USA shows that this disproportionately affects African American women);
- it suggests that all women experiencing domestic violence are helpless, and draws attention away from the failure of agencies to respond to their attempts to end violence;
- the trial in which Battered Women's Syndrome (BWS) is used will focus on experts from both sides rather than on the voice of the woman herself.

Even where BWS is accepted, it is only successful in about a quarter of cases (Gillespie, 1987). Some British lawyers argue that its use is pragmatic in particular cases. However, in the long run, the consequence of this will be that many women will have even fewer options in court.

After discussions with feminist lawyers and activists, Justice for Women decided that diminished responsibility could not be discounted as a defence. Although the problems with the defence were recognized, it is occasionally an appropriate defence if, as a consequence of the violence, women develop psycho-logical problems. However, in these cases what needs to be understood is that the social context of woman abuse is the cause, not any individual woman's personality. Taking this position would change the perspective and content of how expert testimony is given to support women.

Provocation

This defence has been successfully used by violent men for reasons ranging from the woman's 'nagging', being unfaithful, or even 'moving the mustard pot' (Justice for Women, 1993b). In its construction it is an inherently male defence, and precedent has made it increasingly more so.

In order to plead provocation you have to present evidence which shows that the person was provoked, whether by things done or things said or both together, to lose self control.[8] In case law, this loss of control has been defined as having to be 'sudden and temporary' and not motivated by revenge. The case cited in relation to this is *R v Duffy* (1949; 1 ALL ER 932 CA). Here, a woman who killed her violent husband was convicted of his murder and was later hanged. In this case, and many subsequently, juries have decided that the man's violence towards her was her motive rather than a mitigating factor.

Justice for Women has grave misgivings about reforms to the law on provocation being seen as a solution to the current lack of a defence for battered women who kill. In fact, it could merely extend the licence which men already have to kill women. Whilst the campaign has no problem with redefining 'sudden and temporary' to allow for a time gap between the provoking act and retaliation, we doubt that this will aid all women who currently lack a legal defence. Alongside this relaxation of interpretation, however, Justice for Women supports a tightening of the defence in order that neither words alone, nor alleged or actual infidelity, can (uncomplicated by other factors) constitute provocation.

Self-Preservation

None of the above, even with reform, would be an adequate defence; women would still be 'struggling through the loopholes of man made law' (Radford and Kelly, 1991). Justice for Women supports the campaign for a new defence grounded in women's rather than men's experiences and realities: self-preservation. The network has debated this proposal for over a year and an agreed version was reached in 1993. It begins from the understanding that a woman who kills perceives that she has reached a point where it is her life or his, and the history of abuse constitutes evidence to be heard in her defence (see Justice for Women, 1993a and b, for more details). It draws on principles from within feminist jurisprudence and can be seen as an attempt to create feminist law.

The self-preservation proposal has been officially recognized in the Home Affairs Select Committee Report (1993) and by members of political parties. The former, however, clearly had problems with attempts to create feminist law.

> However now that the courts recognise that a history of abuse can result in diminished responsibility, the new defence would imply that the killing was a rational choice. We do not believe that is acceptable. Furthermore, the definition of self-preservation is one unknown in English law (para 96, xxxii).

Justice for Women is attempting to manage the tension between individual women's cases and the broader position by a two-pronged approach. Legal reform is sought through attempts to use individual cases to change precedent and by campaigning for parliamentary action in creating a new defence for murder. Women's organizations and feminist lawyers from other countries have also expressed interest in self-preservation and this demonstrates that making an example of women who kill violent men is not confined to Britain.

Working with Lawyers

Making a difference for individual women's cases can be most effective if Justice for Women are involved from the beginning of a case. When a woman is arrested, she may well not have her own lawyer and/or know any lawyers; in these circumstances the police will offer her representation through the 'duty' solicitor scheme. That lawyer will usually offer to carry on with her case, whether or not she or he has any experience of murder cases or knowledge of domestic violence. This can mean that women are very poorly represented. Early involvement means Justice for Women can check with the woman whether she is happy with her legal representation. Where doubts exist, either a more experienced lawyer can be instructed, or advice offered to her current one. In general, Justice for Women has reasonable working relationships with the solicitors acting for the women they are campaigning for, although there have been some notable exceptions to this.

One aim of the campaign is to work with the woman's legal team in a way that will be productive for all concerned. At the Woman and Law conference, organized by Rights of Women in 1994, London Justice for Women facilitated a workshop entitled 'Campaigners working with Lawyers'. The following issues were discussed:

- Lawyers' accountability to campaigners and how much responsibility can/ should lawyers give to campaigners.
- Encouraging lawyers to recognize campaigners' particular expertise in relation to violence against women and that campaigners can sometimes keep a case going and even open doors that the legal process had shut.
- Enabling lawyers to be willing to consider the new ideas and methods that campaigners are developing. Campaigners are aiming to change the law whereas most lawyers are merely concerned to practice it.
- The need for lawyers to recognize that an understanding of the politics of sexual violence can underpin the legal case.

In at least one support campaign, the woman's barrister commented on the importance of Justice for Women's input, and how rare this was. He also noted that this was due to the reluctance of lawyers to seek advice from those who are not defined as having 'expert' status. In another case, a member of Justice for Women was officially recognized as part of the legal team working on an appeal process. At a public meeting to discuss Emma Humphreys' case during February 1995, Gareth Peirce, Britain's most eminent civil liberties lawyer, maintained that campaigning was a vital component of the creation of justice. She also pointed to the responsibilities that campaigners take on when they are working with people who have been imprisoned for years, and where their history before prison includes abuse and oppression.

Entering into this dialogue with radical lawyers who are aware of the importance of campaigning is producing a two-way exchange of information and expertise, which strengthens both women's cases and the campaign as a whole.

Dilemmas, Tensions and the Future

Whilst the Justice for Women campaign is focused on a particular legal iniquity, it is part of a broader feminist alliance that addresses all forms of violence against women. The changes which are needed are not just legal, but include all aspects of women's oppression and inequality.

Many of the feminist groups who work around violence against women have traditionally struggled to try to ensure that television, radio and newspaper attention does not focus on an individual 'victim's' story. There are sound political reasons for this which include: trying to resist the messages that all women who experience violence respond in the same way; are violated in the same way; by a particular type of man; in particular circumstances; and that the women themselves are the same, that there is a type of woman who becomes a 'victim'.

Justice for Women have tried to find ways to work with the media (with more or less success) that enable individual women's stories to be told (how else can an effective campaign for a woman in prison be run?), but that challenge this stereotyping, and point out that the women for whom the groups are campaigning are not all the same. Not surprisingly, given this history, this has created some tension with other women's organizations.[9] The most effective way of ensuring some control over what gets said, particularly on TV and radio, is for a woman from the campaign to appear. This strategy, therefore, has been used quite extensively, and some of the individual women, particularly in London Justice for Women, have put in long hours to this end. Unfortunately, this can be misread as women wanting to achieve personal fame on the back of a feminist campaign.

However, the media coverage that women's campaigns have attracted has made a difference. Some women are now free and the campaigns organized by Justice for Women (with Southall Black Sisters, Women's Aid, Campaign Against Pornography and other groups[10]) have helped to create new legal precedents. There is an increase in public and media awareness of some of the issues that women face in experiencing violence from known men.

A recurring dilemma is the tendency within the media to exploit women who have a 'sensational' story to tell. Most journalists appear only to see the women as 'victims'. They cannot (or will not) understand that the women are working *in* the campaign, that they have an analysis of the wider context. The danger here is that the women's status as victims is once more reinforced through media representations. In some instances Justice for Women has been successful in challenging this, but in others agreements with the journalists have not been respected.

Another tension is that whilst the media are happy to talk about the 'extreme' situations where women have killed, they are a lot less willing to enter into more complex debates about the issues that women face every day in relationships with violent men.

Justice for Women will continue to campaign for individual women and for statutory legal changes both to the existing defence of provocation and for the new defence of self-preservation. Perhaps one of the challenges for the future is also to find ways to open up the media debate, to try to create a wider and better understanding of women's experience of domestic violence. To put it another way, we need to reach a situation where the first question asked is not: 'Why didn't you leave?' but 'Why did no-one stop him?' In reality, the decision to leave a violent man may well be the most risky decision any woman makes. Most domestic homicides occur when men kill women who are at the point of leaving, or have already left.[11]

Real justice for women requires the creation of a society in which women have the autonomy to live independently of men, with the issue of male violence against women placed high on the political agenda.

Notes

1 These were ways of creating forms of accountability that formal agencies failed to provide. Groups of women supporting a woman who had been victimized would accompany her to 'confront' her abuser. Whilst content varied, the model adopted by most was that the women would encircle the man and tell him he was not allowed to speak, but had to listen. The woman he had assaulted then said whatever she wanted to, and other women could also speak. There are few published accounts of these actions, but they were very different from the more therapeutic model currently endorsed by self-help manuals. In this later version the woman who has been assaulted undertakes the confrontation alone, or by letter, reasserting an individual relationship and meaning rather than the more collective 'calling to account' that 'zap' actions embodied.

2 Both the Maw sisters and Noreen Winchester killed fathers who were violent towards them and June Greig killed her violent husband.

3 1 August 1990, reprinted in Nadel, 1993.

4 In her book, Jennifer Nadel (1993) tells of how she was on her way to work as a Channel 4 news correspondent when she noticed the Court of Appeal demonstration. As a trained barrister she had an interest in legal issues, but had not at this point developed an interest in women's issues. She talked to members of Justice for Women that day, and it was her determination to do something with this story, in the face of continued resistance from her editor, which resulted in some of the earliest in-depth television coverage. Since that time, she has consistently attempted to keep the issue high on the media agenda.

5 See for example: Harriet Wistrich's letter to the *Guardian*, 30 July 1991.

6 Amelia Rossiter was 63 years old when she was sentenced to life imprisonment for murder. She had stabbed her husband during a row in which he had threatened to garrote her. The judge, Mr Justice Boreham, said she had been found guilty of murder on 'the

clearest possible evidence'. She was freed in 1992 on appeal, after serving four and a half years in prison.

7 The event was filmed and the film by Helen Thompson is called *Justice for Women*.

8 The question of whether the provocation is enough to make a reasonable man do as he did is determined by the jury. In determining this question the jury takes into account everything done and said according to the effect which, in their opinion, it would have on a reasonable man.

9 Grass roots organizations, such as Women's Aid, have argued that they simply do not have the time to cultivate relationships with the press, and therefore often feel 'sidestepped' when other organizations appear to get the credit for work around domestic violence.

10 London Justice have made links with a number of campaigns about legal injustices. Some of those which also involve domestic violence are: Justice for Efen Yimaz, a Turkish woman who was killed and whose killer was not prosecuted as she was defined as a prostitute; Rahooni Haroon's campaign (she had her eyes gouged out by her violent partner and he was only charged with GBH); and the Vandana Patel Campaign (in this case the woman was murdered by her violent husband in Stoke Newington police station; the meeting had been facilitated by the local police domestic violence unit).

11 Twenty per cent of all domestic homicides of women occur after separation (Mooney, 1994).

References

BROWNE, A. (1987) *When Battered Women Kill*, New York: Free Press.

GILLESPIE, C. (1987) *Justifiable Homicide*, Bowling Green: Bowling Green UP.

HOME AFFAIRS SELECT COMMITTEE (1993) *Third Report: Domestic Violence*, Vol. 1, London: House of Commons (245–1).

JONES, A. (1980) *Women Who Kill*, New York: Fawcett Columbine Books (Reprinted 1991, London: Gollancz).

JUSTICE FOR WOMEN (1993a) 'A Submission to the Royal Commission on Criminal Justice', London.

JUSTICE FOR WOMEN (1993b) 'Information Pack', London.

KELLY, L., BURTON, S. and REGAN, L. (1996, forthcoming) 'Beyond Victim or Survivor: Sexual Violence, Identity and Feminist Theory and Practice', in ADKINS, L. and MERCHANT, V. (Eds) *Sexualizing the Social: Power and the Organization of Society*, London: Macmillan.

MOONEY, J. (1994) *The Hidden Figure: Domestic Violence in North London*, London: London Borough of Islington.

NADEL, J. (1993) *Sara Thornton: The Story of a Woman Who Killed*, London: Gollancz.

PAGLIA, C. (1993) *Sex, Art and American Culture*, London: Viking.

RADFORD, J. and KELLY, L. (1991) 'Change the Law (2)', *Trouble and Strife*, **22**, pp. 12–14.

ROIPHE, K. (1994) *The Morning After: Sex, Fear and Feminism*, London: Hamish Hamilton.

WALKER, L. (1984) *The Battered Woman Syndrome*, New York: Springer.

WOLF, N. (1993) *Fire with Fire: The New Female Power and How It Will Change the 21st Century*, London: Chatto and Windus.

Part III
Black and Asian Women's Activism

also see p 155.

Chapter 6

The Struggles Continue — An Interview[1] with Hannana Siddiqui of Southall Black Sisters

Gabriele Griffin

The Issue of Domestic Violence

Founded in 1979, Southall Black Sisters is one of the best known Black women's campaigning, advice and support organizations in Britain.[2] Always active beyond the locality of Southall,[3] it came to national prominence in the early 1990s when it campaigned for the release of Kiranjit Ahluwalia.[4]

> We are a local organization whose work has taken on national significance. We receive requests for help from all over the country and what we have to say is relevant to women, particularly for Asian women, throughout the country.[5] *— w'ton - ask Joya*

SBS embodies feminist activism in its work on domestic violence, especially in Asian communities. In 1994, Siddiqui maintained that:

> Domestic violence is still high on the agenda. Over the last year we've seen two Asian women kill themselves, and another Asian woman was murdered by her husband in the local area. It reminded us that there is still a long way to go.
>
> There has been the emergence of some shifts in attitude and practices around domestic violence in British society generally. The cases of Kiranjit Ahluwalia and Sara Thornton highlighted that the public is increasingly becoming aware of domestic violence as indicated by the amount of support from all quarters which was immense. For many years we have been campaigning to reform the law on provocation and self defence. The aim of the campaign has been to ensure that these defences take into account the experiences of women. We now work very closely with groups like the Women's Institute and the Townswomen's Guild as well as Justice for Women to reform the law on provocation.[6]
>
> What we have also noticed is that there were some shifts in attitude

within the Asian community itself. The very people who tried to close us down in the 1980s because of our stance on violence against women are now at least paying lip service to the question of domestic violence, even if they are not doing much about it.[7] But that change is hard to measure. It is not uniform, it does not exist in every area of the country, it is not even uniform within Southall. However, unlike the early 1980s when we did not get support from members of the community, particularly men, we have received more support from some sections of the community, including some men, in the Kiranjit Ahluwalia campaign.

SBS's efforts to raise the issues of domestic violence and other issues relevant to women's rights are now being hampered by the growth of fundamentalism, which has been on the rise in all religions and which has shaped much of the 1990s.[8] Religious fundamentalism inevitably affects women adversely.

The rise of religious fundamentalism is one of the greatest problems we are facing, internationally, in all religions. At the same time we have witnessed the rise of conservative and patriarchal forces. Women have faced the brunt of all the attacks by these forces because they demand a return to the traditional family and traditional family values. In Britain we've got the 'moral majority' or sections of the Christian majority talking about family values and 'back to basics'. The way Christianity has been imposed in schools and how the state actually privileges Christianity speaks volumes. Within the minority communities, the Rushdie affair was a symbol and a catalyst for change, of changing identities, moving from ethnic or racial identities to religious identities which are being imposed either from within the communities or from outside.[9]

Increasingly, religious identities are being treated as racial identities. The need for certainty and for a positive identity to combat racism and discrimination has led the young, and particularly young men, to take on the new identities associated with fundamentalism.[10] This has been fully exploited by the media. Not whole communities are fundamentalist or conservative.

But the rise of fundamentalism and conservatism is certainly a trend we have noticed. Women are at the receiving end again; the rights we have gained over the last decade or so for Asian women are now under threat and we are forced into a position of having to defend them. For example, many institutions such as co-educational schools that may protect women's rights are now under attack. The demand to set up separate religious schools is mainly made in relation to young women.

This has not just come from Muslims but from other religious groups, too.[11] In Southall we have had to fight an attack from Sikh religious leaders with very conservative ideas about women who attempted to opt two local high schools out of the state system and use that route to set up separate religious schools. They hadn't been able to get funding from the state in the way that other state-funded religious schools such as Christian ones or Jewish schools had. We oppose state funding of all religious schools; funding for these schools should be withdrawn. We hold that a separation between church and state is essential. A secular state is absolutely necessary to prevent the privileging of one religion above another. It guarantees a personal right to worship without imposing any particular religion. The idea behind single-sex schools is not to improve women's educational opportunities through education; it's about cutting them off from other influences and possibilities available in coeducational schools. A lot of these women are strictly controlled within the home; the idea is that they need to be controlled in other forums where they mix with others.

Women may be encouraged to go into higher education but that has a specific motive — it's not about women's emancipation. One of the developments relating to women has been the education of girls increasingly being regarded as part of the dowry package.[12] An education makes women potential earners and an extra source of income within the matrimonial household.

The framework is still that of being confined within the traditional family, even though the woman may be educated. She will still be expected to marry, maybe at an older age, but is often put under pressure to have an arranged marriage or a form of arranged marriage. Although there is more freedom around arranged marriages now, the limits and boundaries are still defined by the girls' parents, their families and the communities in which they live.

An increasing number of Asian women approach SBS for help, particularly if they are from Southall itself.

We have a very high rate of Asian women from the local area coming to see us. By reputation we are known as an organization that will provide alternatives for women in the community so many women come to us because such alternatives are not available elsewhere within the community. Instead, community leaders often pressure and persuade women to reconcile themselves with their partners and families, and thereby return to what may well be an abusive relationship. But if they need to get into a refuge they have to go out of the area because it is very easy for them to be discovered if they are still in Southall. We have very good links with Women's Aid refuges, women's centres and particularly Asian women's resource centres, hostels or refuges. And we help women to get into the accommodation and support them through that.

We do a lot of local work but we also have many requests for help from [women] throughout the country because we are known nationally. People often know us better than they know what's available locally. The only thing that we can do if we get asked for advice and information is to give over-the-telephone advice and refer them to a local agency if there is one.

The problem half the time though is that there is no appropriate agency. The general lack of resources makes it very difficult. Sometimes you ring up a refuge and hope that they will do a bit of outreach work even if it's not a specialist refuge. Or you ring a law centre or an advice centre with a good reputation.

The lack of services available to Asian women has caused many to attempt suicide when they find themselves confronted with unbearable situations at home.

There is a high rate of suicide among Asian women, one of the highest rates in the country. Many of the women who come to us have attempted suicide. We find that Asian women don't attempt suicide where there is a history of psychiatric disorder, unlike women in the majority community where women may attempt to kill themselves in the context of such a history. A lot of people would point to the fact that Asian women's social circumstances are such that they lead to the pressures that create depression and suicide.

We would argue that it is a combination of factors which affect Asian women's mental health. They include problems in the community by which particularly young women are hard hit. The suicide rate among young Asian women between 16 and 24 years of age is three times the national average, that of Asian women aged 25–34 years twice as high as the national average. The pressures to have arranged marriages and then trying to survive within these marriages at the early stages are major contributory factors. Many people think that is the only cause of their mental health problems. I think it's more than that. I think it's lack of services and lack of resources. It is also racism and the racial discrimination they face from service providers and society generally. A lot of women are frightened to leave their communities, not only because they will be rejected by them but also because they have to face racial hostility and isolation.

The immigration law in this country can prevent women from leaving violent partners as they may face deportation. These laws don't even allow them to make a claim on the welfare state to survive. I know women who were facing deportation who tried to kill themselves because of all these pressures. That is a form of institutionalized racism.

Then there are all the problems around multi-cultural policies where there is a refusal to intervene and help. These are two sides of one coin: there are problems they face within the family and their low status within it, often reinforced by cultural and religious rules which keep them in a position of subordination, and the failure of service providers and society to offer assistance. This leads young Asian women to think that there is no other way out but to kill themselves.

A lot of women end up going to medical services when they are in a crisis. You often find that services respond inappropriately. Half the time they don't have adequate facilities. For instance, they don't have language facilities, and may depend on the husband or his family to do the interpretation. Not only that, they take on board the interpretation of the woman's problems which is being provided by the husband and his or her family, and link these up with their own stereotypes about Asian women, thus giving them inappropriate services. For example, a 'disobedient' Asian woman may be classified as mentally ill because it is assumed that Asian women are passive and should submit to the demands made by their husbands and families as dictated by their religion and culture.

The response Asian women in crisis often get is medicalization in the form of anti-depressants or hospitalization. But they don't get other kinds of services such as psychotherapy or social work intervention. Their social circumstances are not recognized as a problem. You find that women get inappropriate information when there is intervention, and they don't necessarily get channelled into the right direction so they end up becoming a patient somewhere. This carries consequences with it for Asian women because of the stigma attached to the breakdown of mental health. Husbands may use the issue of mental health in a custody case and say the woman is not a fit mother, attempting to get her hospitalized and using the psychiatric services to back their claims that she is not a fit mother. We have had women like that where it is quite clear that they are not mentally ill but that they have been pigeon-holed as such by their families and professionals alike.

Some women do have mental health problems, and then we work very closely with mental health professionals to get some help. That doesn't always mean psychiatric help. Sometimes there may be a need for that but then there's psychotherapy, for example. However, there are very few such services available to Asian women because many do not have the language facilities or an appropriate attitude which will enable them to meet the specific needs of Black or Asian women. These are very hard to get and there are very few resources. Sometimes women may have to be prepared to travel a very long way to get that help.

Multiculturalism

The treatment which Asian women receive is frequently informed by an ideology of multi-culturalism, that underlies services provision in Britain, and with which SBS has to deal in their daily work.[13]

We have to grapple with the whole question of cultural relativism and multi-culturalism because of the problem of how communities are homogenized through it. Community leaders, who are the most powerful and who are often regarded as representing the interests of the whole community, become the mediators and make demands on outside society and on the state.[14] The result can be that those outside these communities feel that they can't interfere, that they have to tolerate other cultures and that to interfere might even be racist. This view does not recognize power divisions within the community, and that what the community leaders want is not necessarily what the whole community wants.

We have to battle to get women's voices heard. Our wishes, our demands and our interests are not represented by community leaders who tend to be the most conservative, patriarchal and religious forces in the community. Therefore, we demand something different; we do want intervention but it has to be sensitive. There is a need to intervene if there's abuse, if there is violence, if people are being oppressed by cultural practices. These have to be recognized as a form of abuse.

Take arranged marriages: it's very hard to have this practice, when it is forced, recognized as a form of abuse because people with liberal minds think that it is part of certain communities' cultural practices and it therefore cannot be criticized, or that it would be racist to do so. Or they assume that there are certain internal mechanisms in the communities to resolve problems such as the extended family which is assumed functions as a naturally supportive structure. But this assumes that the experience of the family is the same for everyone within it. The extended family can in fact exercise greater pressures on women because they have an even greater number of individuals requiring the women to conform. You find that social workers, professionals and policy makers basically just don't want to intervene in certain areas which they think are too tricky: either they may get accused of racism or they may get accused of being intolerant. Therefore, women's rights are neglected and Asian women don't get the help and advice and the services that they need which are available to women in the majority community.

Resistance

We're campaigning around reforming the immigration laws because they can work against black people in general, but — linking it with our work — they can trap women in violent relationships. For example, we've been campaigning for change of the one-year rule for quite a while but in 1995 we want to mount a nationally coordinated campaign.[15] Within that campaign we want to fight for gender-related persecution to be recognized in this country, which it is not at the moment. We need to make links with women who are sent back to their country of origin and face persecution there because of their gender, because they are divorced or separated women, for example. We want to develop that area of our work.

There are other trends that are going on. The rise of religious fundamentalism and the growth of patriarchal forces is connected with the development of religious and conservative leaders taking over women's institutions like those which have protected women's rights such as refuges for women, centres and helplines. Alternatively they attack women's institutions through, for example, the growth of organized networks or gangs of Asian men, particularly in the North and in the Midlands who hunt down women who have tried to escape.

Young women in particular are seen as in need of control as regards their sexuality and their independence. This is an urgent task for a lot of communities who think their young women are being corrupted by western influences and they are losing control over young women who represent the future of the communities.[16] Therefore the rights of young women in particular have come under attack. So you witness the development of organized gangs of men who track down young women, intimidate them and force them to go back.

I think there are international links and developments around the rise of fundamentalism in other countries which have an impact in this country. In 1989 we helped to found Women Against Fundamentalism which comprises of women from many religious and racial backgrounds. We are also part of a group called the Alliance Against Communalism and for Democracy in South Asia. This is a collection of individuals and organizations who are anti-racist and anti-communalist. The threat of communalism[17] and fundamentalism, is not just a threat against women, but also a threat against civil liberties and human rights, people's right to free speech, etc. We think that fundamentalism is a very reactionary movement, regardless of which religion it comes from. We therefore want to be able to give support to people who are struggling against it, here and abroad. For example, many Hindu fundamentalists in this country have been supporting the Hindu right in India. Following the destruction of the mosque in Ayodhya, many temples in this country were encouraging their congregations to sanctify bricks and send them to India to build a Hindu temple on the site of the mosque.[18] This development also contributed to communal tensions in this country.

Campaigning for Change

SBS refuse the idea that struggles for women are separate from other struggles against oppression.

It is our view that you have to be able to fight reactionary and chauvinistic movements. It's about human rights; it's not just about gender. You need to struggle on many fronts at the same time. You have to fight for civil liberties, you have to fight for anti-racism, you have to fight in relation to class issues and sexuality and so forth, if you are going to fight for the rights of all rather than for the rights of the few.

We are criticized by elements within the left and the anti-racist movement who say to us, 'You shouldn't be washing your dirty linen in public. You shouldn't be talking about problems in the community.' For example, we [were] criticized by some anti-racists for the way we supported Rushdie (as Women Against Fundamentalism) by counterpicketting the anti-Rushdie demonstrations which were held in central London in May 1989. Their argument is basically that we have to live as a minority in this country and if we keep talking about the issue of fundamentalism, we fuel a racist backlash. They argue that our central and most important struggle is the anti-racist struggle.

In our view, however, you have to take on many struggles at the same time if you want to create a progressive movement which is not about the rights of the few but the rights of all oppressed groups. For us it actually enriches any struggle, the women's struggle, the anti-racist struggle, if you take on board the struggles of others and support them as well and make alliances. You learn a lot from each other. For us that's creating a progressive movement which is not about compartmentalizing and saying, 'we fight for the rights of the few now and then later we'll fight for you'. The dangers of not acting like that you see all over the world where people are fighting for one thing and their agenda doesn't include other issues and other oppressions which can make them quite a reactionary force.

Campaigning and coalition-building for the purposes of achieving change rather than just providing a service are central to SBS's work in the 1990s.

We set out as a campaigning group and one of the things we tried not to lose sight of when we [received] funding was campaigning and the need for change. You can help countless individual women but you are not necessarily going to achieve change on a wider scale unless you campaign. You need to use the knowledge that you have gained for that purpose. That is something we have refused to abandon even though there have been disputes within the organization around the issue which led to a split in 1986.[19] Some members of the group wanted to hold on to that principle of campaign work whilst others did not. Amazingly now, we've got all sorts of people, including from the establishment, wanting information from us and wanting to consult with us — something we never expected. We can always utilize the information we have in ways that we think will work in the interests of the women. We are often consulted about how to set up Asian women's refuges, for example. We feel it is quite important to make those interventions because what is the point of having all that expertise if it is not utilized, if it does not create wider change. Therefore we do policy work, and we do campaigning.

Getting funding has had significant impacts on how political organizations, including women's organizations, operate; in SBS's view it has sometimes acted to draw the political tooth of those groups.

I think what has happened, not just with women's organizations but with many other groups such as anti-racist groups, is that funding has destroyed the perspective developed by grassroots organizations that started off with campaigning around a radical agenda. These groups have found that their radical agendas have become increasingly eroded by professionalization, by funding. What we see now is people working around issues as if it were a job, not necessarily as a personal commitment. It's become a nine-to-five job, and if they get paid enough they'll do it, otherwise they won't. You've got consultants now, Black consultants, women's consultants, and commercial organizations taking up issues. There is a whole growth industry around all of this.

You could, of course, argue that in so far as all these diverse people have taken up issues, you have been successful somewhere along the line in raising public awareness. But I think one of the things we have to realize is that the agendas should still be set by the grassroots organizations who know what they are talking about and who have the commitment to those issues. Unfortunately you find that often this is not the case, with people who purport to represent particular issues taking over.

Having said that, some activities that we have seen since the Kiranjit Ahluwalia campaign, particularly among Black and Asian groups, have been very powerful. There was, for example, just after Kiranjit Ahluwalia's release, a demonstration organized by Turkish women's groups in North London where a few women had been killed by their partners. It was a demonstration right through the heart of the Turkish community and it was very good because it reminded us of Krishna Sharma's death when we demonstrated through Southall, raising domestic violence as an issue within the community. Then there was a large demonstration in Huddersfield against 'bounty hunters' and gangs of men trying to hunt down Asian women who've escaped from home. Asian women came from all over the country to participate.

We have seen a lot of developments over the years which have really politicized the women at the SBS Centre and which have reinforced their drive to keep such a place in the heart of Southall. In the 1980s, when there was an attempt to close us down by the Indian Workers' Association, a male-dominated organization in Southall, the women at the centre saved it. They lobbied, campaigned, wrote letters. With Kiranjit Ahluwalia, it was amazing how many women from the community were active. They came consistently to demonstrations and to the Centre to meetings to help out. In the end they felt that her victory was also their victory.

That kind of politicization does not happen in many other groups. A lot of them are service-based. They give advice and provide a service but that's it. There isn't an attempt to bring women together, or to be active in politics. You have to make that effort, you have to organize transport and creches, you have to think of ways of making it possible for women to come in and participate and support campaigns.

You're looking to get women to become politically active in the process, write letters, speak at public meetings and to the press. A lot of women's groups have a real fear of the press and, ok, you can't control it but you can use the media for your purposes. It means extra work, it's not nine-to-five, it's evening and weekend work. The point is that many women are not prepared to do it. Another point is that feminism is dominated by white women who are not interested in Black women's issues. At the same time the anti-racist movement is not interested in gender and therefore does not address Black women's needs. So Black women become invisible within both the anti-racist and the women's movements. This obviously means that Black women have to organize themselves and make the demands appropriate to their situation.

There are problems in all of these movements and it is a question of influence. That's one of the pressures on SBS. We try to influence all these movements so we have to go to anti-racist demonstrations and so on. In contrast, a lot of other groups tend to pigeon-hole themselves and say they only participate in campaigns around a single issue. A lot of our work at the moment is about human rights; we are preparing for the UN conference on Human Rights in Beijing in 1995. At the same time there are public hearings in New York on the government's human rights' records. It wouldn't even occur to a lot of women's groups to use the forum on human rights in New York as well as the women's conference in Beijing, but it's just as legitimate a context in which to press for women's rights as anywhere else.

We have problems around segregation and separatism which create a very narrow-minded perspective about the world. That's not very productive. Generally, very few women's or Black women's groups try to make wider connections or have a wider analysis of women's situation. Some have no analysis at all, they're just busy providing services. But really, what's the point? You should be lobbying for statutory services to increase. But half the time, these groups don't do that. They just fill the gap or take over the services of the statutory sector. So you need to be very careful about what you are aiming to do. You're providing a service but that's not the limit of your aims and objectives. You can use the knowledge gained from casework to create wider change. An organization like SBS is in the best position to do so because we're small, we're grassroots, we pick up trends and respond to them much quicker than a large bureaucracy can. That's part of the effectiveness of the voluntary sector but then you shouldn't stifle it by becoming merely a service provider.

Notes

1 Conducted on 5 December 1994 at SBS's Centre.
2 For further details, see Gita Sahgal's 'Secular Spaces', especially pp. 175–8.
3 For a summary of SBS's history, see *Against the Grain* (Patel, 1990: 7).
4 See SBS's (1992/3b) 'Kiranjit Ahluwalia Wins Freedom' for further details.
5 All sections displayed in this chapter are from the interview with Hannana Siddiqui.
6 See SBS (1993), *Domestic Violence and Asian Women*, section 5.

7   See Gita Sahgal's 'Secular Spaces', p. 174, for some details.
8   For a brief historical exposition of the subject, see Sahgal and Yuval-Davis (1992), pp. 1–25.
9   When Salman Rushdie's book *The Satanic Verses* was declared blasphemous and a *fatwah* pronounced against its author, Women Against Fundamentalism, formed in 1989 (and which includes members of SBS), came out in support of Rushdie. They recognized the politics underlying the campaign against Rushdie as reinforcing the patriarchal domination within fundamentalist communities, against which WAF and SBS had been fighting on behalf of women (see Sahgal and Yuval-Davis, 1992).
10 For a discussion of the rise of gangs of male youths in Southall and its impact on women see Pragna Patel (1990), 'Southall Boys'.
11 For a discussion of the effects of segregated schooling on Muslim girls' education see Saeeda Khanum (1992), 'Education and the Muslim Girl'.
12 For a discussion about the anti-dowry campaign in Southall, see Hannana Siddiqui (1990), 'BMWs and Samosas at the Seaside'.
13 See Anthias and Yuval-Davis (1992), pp. 157–98, for an extended discussion of this issue.
14 See G. Sahgal's (1990) 'Fundamentalism and the Multi-Culturalist Fallacy' for an extended discussion of this issue.
15 See SBS's (1993) *Domestic Violence and Asian Women*, pp. 28–9, for further details.
16 See SBS's (1990) *Against the Grain*, p. 62.
17 See also Clara Connelly (1991), 'Communalism: Obstacle to Social Change'.
18 See G. Sahgal (1992), 'Secular Spaces', especially pp. 171–2, for further details.
19 See 'Mandana Hendessi in Conversation', pp. 11–12, for further details.

References

AFSHAR, H. (1994) 'Muslim Women in West Yorkshire', in AFSHAR, H. and MAYNARD, M. (Eds) *The Dynamics of Race and Gender*, London: Taylor & Francis, pp. 127–47.

ANTHIAS, F. and YUVAL-DAVIS, N. (1992) *Racialized Boundaries*, London: Routledge.

CONNELLY, C. (1991) 'Communalism: Obstacle to Social Change', *Women: A Cultural Review*, **Winter**, pp. 214–19.

KHANUM, S. (1992) 'Education and the Muslim Girl', in SAHGAL, G. and YUVAL-DAVIS, N. (Eds) *Refusing Holy Orders*, London: Virago, pp. 124–40.

'Mandana Hendessi in Conversation', in SAHGAL, G. and YUVAL-DAVIS, N. (Eds) *Refusing Holy Orders*, London: Virago, pp. 10–12.

PATEL, P. (1990) 'Southall Boys', in SBS (Eds) *Against The Grain*, Southall: SBS, pp. 43–54.

SAHGAL, G. (1990) 'Fundamentalism and the Multi-Culturalist Fallacy', in SBS (Eds) *Against The Grain*, Southall: SBS, pp. 16–24.

SAHGAL, G. (1992) 'Secular Spaces: The Experience of Asian Women Organising', in SAHGAL, G. and YUVAL-DAVIS, N. (Eds) *Refusing Holy Orders*, London: Virago, pp. 163–97.

SAHGAL, G. and YUVAL-DAVIS, N. (Eds) (1992) *Refusing Holy Orders*, London: Virago.

SIDDIQUI, H. (1990) 'BMWs and Samosas at the Seaside', in SBS (Eds) *Against The Grain*, Southall: SBS, pp. 37–42.

SOUTHALL BLACK SISTERS (1990) *Against the Grain: A Celebration of Survival and Struggle*, Southall: SBS.

SOUTHALL BLACK SISTERS (1993) *Domestic Violence and Asian Women*, Southall: SBS.

SOUTHALL BLACK SISTERS (1992/3a) 'Rising to the Challenge.' Annual Report 1992/3, Southall: SBS.

SOUTHALL BLACK SISTERS (1992/3b) 'Kiranjit Ahluwalia Wins Freedom', *Women Against Fundamentalism*, **4**, Winter.

Chapter 7

Harnessing Shakti: The Work of the Bengali Women's Support Group

Debjani Chatterjee

We [women] are half of society. If we remain fallen, how will society rise? How far can a person limp, if one leg is kept shackled? The interests of men and our interests are not different, they are the same. Our aims and goals are the same ones as those of men ... We were not created in order to lead passive doll-like lives, this much is certain.

(Chatterjee, 1993)

These words by Begum Rokeya Sakhawat Hussain continue to inspire generations of Bengali women on both sides of the political border that artificially separates Bangladesh and West Bengal in India, as well as the considerable number of Bengali diaspora in the UK and elsewhere in the world.[1] The quotation is taken from the Bengali Women's Support Group's bi-lingual poster: 'Two Great Women of Bengal'. The other great woman we sought to honour in the poster is the poet-politician, Sarojini Naidu.[2] As women achievers who championed women's right to education, Begum Rokeya and Sarojini Naidu led the struggle for women's emancipation and made it an essential part of the movement for India's independence from British rule. Such women have been adopted as role models by the Bengali Women's Support Group.

This group was started in 1985 and the first meeting in Sheffield attracted only four women. Today, we are sixty strong. In our first few years we would meet in each other's homes and, one lunchtime a month, in the basement of a Sheffield voluntary centre catering for mothers and children. For the use of the basement we paid a nominal rent of £5 per year! As word spread about our Group, our numbers increased and it became obvious that not only were we breaking fire regulations, but also we were too many to fit into the room. In 1988, we negotiated the use of 'the Space Centre' above Park Library in Sheffield. In the last few years the Bengali Women's Support Group has won national awards for its work and in 1995 we succeeded in attracting national funding for future projects.

Under a 'Declaration of Intent', our Group's Constitution states that we are 'an anti-sexist, anti-racist, non-party political support group who include South

Yorkshire-wide isolated women and their children, and provide relevant information to all Bengali women and their children in the South Yorkshire area, according to their needs and interests' (Bengali Women's Support Group, 1985: 1). While membership is open to 'any woman who speaks Bengali and shares the aims and objectives' (Bengali Women's Support Group, 1985: 1) of the Group, the Constitution singles out 'isolated women and their children' for particular attention. This was because in 1985 when our Group was founded, we were painfully aware that there were many Bengali women who were suffering all the negative effects of isolation from society, women who were denied the companionship of their peers and compatriots, women who were effectively cut off from participation in the world and whose voices were silenced. Their isolation was physical, emotional, cultural and spiritual. To be isolated in such ways is to be marginalized and undermined. The effect is demoralizing and devastating. Unfortunately, there are many individuals as well as institutions and customs in a sexist and racist society that contribute to the isolation and marginalization of Asian women in Britain. A decade ago the sense of isolation among South Yorkshire's Bengali women was widespread. It affected educated as well as uneducated women, old as well as young women, and women from rural as well as urban backgrounds. There were no Bengali women community workers, youth workers, or social workers around. But we knew that the collective strength of even a small group of us could break the pattern of isolation, act as a pressure group to demand change and begin to make a difference. While great progress has been made within the Group, we know that there are still many more women within the wider Bengali community who are prevented from joining us by chauvinistic elements within our own community who view progressive organizations such as ours as a threat.

The reason for our poster, 'Two Great Women of Bengal', lies at the very heart of the philosophy driving the Bengali Women's Support Group. The poster was designed in 1993 to celebrate International Women's Day, a very important event in our organization's calendar. International Women's Day 1992 had involved drama workshops and we had all enjoyed ourselves immensely, engaging in improvisations and dancing. But when we had a group discussion as to the best way in which we wished to mark the event in the following year, it emerged that we wanted to do something that would have value beyond the month of March and something that would also impinge on the lives of others. A bilingual educational poster was considered a very modest but valuable contribution to redressing the enormous gap that exists in the 'multi-cultural' school curriculum. It causes us both sorrow and anger that South Yorkshire schools show little or no respect for our mother tongue, Bengali, though it is the region's third language; and neither do they offer children role models among Asian women, whether historical or living.

We discussed the probability that no non-Bengali child would be able to name any great Bengalese. We had to reluctantly admit that even if a Bengali schoolchild in South Yorkshire was asked the same question, he or she would probably name Tagore, Nazrul and possibly Sheikh Mujib. Even Bengali girls would not think of naming women and, if specifically asked to name great Bengali women, would struggle to identify any. Our own Bengali communities need their consciousness raising as much as the majority community.

Our poster, when printed, was widely distributed locally among sympathetic teachers, youth leaders, community workers and, of course, members of our Group. It celebrates two Bengali women leaders who were contemporaries and respected each other as sisters in a common struggle, and yet who hailed from different faith backgrounds, Hindu and Muslim, and had very different experiences of education. Sarojini Naidu was encouraged by her academic father to pursue a secular and westernized higher education in India and England. In contrast, Begum Rokeya was denied access to education by her Maulvi father and had to study in secret. Their different backgrounds and experience reflect the diversity in faith, class and education among our own Group members, who hail from Bangladesh and India or are our second generation here and were born in South Yorkshire.

Producing the poster was only one of many different projects in which our Group has engaged. But the concern with children's education recurs time after time. For instance, our Group's first publication, a bilingual anthology called *Barbed Lines*, has a poem about the legendary Sufi saint, Hazrat Shah Jalal, and the editorial note to the piece quotes Komola Bibi's motive in writing this poem as being both to celebrate and 'to keep alive the memory of this great hero for in Britain our children do not even hear his name in the schools and colleges' (Chatterjee and Islam, 1990: 77). In the same anthology again, Rehana Chaudhury urges:

> O mothers of the world, listen.
> Listen with great care:
> now the time has come
> to make men of your
> darling sons
> . . .
> Make him [your son] realise
> he is born of woman,
> teach him respect for women.
> Now the time has come.
> . . .
> I do not want to know
> whether he will become —
> a doctor, a clerk, an engineer
> . . .
> when he grows up.
> I only want to know
> whether he will be a man
> of truth and justice,
> will he honour
> the one who bore him in her womb?

(Chatterjee and Islam, 1990: 105–7)

In 'Awake, Mother, Awake' Monuara Badsha passionately argues that daughters must be given the same opportunities and encouragement as sons: 'In the same way and to the same measure try your best to guide your young daughter to the ideal path. Do not deprive her of the light of knowledge, one day you will see that young girl shine in the world like a bright star' (Chatterjee and Islam, 1990: 21).

A Bengali proverb says: 'An educated woman is sure to become a widow and then she behaves like an unmanageable ox' (Schipper, 1985: 122). Such misogynist views have to be fought against and women's education is a very serious concern for our Group. Education has clearly been identified as the key to financial independence and social emancipation. Our Group, therefore, offers training opportunities from time to time, as well as every encouragement to acquire literacy and other useful skills, the emphasis being on a self-help approach. Residential training weekends, assertiveness training, confidence building sessions and many educational and self-development projects, such as healthy cooking demonstrations, trips to other cities, a wall-hanging project and a bilingual book project, have been organized.

The Bilingual Book Project, with its series of creative writing workshops held in libraries and community centres in Sheffield, Rotherham and Doncaster, has been our Group's most ambitious undertaking. Like Begum Rokeya, Sarojini Naidu, Binodini Dasi,[3] Begum Sufia Kamal,[4] and many other strong women from India, Bangladesh and other countries, we have come to understand that our writing is a way of effecting the changes that we need in society, and that writing is one of the best ways of recording our struggles. It is up to us to take control of documenting our own experiences. In 'Words are Weapons', another Asian sister, Pratibha Parmar rightly states that writing is a way of becoming visible, and that 'we must speak through whatever means are available to us, or we will be condemned to silence, misrepresentation and invisibility' (Chester and Nielsen, 1987: 153).

This need has been at least one important motive behind all our Group's anthologies. 'We all have the ability to create some sense of our lives on paper' (Chatterjee and Islam, 1990: 16), says a contributor to our first anthology, *Barbed Lines*. In our introduction to the Group's second anthology, my co-editors and I state: '*Sweet and Sour* is the fruit of our solidarity. It is our sisterhood which we cherish and find empowering'. (Chatterjee *et al.*, 1993: 11) It is also the anthologies which have won our Group a national and even international reputation, particularly after *Barbed Lines* was awarded the Arts Council's first Raymond Williams Community Publishing Prize in 1990.

Bengali Women's Support Group's efforts at promoting adult education too were recognized in May 1994 when our Group was declared an Outstanding National Adult Education Group Award Winner. A long-time Group member, Suraton Bibi, was featured as an example of an adult education achiever and role model. In her profile of Suraton, Frances Homewood wrote:

> At the age of 9 Suraton Bibi was taken away from school in Bangladesh by her uncle. She was very upset because she wanted to learn. If she had been a boy she would have had a better chance of education.
>
> Several years later Suraton came to England to join her husband who worked in the steel industry. She longed to learn English but was

discouraged by her husband. She helped him to run their restaurant business catering for one hundred and fifty customers at a time. After fifteen years in the country she finally managed to attend English classes.... [when] she made the courageous decision to leave [her husband] ...

During this traumatic time she received invaluable help and support from the other women in the group. Having somewhere to go to find company and attend classes restored her confidence.

(Homewood, 1994: 3–4)

The profile goes on to describe the various educational activities of the Bengali Women's Support Group in which Suraton engaged: creative writing workshops in which she began to write about her childhood in Bangladesh and, after separating from her husband, her life as a single mother in Britain; storytelling workshops in which she 'realised the importance of re-telling her stories of home to her children' (Homewood, 1994: 4); sewing and banner-making classes in which she designed an International Women's Day banner for the Group; and cookery classes after which she 'set up her own catering business providing Bengali food at the group's functions and other events' (Homewood, 1994: 4). At the age of 42, Suraton is now Vice-Chair of the Bengali Women's Support Group and has fulfilled her early ambitions and more. She is still learning and now encourages other women to learn. Her Bengali prose and poetry have been published in the Group's anthologies and her catering helps to support her and her family, including her eldest son who is studying medicine at the University of London.

In 'A Recipe for Survival' (Chatterjee *et al.*, 1993: 27–37), Safuran Ara describes the desperate plight of a Bengali mother of eight children who is trapped in a marriage with a violent husband. Although the social pressures that keep her tied to her husband can be countered to some extent by the friendship and solidarity offered by members of the Bengali Women's Support Group, the woman recognizes that she is also economically tied by her lack of education and her inadequate English. For many years she puts up with her husband's abuse and spending of the child benefit money on gambling and prostitutes. Nor can she contradict him when he tells the hospital that her physical injuries are the result of slipping and falling down the stairs.

An anonymous contributor to our Group's first anthology similarly describes her total helplessness to take control of her own life when she finds herself, newly widowed, in a foreign country and cheated of her property and rights by grown-up stepsons, who throw her out of the house. 'I could not speak any English and I realised how completely helpless one is if one does not know the language' (Chatterjee and Islam, 1990: 102). Ignorant of how to use a coin-operated telephone, but desperately needing to call for help, she finds herself walking to a phone booth and staring at the telephone for a long time before making many attempts to dial the number of a Bengali acquaintance.

Apart from running numerous projects, our Group holds cultural functions which usually coincide with Bengali festive and commemorative occasions such as Bengali New Year and Bengali Language Movement Day. These are important in affirming our cultural identity as Bengalees and, because the Language Movement carried the main thrust of the Bangladeshi freedom struggle, we are sensitized somewhat to the politics of culture and language.

While, as a group of Bengali women, we adopt a deliberate stance in the matter of Bengali cultural activism, can we also call ourselves a 'feminist' group? I recognize that not everyone would agree with me in saying 'yes' — not at this point in our history, even though many of our activities and achievements can certainly be described as feminist. And are our individual members 'feminists'? Our Chair and some members, including myself, would call ourselves feminists, but there are also others who would not accept such a label, associating it too closely with western, and perhaps abrasive, notions of feminism. Being a feminist is also, in a sense, about asserting one's individuality. But for many of us (Bengali women), the family and the community are more important than the self. Many of us would rather not make artificial choices between the individual and the group, between femininity and feminism, and there is a perception in some quarters that western feminism has required that such choices be made.

Our Group may not be consciously 'feminist' at all times, but it does give ample scope for feminist expression. Within our sisterhood, there is room for many different points of view and a variety of approaches. Our arms are wide. We can, on the one hand, appreciate the traditional sentiments expressed so eloquently in 'We Are the Women of Bengal':

> We are like the glory
> and the sacrifice of this earth.
> . . . .
> though our hearts break
> we keep silence,
> lest anyone is hurt.
> Our goodnatured calm endures
> annihilation — again and again.
>
> (Chatterjee and Islam, 1990: 17)

Yet we can also identify with the assertive words of 'A Bengali Woman in Britain':

> A Bengali woman in Britain,
> yearnings unfulfilled, her head unbowed,
> no beggar, she rolls in the dust behind no one.
> . . . .
> A Bengali woman in Britain
> arose one dawn and flew, wings untamed but together.
> She is not insignificant, do not look on her with pity;
> she is no angel . . .
> No elusive goddess, she wants no decorative offerings.
>
> (Ara and Mondal, 1994: 53)[5]

The Yorkshire Post appreciatively described the Group as 'creating a quiet revolution' from a small community room (Roberts, 1994). It is indeed a revolution being nurtured by a quietly subtle and Asian style of feminism, for our Group aims to advance the Bengali community in South Yorkshire: educationally, economically and politically. Underlying this aim is a belief that the key to community development lies in the empowerment and progress of women, and that even a few people, acting together, can change society for the better. In 'What Bengali Women's Support Group Means to Me' I have expressed the hope that

> In the course of time some of us will look beyond the little pond that is our group and take our rightful place in the mainstream of society. I look forward then to a new breed of community leaders who will bring a more caring, selfless and non-competitive outlook to community development.
>
> (Chatterjee and Islam, 1990: 124)

Frances Homewood describes the Group's 'support [for] each other in a common sisterhood' as being 'an unusually feminist stance for women from the Asian community' (Roberts, 1994). She mentions the prejudice that the Group had to face 'from within the Bengali community as well as outsiders' (Roberts, 1994).

I cannot agree that this is an unusually feminist stance for Asian women. What it does reflect is the fact that some of our white feminist sisters have bought the myth of the passive and submissive Asian female. But no contemporary observer can fail to have noticed that the 1990s have seen wide-ranging and often high profile feminist activism on the part of many Asian women's groups in the UK, ranging from the overtly political groups such as the Asian Women Against Fundamentalism and Southall Black Sisters, and literary and cultural groups such as the Asian Women Writers Collective and the Asian Women's Festival Committee. This activism itself has been steadily building up through the 1970s and 1980s.

Susan Hyatt, an American observer, has commented that 'a number of the most interesting minority organisations in Britain today are women's groups, like the Southall Black Sisters in London and the Bengali Women's Support Group in Sheffield ... These organisations have emerged as significant political players, engaging their members in direct action and highlighting how the cultural-relativist positions taken by a "liberal" state can collude with the oppression of women' (American Ethnological Society, 1994: 1107).

The 1990s are a decade of testing for Asian women's activism, as fundamentalist and chauvinist attitudes have hardened. Many Asian feminists also have to make a difficult choice: whether to pursue a purely secular women's movement, or to ground their struggle within the framework of religion, or whether to find the 'right' compromise between the two approaches. Issues of the rights of Asian gay women and of tribal and Dalit or untouchable women have also surfaced. But it continues to be the case that Asian women's strength is not about somehow surviving in a man's world, nor is it about achieving in spite of being women, rather it is now, and always has been, about having the courage to change the world.

The struggles of Asian women in low-paid ghetto jobs have made trade union history here and a number of leaders have emerged from unexpected quarters. The diminutive sari-clad figure of Jayaben Desai leading the striking workers at Grunwick was widely seen in newspapers and on television. She 'became a symbol of courage and determination for the struggle of Asian immigrants, not least for women, who came to see her as the potent figure of militant womanhood' (Chandan, 1982: 34). The defiance of Asian women who have turned against tyrant husbands has similarly made legal history. Tormented wife Kiranjit Ahluwalia became a focus for Asian women to rally around and support when she was seen to be unfairly punished by the criminal justice system for killing her husband. Asian women have spoken out in BBC documentaries against the mercenary abductors who bring back runaway young women to oppressive households. Protests have also been made against instances of exorcisms of so-called 'possessed' Asian women — often undertaken because the women concerned have been depressed, or disobedient, or otherwise not 'conformed'.

At the same time the activities of our sisters 'back home' inspire us too. The feminist activism among the Asian diaspora in Britain parallels the feminist activism of women in India, Pakistan and Bangladesh. The campaigning of women in Pakistan protesting against the notorious Hadood Ordinances,[6] the Law of Evidence[7] and the Shariat Bill;[8] the neighbourhood action of women in India challenging the evils of dowry taking and bride burning; and even the criminal defiance against society by Phoolan Devi, the Bandit Queen, have spoken to us (Alibhai-Brown, 1994) and fire our imaginations and our struggles here.

We can never forget where we came from and our *shonar Bangla* (golden Bengal) is an image that strongly grounds us. Fundraising for flood relief and other needs in our countries of origin naturally occupy us. Apart from street collections and sponsored cultural functions for the upliftment of rural women in Bengal, we engage in more modest activities too such as an annual donation of sarees and children's books for distribution in Bangladesh.

Bengali Women's Support Group tries deliberately to keep in touch with, and to support, the struggles of the women's movement in Bangladesh and India.[9] The issues that have been at the forefront for women in the sub-continent, issues such as the selling of women in prostitution, the low pay and poor conditions in traditionally women's industries, lack of education for girls, dowry deaths, female infanticide and abortions, are issues that have a ring of familiarity for Bengali women in Britain too. This familiarity is all the more sinister for the fact that while these issues are readily identified as 'third-world problems', their existence in Britain remains relatively hidden and denied. As Bengali women in Britain, we all too often remain part of the third world, though living in the first world.

Religious fundamentalism, perhaps the single most baleful phenomenon of our present decade, needs to be confronted and fought wherever possible. While it has swept across the sub-continent in a tidal wave, its currents running through Britain today are no less treacherous. The madness in India which led to the Babri Mosque in Ayodhya being destroyed, resulted also in many temples in Bangladesh and Pakistan being destroyed. We saw that the insanity was at our doorstep too as the Hindu temple in Sheffield suffered an arson attack. In 1993, when the courageous Bangladeshi feminist writer, Taslima Nasreen, exposed the shame of fundamentalism in her novel *Lajja*, she found her book banned, her life threatened and the politicians colluding with her oppressors. A prisoner in her own home in Dhaka, Taslima wrote to thank us for our petitions and solidarity. I know that the support of women abroad and of other Bengali women was very important to her. She wrote to me of the power of international opinion swaying government.

As Bengali women, we have always known that we can exert a *shakti*[10] power, through collective action which neither men (nor even gods!) can withstand. Bengali mythology has empowered womanhood as being the embodiment of Shakti. While Shakti is worshipped as a goddess by the Bengali Hindu, its symbolic power remains forceful for the Bengali Muslim too. Alongside our Eid and Christmas festivities, our Group also celebrates Durga Puja — the most important festival in the Bengali Hindu calendar and a potent reminder of the presence of shakti in our lives. Mother Durga herself, with her combination of grace and power, is an abiding symbol of Bengali feminism. Riding on a lion and slaying the buffalo-demon, Mahishasura, Durga inspires us to harness our own shakti and discover its unlimited potential. Unlike many feminist groups that steer clear of religion, the Bengali Women's Support Group has so far successfully embraced religious pluralism. We take a stand against fundamentalism, but religion in the widest sense remains important to most of our members, whether Muslim, Hindu or Christian.

In 1995, we celebrate our tenth anniversary and can look back with some pride. Many more of our daughters are now attending college and university, many women have acquired training and skills in different fields and several now have jobs and a growing independence. Our friendships have deepened and we have all learnt from each other. We have passed through some very difficult years and no doubt there will be more to come. Nevertheless, we entered the new Bengali century this year with a confident programme of cultural activities, and we also look forward to the next Gregorian century in five years' time with a quiet optimism. Our shakti, now harnessed, can only take us forward.

Notes

1 Begum Rokeya Sakhawat Hussain (1880–1932) was a writer and campaigner for women's education.
2 Sarojini Naidu (1879–1949) was a writer, politician and social reformer.
3 Binodini Dasi (1863–1941), once a prostitute, rose to become one of the earliest and most brilliant actresses of nineteenth-century Bengal. She helped to found the first Bengali actor-owned theatre and was a fearless writer. Her autobiographical writing is contained in *Amar Katha (My Story)* and *Amar Abhinetri Jiban (My Life as an Actress)*.
4 In *Barbed Lines* (1990), Safuran Ara has written: 'It was one of the proudest days of my life when, representing the Bengali Women's Support Group, I met the President of Bangladesh Mohilla Parishad, Begum Sufia Kamal, and, at a public rally in Dhaka, gave her a cheque from our South Yorkshire group along with our sisterly greetings. Writer, freedom fighter and social reformer, Begum Sufia Kamal has touched the lives of Bengali women everywhere' (p. 14).

5   I have freely translated the lines quoted here. The original poem is in Bengali.

6   The Hadood Ordinances were passed in 1979 as part of General Zia-ul Haq's Islamization campaign. Among other 'offences', adultery and fornication were now considered to be serious crimes against the State, punishable by the *hadd* punishment, i.e. public death by stoning. Where no confession could be obtained or the act of sexual penetration had not been witnessed by 'four adult, pious, and forthright males', the court would apply the lesser punishment of whipping and rigorous imprisonment if it was convinced of guilt.

7   The Law of Evidence, *Qanoon-e-Shahadat*, reduced a woman's worth by reducing the value of her testimony to half that of a man's. The Hadood Ordinances made a further erosion when they did away altogether with the testimony of women for the purposes of the *hadd* punishment.

8   The Shariat Bill was passed in 1991 and was mainly concerned with education. One of its effects is the segregation of education along gender lines, with colleges and universities for women encouraging 'domestic' as opposed to 'hard' sciences.

9   In 'Bengali Women's Support Group', Safuran Ara writes:

In our work of supporting Bengali women we have developed co-operative links with Bangladesh Mohilla Parishad. Our members consider that alongside the development of our local community, we must keep abreast of women's progress in our countries of origin and do our bit to contribute. This solidarity among women strengthens and enriches not only international sisterhood, but society as a whole.

(Chatterjee and Islam, 1994: 13–14)

See also 'What Bengali Women's Support Group Means to Me', Chatterjee and Islam, 1994: 116.
Networking contact with the Indian feminist publishers Kali for Women has resulted in plans for a joint postcard publication in 1995 to mark the tenth anniversary year for both Kali for Women and the Bengali Women's Support Group.

10   According to the *Devi Mahatmyam* or *Chandi*, one of the most sacred books for Hindu Bengalees, the gods, who were losing in battle with the demons, knew that their victory was assured if they pooled together all their strength. This collective energy manifested itself as Shakti, the Mother Goddess who has many names.

References

ALIBHAI-BROWN, YASMIN (1994) 'Dear Phoolan Devi', *The Independent*, 20 October.

AMERICAN ETHNOLOGICAL SOCIETY (Eds) (1994) *American Ethnologist*, **21**, 4, p. 1107.

ARA, SAFURAN and MONDAL, DOLLY, (Eds) (1994) *Kavitanjali*, Sheffield: Bengali Women's Support Group.

BENGALI WOMEN'S SUPPORT GROUP (1985) *Constitution*, Sheffield: Bengali Women's Support Group.

CHANDAN, AMARJIT (Ed.) (1982) 'A Woman's Way' *Shakti*, **1**, 2.

CHATTERJEE, DEBJANI (1993) *'Two Great Women of Bengal'*, poster, Sheffield: Bengali Women's Support Group.

CHATTERJEE, DEBJANI and ISLAM RASHIDA, (Eds) (1990) *Barbed Lines*, Sheffield: Bengali Women's Support Group.

CHATTERJEE, DEBJANI, CHAUDHURY, REHANA, GHOSH, KARABI and ISLAM, RASHIDA (Eds)

(1993) *Sweet and Sour*, Sheffield: Bengali Women's Support Group.

CHESTER, GAIL and NIELSEN, SIGRID (Eds) (1987) *In Other Words: Writing as a Femininst*, London: Hutchinson Education.

HOMEWOOD, FRANCES (1994) *From Margin to Mainstream: Profiles of Black Adult Learners in the Yorkshire Television Region*, Leeds: Yorkshire Television.

ROBERTS, ERIC (1994) 'The main thing I have learned is if you are determined enough, you will succeed', *Yorkshire Post*, 9 May.

SCHIPPER, MINEKE (Ed.) (1985) *Unheard Voices: Women and Literature in Africa, the Arab World, Asia, the Caribbean and Latin America*, London: Allison & Busby.

Chapter 8

Asian Women's Activism in Northamptonshire

Anjona Roy

In this chapter I discuss Asian women's activism in Northamptonshire, and have viewed it functioning specifically through a background environment of both fundamentalism and racism.

As always there are difficulties with defining what 'Asian', 'activism', 'racism', and 'fundamentalism' mean. The concept of the word Asian is a western construction, encompassing people born and brought up in Britain who originate, or whose ancestry originates, from South Asian countries either directly, or via Africa, or via the Caribbean. Indeed, the all-embracing term 'Asian' covers a wide range of interests and experiences by differing communities.

I take the word 'activism' to signify personal or collective mobilization for change. To some extent, Asian communities have reclaimed the term 'Asian' as a basis for uniting similar yet differing experiences to achieve change. However, real and distinct differences remain in the constructions of all those who collectively work under this 'umbrella'. The activism of those Asian women who are in positions of complete 'otherness' to their host community in *individually* confronting services, authorities and agencies on a day-to-day basis must not be devalued. For example, as an Asian woman who is employed to challenge and confront policy makers on their decisions abut social and health care provision, I am often put into a situation of overturning engendered and racist generalizations of 'what Asian women are meant to be like' simply by my positioning myself in this way, i.e. as an activist. Similarly, the actions of Asian women on a day-to-day basis, demanding equal and appropriate treatment and services and opportunities which their white counterparts so often take for granted, must also be termed activism. In the context of Asian women's activism, the adage feminists used during the 1970s and 1980s, 'the personal is political', holds true.

Different definitions of racism and fundamentalism have had diverse political impacts over the last 20 years. A popular definition of racism emerged from Judy Katz and other Race Awareness Training theorists during the 1970s and 1980s who described racism as being 'power plus prejudice'. This has been criticized by many Black writers. Thus A. Sivanandan states in 'Challenging racism':

It is the acting out of racial prejudice and not racial prejudice itself that matters. The acting out of prejudice is discrimination, and when it becomes institutionalised in the power structure of this society, then we are dealing not with attitude but with power. Racism is about power not prejudice.

(Sivanandan, 1990: 65)

Fundamentalism as a term straddles the vast expanse of all religions. But within the context of Northamptonshire I find that the term 'fundamentalism' is a tool used by white power bases and Asian community organizations to both control and persecute sections of society. Women Against Fundamentalism use a definition in which

... we [do] not [refer] to religious observance, which we see as a matter of individual choice, but rather to modern political movements which use religion as a basis for their attempt to win or consolidate power and extend social control.

(Sahgal and Yuval-Davis, 1994: 7–9)

In specific instances in Northamptonshire, the County Council has used the term 'fundamentalism' to justify not taking action over the distribution of newsletters to young Asian girls, which misinformed them of the quality and appropriateness of support that they would get from the local Asian women's refuge. The distribution of this literature was done by a local authority-funded and managed project. The purpose of its distribution seemed to be to discredit the Asian refuge and the services it offered, and thus discourage women experiencing domestic violence from seeking help or refuge. The publication also discouraged Asian girls from leaving home, implying that in situations where Asian girls were experiencing conflict with parents, for example, the blame for this lay with the girls. Despite protests from local Asian women's groups and the Asian women's refuge, no action was taken as it was deemed to offend 'fundamentalist' sensibilities.

After the Asian women's group had made complaints about the offending publication, there were considerable pressures placed upon them both by other (male-dominated) community organizations and statutory officers calling into question their right to express an informed opinion. This specific incident had all the hallmarks that Sahgal and Yuval-Davis (1994) identify as 'fundamentalist', in terms of being part of a modern political movement that also consolidates power and extends social control.

Fundamentalism and racism have complex connections and contradictions. Both are social constructs evolved through discourse in a variety of distinct and differing arenas. The cumulative effects of these major societal forces have extreme impacts on the everyday reality of Asian women's lives. Often Asian women are the only group to have a clarity of insight into the complexities of how these social constructs operate. It is only with this knowledge that the latter can be challenged appropriately and, with this vested interest, that they may be challenged effectively.

In the context of Northamptonshire, the Asian communities are small, diverse and disparate. There are a number of communities mainly congregated around urban centres but also significant numbers outside of them (Wright, 1993). In the past, levels of investment into all Black communities from statutory agencies have been extremely low in 'shire counties' compared with inner-city urban centres where Black populations are larger. There have been specific funds available to inner-city Black communities enabling them to develop their services, resources and activities, such as Urban Regeneration monies and City Challenge Grants. There is also a low level of community development work carried out with Black communities despite an identified need for more. By comparison, relatively minimal support exists for women's organizations, with only two funded in the county. In *Women and Community Action*, Lena Dominelli (1990) provides information about how some local authorities have enabled activism on race and gender issues, stating:

> British feminists' ... most recent innovative efforts have occurred through Labour controlled local authorities attempting to [eliminate] 'race' and gender oppression ... These local authorities ... established either Women's Committees or Women's Equal Opportunities Officers to promote women's welfare ...
>
> (Dominelli, 1990: 107)

Within Northamptonshire there have been no such innovations empowering feminists. This may be connected with the absence until recently of a Labour administration in the county. The authority certainly has a Race Equality Officer in some departments, but these officers are few and far between, and extremely overstretched. It would seem logical to assume that if Black populations were larger there would be more incentives for authorities to strategically provide for them or, at the very least, there would be a greater degree of pressure upon them by Black communities to do so.

Larger Black communities in other parts of the country enable expression of difference both between and within communities. Outside of that environment, Black groups struggle with the preservation of an often fragile coalition both in struggles against racism and in the task of constructing positive collective and personal identities for themselves within the constraints of living in a racist society. Where there are contradictions between the construction of positive collective and positive personal identities, the expression of so-called marginal interests can be stifled. Asian women who highlight the differences in their experiences of racism in contrast to the experiences of Asian men can be accused of diluting a Black perspective and dividing Black groups. Certainly when Asian men are accused of not supporting Asian women or enabling them to engage in personal or collective activism, there are clear contradictions between a community identity, which is controlled by men, and the identity of Asian women.

The expression of diversity enables an assertion that communities are not homogenous with identical perspectives, priorities and approach, but multifaceted, containing all the individual interest groups that exist throughout wider society. In larger communities not only is there more space for this expression of difference, but there are more people finding themselves on the margins. Whilst working with Asian women in London, I experienced much more support and community acceptance of women who did find themselves defined, or defined themselves, as having marginal interests. I think that larger population bases may result in more Black lesbians, single parents and other women who do not fit into the norm, surfacing and supporting others to surface.

In 'Women and Collective Action', Filomena Chioma Steady outlines five major stages characterizing the development of the Women's Movement:

1   the period of consciousness raising, mobilization and advocacy;
2   militancy and radicalization leading to direct action;
3   consolidation, institution building, and counter-culture;
4   fragmentation and diversification; marginalization of some groups of women;
5   repression, male backlash, resistance and apathy.

(Steady, 1993: 98)

It could be argued that this model of development and diversification is true for any activism in the west. Larger communities result in an arena where Asian women with a variety of perspectives are able to find a place in which they can support their communities and also can be supported. In smaller communities such as Northamptonshire, there is much evidence and scope for actions and inactions by communities themselves, and for statutory sector authorities to negate the existence of Asian women who do not fit into the norm. This is done by denial, e.g. denying the existence of Asian women who are single parents, or Asian women with drugs or alcohol problems. It is also achieved by the process of essentializing communities, e.g. by accepting the views of one community leader that women from his community do not want to work. The Asian women who find themselves in this way marginalized often engage in work designed to consolidate Black communities to gain a basis on which to build support for themselves in the future. The very inaction of not challenging these groups over their not taking up gender issues is one way of tacitly consolidating the groups.

Just as the experiences of racism and gender will differ between a Black woman with disabilities and a Black lesbian, there will also be a difference in experience of racism and sexism between a Bengali single mother and an Afro-Caribbean single mother. The diversity of Black women's experience does not only exist as a linear progression of dichotomy, but as a matrix of differences. Even the relatively reduced category of 'Asian' is based on immense diversity simply in terms of religion, language, caste and class.

In considering the experience of Asian women in the context of collective activism, I think that one of the influencing factors is the effect of the boundaries of what is considered the norm being extremely closely and rigidly defined in an environment of small communities. In exploring why this occurs, one must look back at the factors affecting not only the social construction of the 'leaders' of those communities, but also of the host community in which they exist. Racism in less urbanized areas is a phenomenon that is increasingly being documented (Dedorian,

1993). In those areas where population densities result in a much lower percentage of White individuals in the community having any kind of personal contact with Black people, there is often no 'in the flesh' challenge to covert or overt racist attitudes or actions. The day-to-day existence in this environment has an impact on the construction of all Black people living there. However, the fears produced in those communities are easily manipulated to empower authoritarian individuals within Black and Asian communities to exert power and control. This is a more powerful force within a small community where there are similarly fewer 'in the flesh' challenges to the definitions of norms and of what is accepted in the community which the conservative and orthodox influences within the community promote.

The national campaigning group Women Against Fundamentalism elaborates how the reaction to individual acts of racism

> ... predictably, provoke(s) the reconstruction of traditionalist religious 'identities' within the threatened religious communities, giving power and succour to religious leaders who seek to promote messages of orthodoxy which are used to control members of their communities, especially women.
>
> (Women Against Fundamentalism, 1994: 1)

For Asian women, identity is an issue that individually and collectively we must learn to manipulate before it is used to manipulate us. Audre Lorde stated in 'Age, Race, Class and Sex: Women Redefining the Difference' that

> as a forty-nine-year-old Black lesbian feminist socialist mother of two, including one boy, and a member of an inter-racial couple, I usually find myself a part of some group defined as other, deviant, inferior or just plain wrong.
>
> (Lorde, 1992: 47)

Later in the same essay she goes on to write about how others have attempted to exploit or manipulate her identity, explaining:

> Differences between ourselves as Black women are also misnamed and used to separate us from one another. As a Black lesbian feminist comfortable with the many different ingredients of my identity, and a woman committed to racial and sexual freedom from oppression, I find I am constantly being encouraged to pluck out some one aspect of myself and present this as the meaningful whole, eclipsing or denying the other parts of myself.
>
> (Lorde, 1992: 52)

The negotiation between a variety of identities is dictated by concerns of self-preservation and trying to strategically position oneself to gain the maximum out of any given situation. This is more central to the realities of Black women who choose to exist out of, or are forced out of, the norm. For these women, not positioning themselves strategically may result in significant effects on their quality of life in terms of community support in a racist environment. Just as religious and orthodox Asian identities are constructed as a reaction to racism, so a single parent Asian woman will often strategically position herself as widowed or with a husband working away from home as a reaction to religious and orthodox identities. Black Community groups and women's organizations similarly exert pressure on Asian women's organizations to effectively choose between sexism and racism as the basis for oppressions.

In Northamptonshire, some Black community organizations have women's groups. Only two Asian community groups have any type of women's section or group. Neither of the groups can be said to offer any kind of service parity when analysing the difference between the services offered to men and the services offered to women. I was informed by a representative of one of those community groups at one point that 'women did not have meetings, but gatherings'.

There is only one independent Asian women's group. The organization, called Dostiyo, has a clear remit within its work that activism entails both individual and collective mobilization of agency for change. This is demonstrated by services delivered on a one-to-one basis with women providing advocacy, information and advice on housing problems, welfare rights, immigration and domestic violence, as well as work undertaken in groups raising these issues, fighting for rights, and enabling women through self-help, training and promotion of women's well-being.

Despite an absence of a substantive organized women's movement in North-amptonshire, Dostiyo Asian Women and Girls Organization tries to progress development of services for women through its pivotal position between women's and Black fora. As an organization it is often caught between criticism from White women and men and professionals from social and health care agencies, *and* criticism from orthodox Black groups. Through what Gayatri Chakravorty Spivak terms a 'strategic use of positivist essentialism' (1988: 205), by taking up issues of the control of Asian women by White men and women and male-dominated community forces, there is an active dynamic of feminist and anti-racist challenge to statutory sector officers and policy makers as well as orthodox interests within communities.

Although the term Asian is a western, euro-centric construction, Asian women of differing faiths, linguistic and cultural backgrounds come together under the umbrella of Dostiyo to use the identity of 'Asian' to make anti-racist challenges without isolating themselves, and also to oppose interpretations of multiculturism that in turn seek to empower orthodox perspectives of all religions that seek to control women. Women Against Fundamentalism elaborate this position, stating:

> Our critique of multiculturalism is not an attack on cultural diversity which we celebrate, but because it can be a doctrine that appeases and increases the power of dominant elites in minority communities who all too freely claim to speak on behalf of a non-existent homogeneous group.
> (*Women Against Fundamentalism*, 1994: 1)

This position is complex to explain and articulate in an environment where Asian women are rarely given opportunities to speak on their own agendas but constantly have to respond to those of others. There often is no space in discourse with Black men or White women to clarify the nuances of these arguments.

Within the context of Northamptonshire, the criticism of Dostiyo by Asian men for example centres on those involved in the organization *as women*, rather than as activists or social-care professionals. We are criticized on grounds of our ability to keep or get men, our sexuality and our fitness to act *in loco parentis* for Asian girls as Youth workers and educationalists. Asian girls constitute a battle-field that traditional male-controlled community groups see as theirs to own. As an organiza- tion, we are accused of being home-breakers when we enable women to escape domestic violence, and of encouraging girls to run away from home when we refuse to judge their actions. Issues of identity, nationality, race, religion and interagency working intersect on the issues of Asian women's rights to self-determination. The tragedy is that, through the discussions between agencies and Black community groups, the individual realities and actions of Asian girls are objectified. The personal statements that are made by Asian girls in taking actions such as leaving home are deconstructed without giving the girls themselves a voice.

The experiences of White men and women professionals failing Asian women and girls as a community is a topical and ever present example of the intersection between racism and fundamentalism. When Black community organizations essen- tialize Asian womanhood and refuse to prioritize issues of domestic violence or conflict with parents by denying their existence or skirting over the critical and complex issues, statutory authorities have a legal and moral obligation to engage and work through these problems with Black communities, particularly when offering services in the area. Often the statutory sector use a strategy of allowing Black groups themselves to define strategies and ways forward. Where there is conflict between the interests of Black communities and a section of Black women in this situation, statutory agencies often wash their hands of the issue. These White women and men professionals have a misconception of the effect of their own power, their own Whiteness in this situation. Warped cultural relativism overtakes issues of quality and equality of service. The reality and responsibility for these decisions will always ultimately depend on White authorities, no matter what level of consultation there is with Black communities. This recognition of power by statutory organiza- tions is a more honest perspective on their Whiteness. Statements are made by fundamentalists that seek to control and divide some Asian girls from the rest of their communities. These statements are defended by statutory organizations using principles of freedom of speech. This 'freedom' assumes that all sections of the community have the same access to resources to produce publications, the same resources to communicate with policy makers to challenge their assumptions. Without a recognition that there are other perspectives other than by those that control, there can be no freedom of speech.

From another angle, there are also White professionals who assume a conflation of religious and Asian professional practice in which the former will always be more important in decision-making processes than the latter. An example of this is the way that in interagency negotiations on guidelines of dealing with sixteen-year-old Asian girls running away from home, no representative from any Asian group in the county, not even from an Asian women's group, was involved. The representatives from statutory agencies thought they acted in terms of protecting Asian girls from their communities. This was based on their assumptions about those communities being potentially fundamentalist and only further objectified the position of Asian girls. Within the context of Asian girls who are in conflict with their parents, it is all too easy for White statutory professionals to move into a position of apportioning blame from a removed and thus 'objective' stance. Thus, for example, parents who remove their daughters from school and face a reaction from their daughters of running away from home, are demonized by 'objective professionals'. Less 'objective' women in the community saw the problem as the inadequate policing of the local bus station that failed to protect the girls from sexual harassment from teenage boys, which in turn provoked the parents to withdraw the girls from school. The White professional lack of analysis into the depth of the problem conveniently shifted responsibility from an authority with a legal and moral obligation to protect all members of the community and with the resources to do so, to an individual problem. No doubt the convenient word 'fundamentalism' was used to justify what was seen as an individual problem rather than an institutional one.

Within these complex intersections of assumptions, power and vested interest, the priority for Asian women must not be about winning arguments, but about winning them in the right way. If Asian women collude with assumptions and reactions from either Asian communities or statutory authorities, they risk undermining their future battles.

One of the issues that is key to statutory authorities' involvement or lack of involvement with Asian women is that of authenticity. There is a tendency by some White statutory sector men and women to view the perspectives of Asian women organizing independently as not 'authentic' and thus not valid in the debate. In doing so, these authorities have their own image of what Asian women 'are really like', which is not based on the latter's material reality. Racist concepts are thus fuelled by the essentializing of Asian women in statements that begin with 'our women are' and the denial of those Asian women and girls who do not conform to norms.

As a woman involved in activism in this context, in order to achieve change, more and more of my time and energy is spent trying to develop an awareness of the perceptions of the embodiments of White statutory authorities in the shape of officers and executives and to theorize the factors influencing their decisions. Part of me thinks that in my Utopian world this would be reversed.

There is a need to theorize racism and fundamentalism as a means of keeping track of why we, as Asian women, propose the arguments that we do at any given time. It is important for us to sustain clarity in analysing the options of which position to take at what time. Activism for Asian women entails taking strategic actions in order to achieve change. These actions will in many senses be determined by analyses of fundamentalism and racism.

References

CHAKRAVORTY, G.S. (1988) 'Subaltern Studies: Deconstructing Historiography', in CHAKRAVORTY, G.S. (Ed.) *In Other Worlds: Essays in Cultural Politics*, London: Routledge, pp. 197–221.

DEDORIAN, J. (1993) *Another Country: Beyond Rose Cottage*, London: NCVO.

DOMINELLI, L. (1990) *Women and Community Action*, London: Venture.

LORDE, A. (1992) 'Age, Race, Class and Sex: Women Redefining Difference', in CROWLEY, H. and HIMMELWEIT, S. (Eds) *Knowing Women*, Cambridge: Polity, pp. 47–56.

SAHGAL, G. and YUVAL-DAVIS, N. (1994) 'The Uses of Fundamentalism', *Women Against Fundamentalism*, **5**, 5, pp. 7–9.

SIVANANDAN, A. (1990) *Communities of Resistance*, London: Verso.

STEADY, F.C. (1993) 'Women and Collective Action: Female Models in Transition', in JAMES, S.M. and BUSIA, A.P.A. (Eds) *Theorizing Black Feminisms*, London: Routledge, pp. 90–101.

WOMEN AGAINST FUNDAMENTALISM (Eds) (1994) 'Editorial', *Women Against Fundamentalism*, **5**, 5, p. 1.

Part IV
Young Women

Chapter 9

Conceptions of Power of/between Black and White Women

Debbie Weekes and Terri MacDermott

Introduction

This chapter explores the differing conceptions of power employed by Black and White women when understanding themselves and others. Our aim is to illustrate the ways in which we think that the contemporary usage of a feminist/Foucauldian model of power is inadequate on its own for understanding the totality of female experience. We want to show how a Foucauldian definition of power, as detailed in Radtke and Stam (1994), is inadequate for conceptualizing and describing the structuring of both social life and individual experience. We explore some possible reasons why 'feminism' has not moved beyond the recognition of difference. In the conclusion, we outline an alternative conceptualization of power built around the notion of a 'racialized gendered identity'. We are aware that attempts to incorporate classed and racialized differences within the concept of 'woman' have already been made by Black feminists since the beginning of second-wave feminism (Amos and Parmar, 1984; Carby, 1982; Dill, 1987; Ladner, 1972; hooks, 1982, 1989, 1991, 1993; Parmar, 1990), but we would like to argue that feminism in the 1990s needs to move beyond the recognition of difference. We consider this is to be a central issue for a feminist activist agenda of the 1990s.

Methodology

The decision to research the ways that both Black and White women conceptualize power stems from our own positions as a Black and a White woman working within a university, and our own attempts to understand the social structuring of our friendship. We decided that our positions as researchers should racially match those of the women we interviewed, especially considering that our aim was to explore racial dynamics within feminist discourse and to reject traditional ideas of womanhood by examining the ways in which Black and White women identify racialized and gendered signifiers of their experiences.

Some theorists refuse the notion of 'insider' knowledge that a Black researcher can bring to interviewing Black respondents, due to the rejection of the idea of a singular 'truth' (Phoenix, 1994; Rhodes, 1994). It has also been recognized that 'there are dimensions to Black experience invisible to the White interviewer/ investigator who possess neither the language nor the cultural equipment, either to elicit, or understand that experience', and that racial matching of interviewer and interviewee may be regarded as 'a defence against intrusion by the preservation of a share of experience to which members of the dominant groups are denied access' (Rhodes, 1994: 549). We believe that the debate around the relationships of power between researcher and researched is important, especially as we will be analysing how Black and White women conceptualize power among themselves. Due to the subject matter of our research, we felt it necessary to minimize, *as far as possible*, the power relations between ourselves as researchers, and the women we inter- viewed. Ultimately, of course, the interpretation of data has remained with us. In line with Rhodes's assertion that this interpretation may be subject to a 'white cultural and ... intrinsically racist filter', we have attempted to explode these dynamics by looking at the ways in which the women we interviewed articulated ideas about power.

We interviewed 12 women, six Black women and six White women, in semi- structured interviews. We use a (W) to indicate the White women's responses and a (B) to indicate those of the Black women. The questions we asked covered the following areas:

1. feminism, the women's movement and racism;
2. concerns that women have;
3. how women see themselves as different/similar;
4. how things could be improved;
5. the impact of social class and race.

The White women were selected mainly through a local school. The Black women were selected through the university and a local community centre. The same questions were asked of each sample. All the names used in this chapter are pseudonyms. We are not asserting that the voices of these women represent anything other than the insight that each gives on any particular issue at a specific moment in time. We would, however, like the 'voices' to be heard and for the reader to consider the possibility that the Foucauldian definition of power is not adequate on its own to understand the various ways that the female experience is structured. We do not wish our examination of power to become tied up within a discourse of racial matching as we think it is also vital to theorize the relationships of power that create concern about 'truth' within the research process in the first place.

Power according to Foucault

> Power, as the capacity of men to oppress, dominate, exploit and subordinate women ... is well explored in feminist accounts. But they rarely explore women's *power over* children, other women or, more rarely, men.
>
> (Vickers, 1994: 185; original emphasis)

In recent years, feminism has tended to adopt a Foucauldian conceptualization of power (e.g. see Radtke and Stam, 1994). Power is no longer seen only in terms of a commodity that one holds at the expense of another. Power is now also conceptualized as a multiplicity of relationships and forms of resistance. Foucault (1980, 1982), in his definition of power, focuses specifically on the non-economic form of power related to epistemic concerns and subjectivity. To quote Foucault:

> Power must be analysed as something which circulates, or rather as something which only functions in the form of a chain. It is never localised here or there, never in anybody's hands, never appropriated as a commodity or piece of wealth. Power is employed and exercised through a net-like organisation. And not only do individuals circulate through its threads; they are always in the position of simultaneously undergoing and exercising this power. They are not its inert or consenting target; they are always also the elements of its articulation. In other words, individuals are the vehicles of power, not its points of application.
>
> (Foucault, 1980: 98)

The exercise of such power requires no external surveillance or coercion; 'rather, because the individual is constituted through power, the exercise of power can occur through a process of self-discipline or self-regulation' (Radtke and Stam, 1994: 4). The exercise of this power is implicated in the mechanisms and procedures for producing knowledge and therefore in knowledge itself; 'consequently, all social practices are shaped by power, including, at least according to some authors, the reproduction of traditional gender arrangements' (Radtke and Stam, 1994: 4). Crudely put, this relationship is illustrated in Figure 9.1.

To reiterate the above point, power is conceived of as only existing in its exercise. From this perspective, power is neither one-directional, nor does it flow from a single source to shape, direct, or constrain subjects. Rather:

> Power is in reciprocal relation to subjectivity, where subjectivity can be defined as individual self-consciousness inscribed in particular ideals of behaviour surrounding categories of persons, objects, practices or institutions. Subjectivity is constituted through the exercise of power within which conceptions of personal identity, gender and sexuality come to be generated. Men and women actively exercise power in positioning themselves within, or of finding their own location amongst, competing discourses, rather than being merely 'positioned' by them.
>
> (Kerfoot and Knights, 1994: 70)

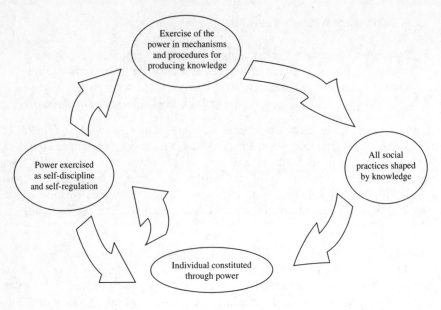

Figure 9.1 A feminist/Foucauldian model of power.

Cooper (1994) articulates the feminist/Foucauldian challenge to the orthodox interpretations of power within four 'frames of reference', which can be summarized as:

1. Power is a phenomenon that is exercised rather than a commodity that can be
    possessed. Thus 'power is not a resource that belongs to individuals or groups,
    where, if some have more, others will automatically have less, but is rather
    "incorporated in numerous practices". *People exercise power through the effect
    their actions have on others' actions'* (Cooper, 1994: 437; our emphasis).
2. Power is productive rather than purely repressive. Power is seen to be productive
    'through its various mechanisms or "technologies", *power shapes, creates and
    transforms social relations, practices and institutional processes'* (Cooper,
    1994: 437; original emphasis). Foucauldian feminists have tended to concen-
    trate on the ways in which various regimes have constructed knowledge, bodies
    and subjects, rather than on the nature of the power relationship itself.
3. Power is not centralized in a state or single apparatus but present throughout
    social relations. Cooper illustrates this as a 'bottom up' analysis. Power is not
    seen to originate from a single source such as the sovereign or the law, 'but runs
    through the capillaries of society' (Cooper, 1994: 438).
4. The combination of the first three, power as an exercised phenomenon, as
    productive and as all-encompassing throughout society, adds to a total picture of
    power through which we live, breathe and think rather than as an identifiable
    'form' or relationship that can be negotiated or fought with. Within a Foucauldian
    conceptualization of power, power is not an entity that can simply be overthrown.

Feminism: The Universality of Womanhood

Some feminist conceptualizations of womanhood have implied a dichotomous relation of women to men. In the need to value the previously devalued part in the male/female dichotomy, western feminism of the 1970s and early 1980s posited an essential category of woman in order to imply the unity of 'sisterhood'. Sexual difference has been paramount in feminist theorizing about 'woman' and has viewed gender relations as symptomatic of this (Anthias and Yuval-Davis, 1992: 97). This is reflected in some of the comments made by the White women interviewed, comments such as Alison's (W) that 'feminism is for me to see all things from the women's perspective, to believe in and support all women, to spend most of my time with women'. However, as Butler (1990) points out: '*Woman* is not a unitary category. Yet, this does not mean that the noun "woman" is meaningless. It too has its own specificity constituted within and through historically specific configurations of gender relations' (Butler, 1990: 131). Butler further suggests: 'it would be wrong to assume in advance that there is a category of 'women' that simply needs to be filled in with various components of race, class, age, ethnicity and sexuality in order to become complete' (p. 5). Assumptions of the universality of dualism imply categories which are both static and stable and as a result propose an analysis of gender which is ahistorical and deterministic (Gordon, 1991: 94). The binary relationship of male to female as a basis of theorizing about the oppression of women assumes a shared commonality of subordination that leaves the dimensions of class and racial privilege intact. Such a construction of what constitutes 'womanhood' has coercive and regulatory consequences although, within some feminist contexts, it has been constructed as serving the purposes of emancipation (Butler, 1990: 6). The ambivalence women experience when seeking to discuss differences among themselves is evident in the responses of some of the women we interviewed. They made comments such as 'yes they do experience the same inequality that White women do and some more' (Bev, W) or 'no differences fundamentally apart from the obvious differences' (Toni, W) or Jane's (W) comment that she feels 'that Black women probably experience that same sexism as White women but the difference between us is that they have the added pressure of racism'. These women find it difficult to consider how the existence of power relations shape the experiences of Black women differently from those of White women. However, Brah (1992) has argued:

> Our gender is constituted and represented differently according to our differential location within the global relations of power. Our insertion into these global relations of power is realized through a myriad of economic, political and ideological processes. Within these structures of social relations we do not exist simply as women but as differentiated categories such as *working-class* women, *peasant* women, *migrant* women. Each description references a specificity of social condition. And real lives are forged out of a complex articulation of these dimensions.
>
> (Brah, 1992: 131)

The difference of social condition referred to here, emphasizes the social construction of different categories of women. Brah asks for a categorization that recognizes the multiplicity of the 'forms' of 'woman'. As can be seen from the quotes below, there was a diversity of knowledge and views among our interviewees on how the women's movement and racism interrelate.

> I am not aware that the women's movement has ever made a stand on race, or any other issues than gender. (Bev, W)

> I think women hoped for equality within the women's movement. However, eventually this didn't seem to happen. I feel the women's movement eventually became a White middle-class women's arena. (Ada, W)

> Although racism has not always been given equal priority, especially in the early days of the second wave, and accusations of racism can and have been levelled at a wide range of feminists at the levels of debate and theory and at the level of activism, there have been attempts to tackle racism. However, it does seem to me that although White feminists may be working on an individual level in a variety of ways, their involvement in a wider sense is not what it should be. (Ruby, W)

> There was the sort of propaganda about supporting women everywhere and Black women getting involved in feminism and feminism shouting about the rights of women everywhere but in actual fact in its own structure and practice it worked against Black women quite often and didn't support them. (Imani, B)

> I don't think racism was on their agenda ... it [feminism] can be divisive in the sense that it pulls Black women away from the fight against racism and it persuades them that the most important thing to be fighting is sexism, and they then identify, quite rightly, as a woman but at the exclusion of recognizing their Blackness. (Aisha, B)

Difference: The Politics of Identity

White feminists have publicly acknowledged the existence of 'difference' (Barrett and McIntosh, 1985; Ramazanoglu, 1989). However, this has not gone any way to restoring Black women's previous marginality. Instead it has sometimes served to reinforce it, as one definition of difference implies a notion of 'the other' which deviates from the norm (Gordon, 1991). In our Black sample the differences between Black and White women are conceptualized along race divisions. The similarities were not necessarily an important part of this conceptualization, which immediately set up a dichotomous, and at times, essentialist analysis.

> White women cannot appreciate or feel any empathy with Black men in the same way that I can ... they might feel that they don't have as much of a

power base as White men, but they sure as hell got more of a power base than Black women and Black men for that matter. (Aisha, B)

We know 'struggle' from very young years and throughout our lives. White women mainly experience 'discomfort' at stages which causes them to become reactionary in the then and now. (Maxine, B)

This group of Black women recognized both the power dynamic between themselves and White women, who were also defined monolithically, and also their common- ality with Black men, rendering a feminist analysis of sexual/gender based oppression problematic. When the consideration of racialized identity became gendered within the Black sample, differences were not acknowledged within the group of women. Issues of class were not necessarily regarded as applicable to Black individuals. Imani (B) saw race as the most dominant signifier of Black experience, thus locating this experience within a genderless/classless framework.

I think about difference I suppose but not about class ... I understand the class thing when it's applied to White people in this country ... but I don't really understand it in relation to how I see myself and other Black people. (Imani, B)

I have no social class. Regardless of what class I may be seen as, my race puts me in a class of my own. You see, even if I was Whoopi Goldberg, Denzil Washington, or even Diane Abbot, Britain's first Black MP, my social class would still be limited for me because of race. (Wema, B)

Working class would ... be my original classification by virtue of my parentage. However, I'm taught that by virtue of my education/training, I'm now middle class, My problem with the above is that this society will disregard both labels and see/treat me as second class, ... dependent on the circle I happen to be in at the time. (Aisha, B)

The Black women in the sample clearly thought that economic definitions of class are irrelevant to Black experiences. Dominant conceptions of class tend to refer to its economic dimensions, whereas the Black respondents articulated a definition of class in terms of citizenship. Class is not only gendered but also racialized and is experienced by Black individuals in terms of their social positioning as second-class citizens. However, one Black woman recognized the power differential between herself as a lecturer and a working-class White woman:

Objectively speaking, as a Black woman, my lifestyle, ... standard of living, degree of control over one's working life and domestic life ... has got to be greater than that of a White working class woman, so there's a sense in which her inequality may be even greater. (Maya, B)

Within the sample of White women, class was articulated as a huge signifier of their gendered experiences. It is clear that their ideas of class were based upon the traditional Marxist definition of resources. In terms of our consideration of power, we believe this rejects the Foucauldian notion of its multiplicity and 'web-like' nature:

> There are differences which are not simply predicated on race. I am perhaps more similar to some Black women than I am to some White women ... All women experience structural inequalities of many different kinds and not all women will experience all of them all of the time ... Not all Black people experience racism in the same way. (Ruby, W)

> I feel that I am most affected by my class but that could well be that my level of race awareness is not very high, my racism. (Alison, W)

> I think your social class has a big impact on your life. All the different cultural influences as well as economic influences that effect you, language, accent, religion, family and the knowledge of your roots. I would say that being brought up a catholic and a socialist has been formative in my life. (Toni, W)

Equally Ruby (W) recognizes the advantages that she has as a middle-class woman:

> I occupy a relatively privileged position in this society. I have been fortunate to experience a university education. I have a professional job and all these things do not allow myself to be classified as 'working class' as I understand it. I also recognize that there is a wide gulf of experience that excludes me, as I exclude myself, from describing myself as 'working class'.

Ada (W) gives a very powerful description of the impact that class has had upon her life:

> I was one of seven children brought up alone by my mother. Also I was the only one that got through college, and university. I had to go without money, clothing and other things to actually do this and it was only possible for one family member to be funded to go through college. Other members had to earn a wage to help support the family.

In the main, the Black women in the sample rejected attempts by White feminists to theorize the Black female experience. Maya (B) felt that the interrelation of race, class and gender, rendered certain analyses, such as focusing on clitoridectomy, as problematic. Their objections to mainstream feminism supported their belief that White feminists failed to consider a wider, globalized and interrelated analysis, which did not position gender as the main signifier of all female experiences:

> When you have to go to the field and till the land, your husband's beating you, he's sleeping with so and so, you've got to bring in the food. He might be doing it but at least he's around to help you look after the children. I'm

not condoning it but it's about reality ... their [White] women were down the pit, their children cleaning chimneys, pregnant [women] pulling great truckloads or whatever, and you go to those women and say 'let's talk about interpersonal relationships' ... why focus on clitoridectomy? Why focus on arranged marriages? What do you think the royal family's about? (Maya, B)

However, this statement specifically links racialized experiences with 'truth', reinforcing an idea of difference, which could be read as essentialist. It implies that Black racialized experiences cannot and should not be theorized by White feminists. Brah, however, suggests that 'black and white feminism should not be seen as essentially fixed oppositional categories but rather as historically contingent fields of contestation within discursive and material practices in a post-colonial society' (Brah, 1992: 126).

Conclusion: Power and a Racialized Gendered Identity

A specific form of racial gendered identity has been constructed. This racialized gendered identity is primarily structured through a reification of difference, and a view that Black women are not seen as having the sheltered and pampered existence that is so often associated with White women. For Black women, this produces a proliferation of struggles and the constant question of how and what to prioritize.

As a Black woman I always feel that I've got two hills to climb ... If I get to the top because I'm a woman I'm not necessarily at the top because I'm Black. I've had to fight more battles because I'm Black than because I'm a woman, people are much more willing to accept the female side rather than the Black side. (Anita, B)

Colour is always an issue as White women are perceived as women first. Black women however are seen from the aspect of their colour/culture before being addressed as women. Also labels such as 'aggressive' are more likely to be attached to Black women whereas it is said to be 'assertive' for White women. (Maxine, B)

A multiplicity of struggles, however, also exists for White women and we must avoid the danger of assuming a homogeneity of White gendered identity. We have already outlined a feminist/Foucauldian understanding of power. We now want to show why we believe it is conceptually weak. Alison (W) described the differences in power between Black and White women in arenas such as education, social background, housing, etc. Each of these is a form of resource. Indeed, the concept of power offered by the women interviewed is one of access to or lack of resources. Hartsock (1990) criticizes the Foucauldian concept of power for its lack of social structure, making domination very difficult to locate. While on the one hand Foucault argues that individuals are constituted through power, he also argues that individuals are not constituted by relations of domination by one group over another. However, without an acknowledgement of these differences political action becomes difficult to envisage. As Hartsock states:

> Our understanding of power needs to recognize the difficulty of creating alternatives. The ruling class, race and gender actively structure the material-social relations in which all parties are forced to participate; their vision, therefore, cannot be dismissed as simply false or misguided. In consequence, the oppressed groups must struggle for their own under-standings which will represent achievements requiring both theorizing and the education which grows from political struggle.
>
> (Hartsock, 1990: 172)

The Black and White women we interviewed recognized alike that White women are in a more powerful position than Black women. Each identified resources as the reason for this. For them, resources equal power. Resources, however, go beyond the material to encompass a whole host of other, subjective resources such as the feeling of 'belonging', security, freedom from fear of attack, a sense of history and a sense of future, a sense of value and humanity, and a sense of a social recognition of that value and humanity. When asked what particular concerns they had as women, each of the White women, not unreasonably, replied along the lines of 'economic security, child care, poor housing, unemployment. Lack of sufficient funds to lead a decent standard of living, having enough money to clothe myself and my son' (Ada, W). When asked about the impact of racism, none recognized that it had an impact on the construction of their own White identity. Neither did they recognize the impact upon the social structure between this 'racialized' White identity and a Black identity constructed as 'other'. 'I am White and I haven't suffered racism in an obvious or up-front way' (Toni, W). Ruby stated: 'I am a White woman in a White racist society . . . White women do not experience racist oppression. They, or at least some of them, can experience pain for and awareness of Black women's experience of racism but there is a limit to our understanding.' Bev (W), when asked which affected her most, race or class, replied: 'class because I am White, living in a White society. My class is what differentiates me from other White people.' There is no recognition here of her identity as a White person in a society which is described as a 'White society' but has Black members. Bev (W) states: 'I want to be accepted for my colour just as a Black woman would, I do not want to suffer prejudice from Black people. I would like to be better integrated into a Black, mixed race community . . . I don't like it when Black people are separatist, I understand it but it offends me.' Jane comments: 'I am a White woman and I have never been subjected to racism', and states further that 'class affects me more because the fact that I am White means I suffer very little in terms of racism.' What is obvious is that all women privilege some aspect of themselves as significant in differentiating their 'self' from others. The aspects they see as significant in each context is, in some respects, colour specific. White women may, in the first instance, consider what differentiates them from other White people, thus failing to see people of different colours as significant for a White person's self-image, while Black women may, in the first instance, consider colour as the dividing characteristic. So what does this mean for racialized gendered identities? Pajaczkowska and Young (1992) have argued that White racial identity is an 'absence'. As some quotes have shown, the White women do recognize their racial identity in that they say they are White. However, they do not understand themselves as constructed through an interracial social relation and some do not self-consciously recognize the implications of their colour on their lives. Pajaczkowska and Young argue that this is because White is 'dominant'. There is very little awareness of the 'White' racial identity. Only two comments from our White sample show any recognition of an identity as White and where this positions White women in relation to Black women. Toni (W), when asked what her concerns as a White woman are, replied, 'that I continue to recognize that I have a "racial identity"'.

Alison (W) also recognized that racism has an impact on both parties (so to speak): 'I need to be concerned with my own racism, the way I've benefited from imperialism.' This reflects Pajaczkowska and Young's assertion that

> An identity based on power never has to develop consciousness of itself as responsible, it has no sense of its limits except as are perceived in opposition to others. The blankness of the identity of empire covers an ambivalence which is often unconscious, and which, consequently, can be most readily perceived in the representations it creates of the colonial 'other'.
>
> (Pajaczkowska and Young, 1992: 202)

The White woman's concept of womanhood may be devoid of race, whereas race is integral to the Black woman's concept of womanhood. This means that we need to build a conceptualization of womanhood which works through racialized identities. Radtke and Stam (1994) ask:

> If power concerns a relationship between social forces (and not just between power and its subjects) then it seems plausible that those exercising power (the forces or agents of domination) are also affected by its exercise ... How do those exercising power change? What effect does power have on their bodies, choices, identities *etc.*?
>
> (442)

We have constructed two diagrams (Figures 9.2 and 9.3) to illustrate the different ways in which Black and White women construct racialized gendered identities. These diagrams encapsulate the power as absence/power as difference dichotomy within the identities of these women and further illustrate the different signifiers (either race or gender) which shape their respective experiences and the subsequent dichotomous conceptions which arise out of these.

For example, the White women in the sample failed to acknowledge a White racial identity when conceptualizing across gender, irrespective of the impact of race upon Black female identity. Gender is clearly the main signifier of the White female experience, thus developing a male/female dichotomy, indicative of western feminism's concept of womanhood. However, differences within the group 'women'

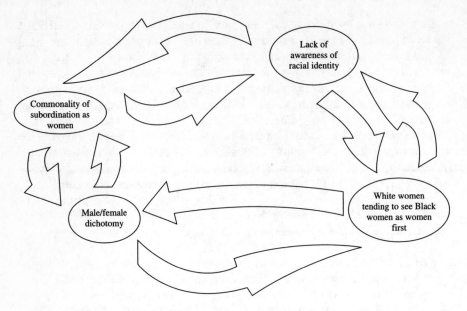

Figure 9.2 A white racialized gendered conception of womanhood.

were recognized in terms of class division. The adoption of this White eurocentric perspective fails to allow the articulation of Black womanhood in two specific ways. First, it reinforces a universality of womanhood in which the experiences of Black women become significantly marginalized. Second, this genderless nature of the Black female identity is additionally exemplified by White and Black women's homogenizing of the category 'Black' which is irrespective of gender difference.

For the Black women, race was clearly the main signifier of experience. Often race and gender would be separated, i.e. Black first, woman second. However, it is important to recognize that concepts of Black womanhood, often marginalized through White feminism, either assume a universality of 'woman' or an individualized self-other dichotomy that ignores the effect of racism. This then renders Black racialized identity without an analysis of the power as difference dichotomy, which seeks to reinforce the difference between Black women and White women. However, as Hall (1990) has argued, prioritizing ethnicities to the point of essentialism can lead to the reinforcement of other oppressions in not challenging existing gender inequalities or class structures. This can be seen in the ways in which at least half of the Black sample regarded class as irrelevant to their experiences. The perspective of mainstream feminism conceptualizes racialized identity within a western individualized, self-other framework that excludes the globalization of racialized identities (Bourne, 1983: 21). We do not wish to pose an essentialist argument, but it cannot be denied that essentialism, when adopted by oppressed groups, can often increase political mobilization (Spivak, 1987: 205; Fuss, 1989: 31). Racism creates racialized identity as the main signifier of experience that influences the dichotomous conceptions of Black women, almost to the exclusion of

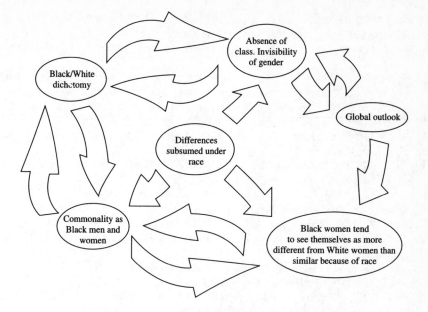

Figure 9.3 A black racialized gendered conception of womanhood.

acknowledging gender and class difference. The category 'woman' becomes problematized under these conditions of racism. We would like to suggest that the eurocentric nature of the White racialized identity fails to take account of globalized social relations. This leads on to our final assertion, that, in order to progress beyond the recognition of difference, feminism needs to integrate the wider, global relations of power and the impact that these may have on the structuring of the variety of female experiences. Perhaps the integration of global analyses of power within feminism can begin to go beyond the recognition of difference to a consideration of the deconstruction of the problematic definition of 'womanhood', which, in turn, can adequately account for the changing social relations of gender and race, and recognize that prioritizing oppressions may not necessarily reinforce essentialisms but rather, be implemented as a political strategy, based on the imposition of racial or gendered signifiers.

References

AMOS, V. and PARMAR, P. (1984) 'Challenging Imperialist Feminism', *Feminist Review,* **17**, pp. 3–21.

ANTHIAS, F. and YUVAL-DAVIS, N. (1992) *Racialized Boundaries: Race, Nation, Gender, Colour and Class and the Anti-Racist Struggle*, London and New York: Routledge.

BARRETT, M. and McINTOSH, M. (1985) 'Ethnocentrism in Socialist Feminist Theory', *Feminist Review,* **20**, pp. 23–47.

BOURNE, J. (1983) 'Towards an Anti-Racist Feminism', *Race and Class: A Journal for Black and Third World Liberation,* **25**, 1, pp. 1–21.

BRAH, A. (1992) 'Difference, Diversity and Differentiation', in DONALD, J. and RATTANSI, A. (Eds) *Race, Culture and Difference*, London: Sage, pp. 126–45.

BUTLER, J. (1990) *Gender Trouble: Feminism and the Subversion of Identity*, London: Routledge.

CARBY, H. (1982) 'White Women Listen! Black Feminism and the Boundaries of Sisterhood', in CENTRE FOR CONTEMPORARY CULTURAL STUDIES (Eds) *The Empire Strikes Back: Race and Racism in 70s Britain*, London: Hutchinson in association with the Centre for Contemporary Studies, University of Birmingham, pp. 212–36.

COOPER, D. (1994) 'Productive, Relational and Ubiquitous: Conceptualising Power Within Foucauldian Feminism', *Sociology*, **28**, 2, pp. 435–55.

DILL, B. (1987) 'The Dialectics of Black Womanhood', in HARDING, S. (Ed.) *Feminism and Methodology*, Milton Keynes: Open University Press, pp. 97–109.

FOUCAULT, M. (1980) *Power/Knowledge: Selected Interviews and Writings 1972–1977*, (edited by C. Gordon), New York: Pantheon Books.

FOUCAULT, M. (1982) 'The Subject and Power', in DREYFUS, H. and RABINOW, P. (Eds) *Michel Foucault: Beyond Structuralism and Hermeneutics*, Chicago: University of Chicago Press, pp. 229–52.

FUSS, D. (1989) *Essentially Speaking: Feminism, Nature and Difference*, New York: Routledge.

GORDON, L. (1991) 'On Difference', *Genders*, **10**, pp. 91–111.

HALL, S. (1990) 'Cultural Identity and Diaspora', in RUTHERFORD, J. (Ed.) *Identity, Community, Culture, Difference*, London: Lawrence & Wishart, pp. 222–37.

HARTSOCK, N. (1990) 'Foucault on Power: A Theory for Women', in NICHOLSON, L. (Ed.) *Feminism/Postmodernism*, London: Routledge, pp. 157–76.

HOOKS, BELL (1982) *Ain't I a Woman Yet: Black Women and Feminism*, London: Pluto.

HOOKS, BELL (1989) *Talking Back: Thinking Feminist, Thinking Black*, London: Sheba Feminist.

HOOKS, BELL (1991) *Yearning: Race, Gender and Cultural Politics*, London: Turnaround.

HOOKS, BELL (1993) *Sisters of the Yam: Black Women and the Self-recovery*, London: Turnaround.

KERFOOT, D. and KNIGHTS, D. (1994) 'Into the Realm of the Fearful: Power, Identity and the Gender Problematic', in RADTKE, H. and STAM, H. (Eds) (1994) *Power/Gender: Social Relations in Theory and Practice*, London: Sage, pp. 67–89.

LADNER, J. (1972) *Tomorrow's Tomorrow*, Garden City, NY: Double Day.

PAJACZKOWSKA, C. and YOUNG, L. (1992) 'Racism, Representation and Psychoanalysis', in DONALD, J. and RATTANSI, A. (Eds) *'Race' Culture and Difference*, London: Sage, pp. 198–220.

PARMAR, P. (1990) 'Black Feminism: The Politics of Articulation', in RUTHERFORD, J. (Ed.) *Identity, Community, Culture, Difference*, London: Lawrence & Wishart, pp. 101–27.

PHOENIX, A. (1994) in BHAVNANI, K-K. and PHOENIX, A. (Eds) *Shifting Identities Shifting Racisms: A Feminist and Psychology Reader*, London: Sage.

RADTKE, H. and STAM, H. (Eds) (1994) *Power/Gender: Social Relations in Theory and Practice*, London: Sage.

RAMAZANOGLU, C. (1989) *Feminism and the Contradictions of Oppression*, London: Routledge.

RHODES, P.J. (1994) 'Race of Interviewer Effects in Qualitative Research: A Brief Comment', *Sociology*, **28**, 2, pp. 547–58.

SPIVAK, G. (1987) *In Other Worlds: Essays in Cultural Politics*, New York and London: Methuen.

VICKERS, J. (1994) 'Notes Toward a Political Theory of Sex and Power', in RADTKE, H. and STAM, H. (Eds) *Power/Gender: Social Relations in Theory and Practice*, London: Sage, pp. 174–94.

Chapter 10

Invisible Women: Young Women and Feminism

Debi Morgan

> I started the network for survivors because I knew that I was not the only one, that there were other young women out there feeling isolated, lonely and that nobody really cares about them or what has happened to them. As survivors [of child sexual abuse] there is a lot of support we can give to each other. (Rachel, age 16)

Young women like Rachel are speaking out about their experiences, their needs and issues of concern to them, and are taking action as individuals and as groups. We are not used to hearing about this activity, even though it is happening all around us. Instead we are subjected to unrepresentative images of glamorous young women in fashion magazines on the one hand, and young women getting pregnant in order to get housing or lone mothers dependent on welfare benefits on the other hand. Young women are relatively invisible within society and this lack of prominence is reflected within feminism and Women's Studies. Issues such as race, class, sexuality and disability are at least on the feminist agenda, older women's issues and experiences surface occasionally, but 'young women' as an area of study remains neglected; young feminists themselves are not an integral part of the women's movement. Although young women are benefiting from the changes that feminism has made to their lives and they see equality as both desirable and obtainable, they are not making the connections between their lives, their experiences and feminism. Feminism has failed to develop a politics that addresses young women.

My aim is to highlight some of the feminist activism of the young women with whom I work as members of a local Youth Council. I want to explore how they see themselves and their lives in relation to feminism and to consider which factors have motivated them to become activists. At present, young women are not a significant part of feminist discourse. I want to explore why this is so and examine the implications for feminism. Young women are alienated from feminism and I shall put forward arguments about why we can no longer afford to ignore young women, how we need to be investing in them and making these connections because not only do they have a lot to offer, but feminism will be stronger with them. After all, they are the future.

It is difficult to define exactly when you stop being a girl and become a young woman, or indeed at what age you stop being young. What is becoming increasingly clear is that the whole process of becoming an adult is extremely complex, that it is a very different experience for young women than for young men and that young women's experiences of adolescence have been neglected (Lees, 1993). For simplicity, I have used the guidelines of the Youth Council and taken 'young women' to refer to those who are between 13 and 25 years old.

Young Women as Activists

I have chosen to highlight the activities of three young women of whom I am aware through their involvement with the local Youth Council. They cross a range of ages, different races, classes and sexual orientations, varied educational experiences and a variety of issues and needs. I have changed their names to preserve confidentiality and to protect their identities because they do not necessarily want their friends or parents to know about their activities. This reticence is indicative of the difficulties that these young women face: two of them are still living at home and their parents are not aware of the full extent of their activities — the women fear that restrictions would be put upon them if they knew.

Amanda

Amanda is 19 years old and is currently studying full-time for a degree. She is concerned about issues relating to women, human rights and the environment. As an active member of the Student Union Women's Caucus she is involved in producing newsletters, organizing meetings and representing female students. She is also active within the local Youth Council where one of her major contributions has been raising awareness of Toxic Shock Syndrome, a condition that can be related to tampon use and where you are more at risk the younger you are. Working together with a group of young women she has produced a leaflet, a poster and a workshop pack, and has been raising the awareness of other young women in the area. Another area of activism in which Amanda has been involved is setting up a local voluntary organization for lesbian, gay and bi-sexual young people.

Naeema

Naeema is 23 years old. She left college after completing a BTEC in Business Studies and is now a receptionist for a local car dealer. She would like to return to studying in the future and is currently looking for work in the voluntary sector. Issues concerned with young people, racism and sexism, are of particular interest to her and have been major factors in her becoming a representative on the local Youth Council, a member of the British Youth Council's membership development group, and an active member of CEMYC (Council for Ethnic Minority Youth Committees), which represents Black young people nationally and internationally. As a result of her work for CEMYC she travels to meetings, conferences and seminars in many different countries.

Rachel

Rachel is 16 years old. She recently started 'A' levels but had to give up when her home situation deteriorated to the extent that she had to leave and was homeless for a while. She is now living back at home and is working part-time in a supermarket. She will return to studying in the future but right now she is working on leaving home by becoming a Community Service Volunteer (CSV). As a result of her own experiences of sexual abuse, she has set up a national network for young survivors, producing a regular newsletter and distributing information. She approached the Youth Council when it started to become too big to run from home. Her aim is to provide a support network for young women like herself and also to raise people's awareness of sexual abuse and its effects. Rachel is also a volunteer with a young women's group at a local youth club.

All three of these young women are activists, yet Naeema is the only one who sees herself as such. Amanda feels that she ought to be doing more, whilst Rachel does not really see herself as doing anything useful. Both Amanda and Rachel have low self-esteem and they do not credit themselves with the contributions they are making, yet they are achieving much between them. Given greater self-esteem, support and resources how much more could these young women achieve? Naeema acknowledges her own worth. She is clear about what she is trying to achieve and has taken opportunities as they have arisen, resulting in her already having a national reputation for the work she is doing. Being older, more confident and having her own income have been important factors in contributing to Naeema's achievements.

Parental support has quite an impact when you are young — especially if you are still living at home. Naeema's parents know about most of the work she is doing. They support her but she is expected to put her family first, which creates conflict at times. Her older sister is married and has two children, and this means that Naeema is able to have more freedom and is not under as much pressure to conform to her parents' expectations than if she was the eldest girl. Amanda's parents know about some of her activism, but the area around her sexuality is not one she finds easy to share with them. Living in student accommodation has given Amanda extra space and time, which she is still adjusting to. Rachel lives with her mother, sister and brother and is desperate to leave home. Her mother knows very little about Rachel's activism. Living in a small village without transport adds to Rachel's isolation and dependency.

Personal experiences have motivated them but have also sometimes had a negative effect. Rachel's experiences of being abused by her father as a child have had far-reaching effects on her life, on her relationships with the rest of her family, her social relationships, her self-esteem, her education and her mental health. She is angry about her past and wants to make changes. She feels that there is not enough said or done about abuse. By reading and talking to others about the subject she hopes that she will be able to work through her own experiences and put them into a context which helps her to both cope with her own situation but also make changes that will help others. Naeema has been motivated by experiencing both racism and sexism. Within her community there are different expectations for young women and young men. She abhors this discrimination and feels that Asian young women need more choices and encouragement. Both of Amanda's parents have disabilities and she believes that this has contributed to her being more aware than her contemporaries of oppression and inequalities.

Both Amanda and Naeema sees themselves as feminists. Teachers and youth workers have provided positive role models for Amanda, influencing, supporting and encouraging her. She feels that she has a responsibility to work actively for her beliefs. Being at university has opened up opportunities with access to feminist ideas and action groups. She reads feminist literature and has chosen Women's Studies as one of the optional modules within her degree course. Amanda feels that her views make her different from most of the other female students. She describes herself as a 'closeted feminist'. Naeema believes that racism and sexism are interwoven and that there is a need to address race issues within feminism and sexism within Black organizations. She feels that she has easier access to Black organizations than feminist ones at the moment but thinks that they are both important. Rachel does not see herself as a feminist. Her contact with feminism has been minimal and she sees organizations such as GreenPeace and Amnesty International as having had the most influence on her ideas.

Young Women's Experiences

When Michelle Fine and Pat McPherson invited four teenagers for a series of dinners to talk about being young women in the 1990s, they were struck by how powerful feminism had been in shaping these young women's lives and the meanings they made of them and how inadequately their feminism dealt with key issues of identity and peer relations (Fine, 1992).

Being a young woman in the 1990s is challenging. HIV and AIDS, changing family structures, the emphasis on education and having a career and the demands of living in a consumer society are just some of the issues that young women have to contend with. Whilst new possibilities have been created, the pressures on young women have also increased. McRobbie describes young women as having been 'unhinged' from traditional gender roles and expectations (1993: 408). For Naeema, this 'unhinging' has given her opportunities to be involved in international work, but at the same time it has caused conflict between her and her parents which she is struggling to resolve. As the future becomes less predictable, independence and assertiveness are becoming not just desirable but essential.

Many young women, although they may express feminist views, reject feminism as being not relevant to them. The image of feminism has been polarized to the extent that feminists are seen as having radical views and being anti-men (Sharpe, 1994: 284). Rachel does not identify with feminism for this reason. In her study of young women Sue Sharpe found that many who do accept and support feminist views over-estimate the advances that have been made. They feel that equality has been achieved and therefore the women's movement is redundant.

There are many other young women who, like Amanda, Naeema and Rachel, are politically aware and active, defining their sexuality, organizing women's groups in schools and colleges, forming bands, starting magazines. But even when young women do identify themselves as feminists, they are often rejected by their peers. Amanda describes herself as a 'closeted feminist' because she is unable to express her views amongst her student friends. Other young women have found older feminists to be oppressors:

> We had already recognised our oppression as young women in the wider society — laws, parents, schools and so on. But we hadn't realised we were also oppressed by older feminists ... your ageist assumptions deny us our ability to think for ourselves, to create and make our own decisions. In your minds, you place our feminism on another level, below that of yours.
>
> (Hemmings, 1982)

Young Women and Feminist Theory

Being at the margins of feminist theory is inevitable when young women are excluded from the process of analysing practice and creating theoretical frameworks. They are unable to influence ideas, raise issues and concerns, or even challenge their marginality. They are not relating their experiences and documenting their lives. Therefore, young women have to rely on other women to do it for them. There are few women who have taken the opportunity to write about young women and the outcome is that there is little research and limited literatures available.

The most striking feature of the existent literature on young women is the paucity of written material. Sexism in education, young mothers, and young women's sexuality are the main areas of study. The literature on adolescence invariably focuses on male adolescence (Nava, 1992; McRobbie, 1993). I could find no body of research or documentation of young women's activism and agreed with Michelle Fine's conclusion:

> young women's political outrage simply does not exist as a category for feminist intellectual analysis
>
> (1992: 177)

There is hardly any literature which has been written by young women themselves.

Youth work with girls and young women, which has grown in prominence since the 1970s, is probably the most comprehensive body of literature that focuses on young women and I found this, too, was disappointing. The majority of this literature is in the form of short articles in youth work journals written by women working in the field. The more theoretical and analytical texts have been written by the same few women and are quite dated. There is hardly any material that focuses on Black young women, young women with disabilities, or young lesbians; and within the more general literature on Black young people, and young people with disabilities, young women do not feature prominently and there is no analysis of gender differences. Equality issues and more current feminist issues, such as difference, positioning and identity politics, are not even finding their way into youth work literature. Most of the writing on work with girls and young women was written during the 1980s, and very little has been written since 1990. The few texts to have emerged recently are reflecting current concerns about youth being seen as problematic, such as single mothers, prostitution and young women at risk or in trouble (Mountain, 1989; Green, 1992). Yet in reality these issues affect only a small minority of young women. For example, according to Save The Children only 2 per cent of young women under 20 in the UK are single mothers (Whalen, 1993).

Women's Studies is one way of accessing feminist theory. Women's Studies in Britain has grown over the last 15 years. The majority of courses are either postgraduate, or within Adult Education, or the Worker's Educational Association (WEA) and tend to attract older women (Griffin, 1994). Few young women have the opportunity to do Women's Studies. However, there are increasing opportunities to include Women's Studies modules on other courses such as the Youth and Community training (Morley, 1993) and on first degrees like the one that Amanda is doing. One way of making feminism more accessible to young women would be incorporating Women's Studies modules into schools and colleges.

With little relevant literature and limited access to Women's Studies young women can find it difficult to access the women's movement. For some young women it is harder than for others:

> .... most of us have sought out the women's movement, with some considerable difficulty. It doesn't exactly reach out and grab you, especially if you live in the provinces, or are Black, or are working class.
>
> (Hemmings, 1982)

Amanda, being a student, has opportunities to access the women's movement. Naeema has found Black organizations more accessible to her than feminist ones, whilst Rachel, who lives in a small village, has no access as such. Even when contact is established, there are barriers to overcome:

> In fact, at first when we did find the women's movement most of us were completely intimidated by the structure and the jargon.
>
> (Hemmings, 1982)

Making Connections — The Way Forward

Young women are expressing feminist views but at the same time they are rejecting the stereotypical image of feminism. Although their knowledge of the women's movement is fragmented, they have more knowledge of its existence now (Sharpe, 1994). Young women like Amanda, Naeema and Rachel are taking action, often outside of the women's movement and with little support. Young women are situated right at the margins of feminist theory because they are not actively involved in creating it. Feminist theory will continue to be deficient until it recognizes, validates and incorporates young women's experiences. Until feminism incorporates their perspectives, young women will feel that it is irrelevant to their lives and will continue to see feminism as the concern of others. It seems to me that there are two strategies needed here. If feminist theory does not adequately reflect reality, the first strategy needs to address this deficit by enriching theory and making it more comprehensive. The other strategy comes from the need to appreciate the value of young women and, through recognizing the benefits to feminism, to invest more directly in young women themselves. There is of course a direct correlation between the two because when we start incorporating young women's experiences we will be investing in them.

Enriching Theory

Studies of young women's experiences of adolescence
The effects of gender on the growing up process has not been comprehensively studied (Sharpe, 1994). This would help make feminism relevant to young women whilst providing important research material.

Young women's lives need to be documented
Society is changing all the time and it is easy to get out of touch with the reality of young people's lives. Recording young women's experiences would incorporate young women into feminism and would validate their experiences, achievements and contributions.

Investing in Young Women

Young women are an untapped resource
Take Rachel for example: her experiences of sexual abuse are recent. Sexual abuse is an area in which feminists are outraged and there needs to be more study, more analysis and most importantly, more action. Young women like Rachel need support, but at the same time they have experiences from which we can learn, and they have the determination to take action if they have support and encouragement. Rachel approached the Youth Council because she recognized that she needed support and she knew from previous experience that she would be listened to and her experiences would not be dismissed.

Feminism needs to recognize and theorize the differences among women, including young women
Young women are not a homogenous category. Failure to theorize differences helps

to maintain the image of feminists being older women and images of young women being White, middle-class, able-bodied and heterosexual.

Using power differentials to our advantage

Young women often lack knowledge, resources and confidence and could benefit from other women helping them make changes. The Milan Bookstore Collective emphasize that women are not all equal and that by bonding with women who are more powerful we can use this differential to our advantage. This could be an effective way of empowering young women. There are numerous ways in which we can have contact with young women: they are our daughters, nieces, friend's daughters and neighbours. Some of us work with them as teachers, youth workers or social workers. Louise Morley, who teaches Community and Youth Work training, recognizes the strong position of the women she teaches to disseminate feminist ideas in the wider community and how important it is that they engage with their professional role from an empowered position (1993: 127). Jennifer Marchbank is a youth worker working with a girls' group in Scotland. She describes her youth work with young women as 'the ultimate feminist action' as she assists them in the development of their abilities, to analyse and question the world in which they live their lives, and to actively choose how to live their lives (Marchbank *et al.*, 1993: 161).

Creating positive images

Positive images of young women instead of the negative images that exist would challenge stereotypes of promiscuous welfare mothers, anorexic adolescent girls and tall, blonde models. These would provide positive role models for young women and would also highlight differences between women.

Providing a platform

Young women need to have platforms from which their opinions can be expressed. Students can use their Student Union, and members of other organizations often have a framework for representation, but for young women like Naeema and Rachel, who do not belong to any organizations as such, local Youth Councils, although they are few and far between, can provide excellent opportunities for young women. Naeema is chairperson of her local Youth Council and believes that it has been the most influential thing in her life in terms of her activism. Through her experiences of being involved in decision making at local level, she has been able to go further and represent young people nationally and internationally. She has had opportunities to explore different issues, learn skills such as public speaking and report writing, and believes that her personal development has been enhanced in a way that could not have been achieved elsewhere.

Positive role models

There are many young women who are already active feminists. These young women could provide positive role models for other young women. There needs to be some way of identifying them and developing a communication system whereby young women have easy access to information about them.

We are all learning
Everyone is at a different point of the learning curve. Those new to feminism need to be welcomed and encouraged. Space needs to be made to explore issues without fear of hostile treatment, quick judgements or dismissals.

Conclusion

There is a cycle that exists where, because little is written about young women due to their marginalization, few young women identify or engage with the feminist movement. This leads to little research, academic study or recording, which in turn leads to further marginalization of young women. We have a responsibility to young women and to ourselves to break into this cycle. By valuing young women, acknowledging and supporting the activism in which they are engaged, focusing on issues which are pertinent to them and increasing opportunities for young women to engage in feminism, we can make feminism relevant to more young women. Amanda, Naeema and Rachel are just three young women who have enormous potential and who are currently engaging in feminism in their own ways. How can we justify continuing to exclude young women? If the changes that we are seeking are for the benefit of us all, surely it makes sense to work together.

References

FINE, MICHELLE (1992) *Disruptive Voices: The Possibilities of Feminist Research*, Michigan: University of Michigan Press.

GREEN, JUDITH (1992) *It's No Game: Responding to the Needs of Young Women Involved in Prostitution*, Leicester: National Youth Agency.

GRIFFIN, GABRIELE (Ed.) (1994) *Changing Our Lives: Doing Women's Studies*, London: Pluto Press.

HEMMINGS, SUSAN (Ed.) (1982) *Girls Are Powerful: Young Women's Writing From Spare Rib*, London: Sheba Feminist Publishers.

LEES, SUE (1993) *Sugar and Spice: Sexuality and Teenage Girls*, London: Penguin.

MARCHBANK, J., CORRIN, C. and BRODIE, S. (1993) 'Inside and "Out" or Outside Academia: Lesbians Working in Scotland', in KENNEDY, M., LUBELSKA, C. and WALSH, V. (Eds) *Making Connections: Women's Studies, Women's Movements, Women's Lives*, pp. 155–66, London: Taylor & Francis.

McROBBIE, A. (1993) 'Shut Up and Dance: Youth Culture and Changing Modes of Femininity', *Cultural Studies*, **7**, October pp. 406–26.

THE MILAN WOMEN'S BOOKSTORE COLLECTIVE (1990) *Sexual Difference: A Theory of Social Symbolic Practice*, Bloomington and Indianapolis: Indiana University Press.

MORLEY, L. (1993) 'Women's Studies in Community and Youth Work Training', in KENNEDY, M., LUBELSKA, C. and WALSH, V. (Eds) *Making Connections: Women's Studies, Women's Movements, Women's Lives*, pp. 118–29, London: Taylor & Francis.

MOUNTAIN, ANITA (1989) *Lifting the Limits: A Handbook for Women Working with Young*

Women at Risk or in Trouble, Leicester: National Youth Bureau.

NAVA, M. (1992) *Changing Cultures: Feminism, Youth Culture and Consumerism*, London: Sage Publications.

SHARPE, S. (1994) *Just Like a Girl: How Girls Learn to be Women: From the Seventies to the Nineties*, London: Penguin.

WHALEN, A. (1993) *Try on my Shoes: Youth Work with Young Women in the 1990s*, London: Save The Children.

Part V
Lesbians Organizing Together

Chapter 11

Lesbians Organizing Together (LOT) in Dublin

Maria Power

Introduction

LOT (Lesbians Organizing Together) was formed in August 1991. Literally and actively, Lesbians Organizing Together is what LOT represents today. It is young in developmental terms, precisely it is four years old in September 1995. In essence, LOT is an umbrella type organization which provides coordination and support to lesbian groups and individuals. LOT is owned by all its members and every member has a say in the major decisions of the organization.

To reach the age of four is quite an achievement for a lesbian organization that is as diverse as LOT. LOT is not only surviving, it is expanding and having very positive effects on and for Irish lesbians. It is an achievement because most lesbian and many other women's voluntary organizations have on average lasted anywhere between 1 and 2 years. Their demise has come about for any of a multitude of reasons but most commonly the diversity of ideologies and work practices have been at the core of the famous 'splits'.

By using different structures and combinations of decision-making processes, LOT has tried to facilitate continuity. This has had its difficulties, debates and frustrations but these have been outweighed by the positive outcomes and positive effects on lesbians, both volunteers and staff. Almost without exception the experience has been empowering for all lesbians who have come into contact with or have been actively involved in LOT. I would suggest that activism through LOT is powerful and empowering for all of us.

Origination and Formation of LOT

The original idea for LOT came about in June 1991 from a couple of lesbians — Pauline Tracey and myself. We were frustrated that there was very little activism focused on lesbians in Dublin at that time. The one lesbian group that did exist was the Dublin lesbian help line. This group is still here today, 13 years on from its formation and it is going strong.

There was a significant amount of activism during the late 1970s and 1980s. Some of the main events were the formation of Irish Women United in 1975 and the Women's Conference on Lesbianism in 1978. These events were the foundation for what exists today. In the early 1980s, there was a women's centre in Dame Street, which was very important for lesbians at that time. Unfortunately misappropriation of funds and different ideologies made it untenable to continue. It was these experiences and the void regarding lesbian activism that existed in 1990 that provided the impetus for a new lesbian organization in 1991. The time was right, energy was high, it just needed focus. Today it is the lesbians of the 1970s, 1980s and 1990s that organize together, drawing on a wealth of talent, experience and skills.

The main group that was active in Dublin in 1990 was GLEN (Gay & Lesbian Equality Network). This group had as its focus Law Reform, namely the decriminalization of homosexuality for gay men. The campaign was successful and resulted in the law being repealed with an equal age of consent of 17 in June 1993. Though this group is well organized, it is primarily focused on issues of greatest concern to gay men, rather than to lesbians. The group's active membership is also predominantly gay men with an average of 1–2 lesbians participating at any given time. It is for this reason that a group of lesbians wanted to work on issues for themselves that were of concern to other lesbians.

Early in 1991, it was the couple of dissatisfied lesbians who sat down, talked for hours over numerous cups of coffee and then came up with a proposal for a new lesbian organization — specifically run by lesbians for lesbians on issues of concern to lesbians.

The forum for the origination of LOT happened when a group got together to prepare for a workshop on 'Homophobia'. The workshop was hosted by The Council for the Status of Women (CSW) for its delegate membership. This workshop was brought about by Lesbian delegates from Cork and Dublin lobbying the CSW for a greater awareness of homophobia and lesbian lives. The CSW is the largest women's organization in Ireland. It is Government funded by the Department of Labour and its main focus is highlighting women's concerns on matters of public interest. The CSW has a high public profile; therefore, hosting a workshop on homophobia was seen by most lesbians as significant. At this meeting, which was attended by approximately 30 lesbians, it was suggested that a new lesbian group be formed in Dublin and there was a proposal put forward about how this might proceed.

The first meeting of LOT was held on 8 August 1991. About 35 lesbians attended, which was a great show of interest in the proposal. From there it was agreed to meet monthly, set up structures, appoint coordinators and name the new organization.

Structures and Evolution by Consensus — 1991–1994

The structure that was proposed was an 'umbrella' type structure. The thinking behind this was:

- that there was an enormous amount of talent and skills in existence in the lesbian community and it was high time that we used such attributes for our own needs as lesbians;
- to encourage lesbians to engage in activities that they liked and wanted to do for themselves;
- this structure allowed for and attracted the wide diversity of strengths, talents and roles that are required to run an organization;
- it allowed for collective activity in areas about which lesbians feel strongly, for example: partnership rights, better creche facilities, better support services. Similarly, other groups of lesbians are often more attracted to organizing social activities;
- the organization would support any group or activity that was organized by lesbians and/or for lesbians. This allowed activities to be initiated by a group or an individual lesbian who wished to pursue an idea of her own. Support is in the form of funding, meeting space and administration.
- the organization would offer lesbians an opportunity to manage the organization in several different roles and in a way that lesbians themselves would see as appropriate.

The following points were agreed:

- First, that it would be an umbrella structure, which would be jointly coordinated by two lesbians.
- All activities, if more than one person was interested, would be organized collectively by groups.
- Where only one person was interested in a particular activity, it would be a short project with support from the organization.
- Each group would set its own agenda and develop its own policies, thereby promoting autonomy and empowerment of individuals on the ground. Policies for the organization as a whole would only be introduced as and when needed.
- There would be a monthly meeting open to all lesbians and each group would commit a representative to talk about their activities.
- That monthly meetings would be the forum where all LOT decisions were made and everyone there had a say. All major LOT proposals had to be ratified by the monthly meeting where the issue could be discussed openly and then a decision made by consensus.
- The meeting aims to have all decisions made by consensus but a voting policy is in place if a certain process and time has been followed and no agreement is reached.

Evaluation and Planning Day

This is an annual event and is usually held towards the end of January. The idea of the day is to spend the morning evaluating the past year, voting on any major policies that have been proposed and spend the afternoon planning for the coming year. Again, this day is open to everyone though only members can vote. It is an exciting day as it allows everyone an opportunity to reflect, talk about any problem areas and also pat themselves on the back for all the good work that has been done all year. Approximately 50 women attend and collectively agree the priorities for the coming year. As everyone knows, not everything can be done in one year and one cannot keep everyone happy all of the time. This day allows all women who are interested to have a say on what the needs of the community are and what the priorities should be. Subsequently, resources and energy are given to projects, ensuring that *visions are realized*.

One organizational change takes place on that day. The coordinators who have been in that role for the previous year step down. Names for the coming year are proposed by persons interested in going forward (the previous year's coordinator can go forward again for a second year, which is the maximum time allowed). Where more than two names are proposed a vote takes place to elect two coordinators.

It is a day when many more women get involved in LOT either in groups or projects they are interested in. The day is facilitated by an outside facilitator and is opened with the launch of the Annual Report for the previous year.

Ideology and Ethos

LOT is primarily about encouraging lesbians to come out and to work for themselves. That work can be organizing discos, lobbying political parties or providing support services. The objective is to encourage lesbians to be active on issues that concern us as lesbians.

The aims of LOT are:

- to promote unity by coordination and support for lesbians and lesbian groups;
- to encourage and support the coming out of all lesbians;
- to promote a positive identity and/or positive image for lesbians;
- to provide a platform for issues to be raised and addressed, new groups to be formed and ideas to be explored for the lesbian community at large.

The ethos is over-ridingly lesbian feminist, though some women in LOT describe themselves as gay. It is primarily about 'empowerment' of lesbians. This is done through encouraging lesbians to:

- work for themselves (in groups or individually);
- get involved in decision making;
- take on new roles;
- engage lesbians for paid work that might be required;

- explore lesbianism and outness in a safe environment;
- take on paid work with a lesbian organization;
- be conscious of issues of class and parallels of other minority interest groups;
- make decisions about what we want for our future.

One of the significant results to date is the increase in confidence and self esteem and the increased sense of security in being lesbian that many lesbians have got from being involved and active in LOT.

Training

Another principle that LOT strongly supports is the provision of training specifically for lesbians. All training is carried out in a safe environment with qualified lesbian trainers where possible. It is the lesbian trainers who have given so much of their time, free of charge, who have contributed to LOT being as strong as it is today.

The training to date has included

- Facilitation
- Group work
- Media training
- Presentations and public speaking
- Writing workshops
- Leadership training which included teamwork, chairing meetings, group dynamics
- Communication skills
- Feedback/evaluation and planning
- Conflict resolution
- Outreach role plays

Most training takes place over a weekend and sometimes runs over a number of months where resources permit. Some of the training mentioned is repeated annually and new areas are always being planned for the following year. New training might be more group training, i.e. perhaps a residential weekend for all members of LOT. Another area of interest is enterprise development training for lesbians. In all cases costs are kept to a minimum and are usually absorbed by the organization so that all members can avail themselves of training. LOT believes that training allows lesbians to explore more fully their potential in a particular area of interest and in turn invest in the future of LOT.

Major steps

Up until 1993, though we had made great progress in deciding structures and processes, we still did not have a regular office space. We were moving from hired rooms over pubs to political party offices, to student unions, to illegal derelict buildings. As regards finance, the Social and Entertainments group was running discos and the Finance group was successful at accessing some small grants.

It was finally proposed at a meeting in April 1993 that we should commit ourselves to paying rent and having a regular meeting space. This was to prove to be one of our first major and most difficult decisions. Many of the lesbians involved panicked. They were not ready for commitment — how would we pay rent, were we ready as an organization? After much discussion the decision was made to go ahead with only one abstention vote.

We got our first office in June 1993. It was a tremendous feeling. It was the first time in most of our lesbian lives that we had our own space, our own literature and paraphernalia on the walls and it was all positive about ourselves. It was the first time we did not have to keep looking for meeting spaces either coyly or indirectly. The space was safe, the energy was high and our pride was obvious.

The office space is used by groups every day and every night except Sunday nights — all year round.

The next major issue was introducing our first LOT policy around membership and voting. These meetings were difficult and at times traumatic. I will discuss the difficulties later but for now this was the policy adopted in May 1993:

> *Membership* is open to women who identify as lesbian, bisexual or who are exploring their sexuality and straight women who identify as allies. The onus is on straight women to identify as allies. To become a member, one must be involved in LOT (groups, staff or monthly meetings) for at least three months.

> *Decisions* will be made by consensus if possible. If this is not possible a further meeting will be allocated for discussion, after which voting can then be held. The voting after a second meeting must be carried by at least 60 per cent. If it is not, a third meeting can be held for discussion, voting carried out for the second time can be carried by a simple majority at this stage.

All members can vote. Allies are not entitled to vote on major policy issues but have equal rights to voice opinions and participate in discussions and decisions at other meetings. Key roles in the organization including that of coordinator can only be taken up by women who identify as lesbian.

Other policies on violence between women, finance policies, social and entertainments policies, etc., were adopted with a bit more ease.

Another major decision was taken in 1994. This was that LOT would become an Employer and manage a Community Employment Scheme. A CE scheme is a Government-funded scheme that pays low wages for 20 hours work a week. It is aimed at individuals who are unemployed. Many voluntary organizations in Ireland avail themselves of these schemes so that workers can be employed who otherwise could not be funded. The advantage to the individual can be valuable work experience and training programmes to support their development. For LOT, the CE scheme is an enormous extra resource. By January 1995, LOT will have 11 staff including a full-time Team Leader. Staff are allocated to various areas of work in the organization and work ranges from administration, supporting a help line, supporting LOT groups, to developing a library and resource space for lesbians. The scheme eases the day-to-day work demands on volunteers and also assists the organization in becoming a more stable and identifiable group in the voluntary sector in Ireland. LOT contributes significantly to the issue of lesbian visibility in ways that may be much more difficult to do on an individual basis.

Difficulties for an Organization Like LOT

In most organizations there are difficulties, but in LOT some are specific to the type and size of the organization. The organization has a membership of 200+, of whom approximately 50 women are regularly active. Members' experience varies from lesbians who have been politically active for years and are very strong in their feminist beliefs, to others who are not familiar with such ideology. Some women are very out while others are just at the beginning stages of coming out. Political issues often arise and, because the range of experience and opinion of members is wide, much time can be spent working through process and reaching consensus. This working through — though very often empowering — can be exhausting. It is an important issue as most women volunteering have limited energy and an organiza-tion must be careful not to lose the balance between process/ownership of decisions and losing the membership from burn out.

An example of a difficulty was the policy on membership. Opinions varied from opening the membership to everyone to being lesbian only. The debate took three 3 hour sessions with a consultant facilitator. The sessions were intense, passionate and frank. The outcome was eventually voted on because not everyone agreed to all of the proposal. The downside is that although we have an agreed policy, it is not to everyone's satisfaction. However, it is a workable solution.

Difficulties continue to arise from time-to-time. More importantly, collectively we are much better at dealing with issues and conflict. This is due in part to learning from experience, including conflict resolution and communication skills as part of our regular training, and in part to structures being changed and mechanisms put in place to allow open discussion on important issues.

Practically, this was done by setting up a structure commonly used in Community Development called a Steering Committee (or Management Commit-tee). This committee has a representative from each group and has responsibility for day-to-day decisions. Policy and major decisions are still left with the monthly meeting. This means that there is 'transparency' of all decisions and at the same time it allows smaller groups to make decisions or recommendations to the organization.

Changing the structures and improving the decision-making process was a tense and nervous task but working through it made the organization stronger because more women assumed ownership for the outcome. The nervousness was particularly around the issue of ensuring democracy and ownership by all. However, streamlining the decision-making process has also allowed more time for discussion by the wider group at monthly meetings. The monthly meetings have become more inclusive. (Appendix 1 shows the structure of LOT as it was adopted in August 1991. Appendix 2 shows its development, and Appendix 3 indicates the decision-making structure.)

Another area that sometimes causes difficulty is working with gay men. This is usually a gender issue. It has become more apparent as LOT is a lesbian-only organization and encourages lesbians to speak for themselves. Difficulties arise where gay men speak on behalf of lesbians without consultation — this is beginning to anger lesbians more and more. LOT encourages lesbians to speak out for themselves in ways which they themselves are ready for.

In conclusion I would say that difficulties are part of the normal process of organizations. Issues and conflicts that are dealt with well are often agents of strength and bonding for members of an organization. As LOT stabilizes and becomes more secure, support of each other and of each other's visions is vital. This attitude and feeling of goodwill towards each other will see us a long way through and allow for constructively dealing with differences.

Currently — What Exactly Gets Done and by Whom

LOT Groups

A number of groups have become part of the LOT structure. Some were already in existence but most were formed by different interest groups of lesbians after the formation of LOT. The groups are: LEN (Lesbian Equality Network), First Out, Dublin Lesbian Line, Publishing Group, Social and Entertainments, Finance Group, Outreach Group, Staff Group.

A brief outline of the work of each group follows.

LEN (Lesbian Equality Network)

This group came together to ensure that at a time when a lot of publicity was being given to homosexuality in Ireland, lesbian issues would be focused on and included in legislative changes/developments. This group corresponds regularly with Government Departments, organizes training to assist lesbians to deal with the media and gets involved in workshops/discussions on equality and the law. The group has also produced leaflets, and, more recently, has made a submission to the Department of Equality in relation to their proposals regarding the Equal Status Bill which is expected to be delivered in early 1995.

First Out

This is a support group which facilitates discussion in a safe way for women who are questioning their sexuality. The group meets fortnightly, once during the week and once at the weekend. The meetings are conducted by trained facilitators and each week a different topic is chosen for discussion. Among the topics covered during 1994 were: 'Coming out', 'Fears & Concerns of Being Lesbian', 'Sex, Religion, Mothers'. On average a First Out meeting is attended by 10–12 women and for 1994, approximately 260 attended First Out meetings.

The volunteers of First Out attend training sessions at least once a year and twice if it is deemed necessary.

Lesbian Line

This telephone help line has been in existence for 13 years. It is still one of the main backbones of the lesbian community. Like the above group, volunteers are trained on a regular basis to work on the line. During the past couple of years, the line has hosted workshops on various topics such as 'Violence in the Lesbian Community' and has also undertaken research of the line calls. The main findings were that there was a change in callers to younger lesbians and also that there was a significant increase in the number of married women who call the line.

At the time of writing, the line is available only one night a week for two hours. There are plans to have a second night a week. The members of the line will train LOT staff to assist with help-line calls that now come into the LOT office during office hours.

Publishing Group

The main activity of this group is to produce two pages of articles of interest to lesbians on a monthly basis. This is produced with the monthly newspaper *Gay Community News*. The two pages are simply titled 'Lesbian Pages' and the information that is collated, edited and produced is carried out by a group of lesbians. What must be mentioned is that agreement to having the two pages included in GCN was hard won. It took a lot of negotiation between LOT members and the NLGF (National Lesbian and Gay Federation), which is predominantly male and controls the production of GCN. The results have proved worthwhile, although it is a long way from being equal in terms of a community newspaper. The group is looking at expanding its brief with the assistance of LOT staff. Some of the possibilities include the development of an archive/resource library.

Social and Entertainments Group

This group is sometimes the life and soul of the organization. It organizes many social activities — mostly discos as they are the most reliable and regular income generator. However, other activities that often do not make money have been pursued. These are pub quizzes, which are great fun, a bingo night, comedy and cabaret nights and theatre/sketch evenings. Two of the main events of the year are: The Wild and Wonderful Women's Weekend, which is an annual weekend of events day and night, and is usually held in mid-September. It includes sports, discos, sketches, lunches, workshops, videos and music. The other great evening is the LOT Christmas dinner, which is attended by a maximum of 100 women as this is the most the restaurant will hold. It is a great evening and though the price is not subsidized only the cost is charged. Long may the social and entertainments group survive as it is much needed.

Finance Group

Well, not the most exciting of groups in terms of the title but as a group it is essential, concerned as it is with the financial management of the organization. In the past it concentrated on ensuring good accounts were kept, completing funding application forms to different trusts and government bodies and monitoring the yearly budget. All funding requests come through this group who make the decisions based on funds being available and the activity being lesbian-related. If requests are for large amounts then the monthly meeting approves the expenditure. This would be the case for most training budget requests.

During 1995, it is hoped that the group will concentrate on core funding and persuade the Government to give core support to the overall LOT project and all its activities.

Outreach Group

This was a new group formed in 1994 as a result of a proposal at the annual Evaluation and Planning day in January. The aim of this group is to go out and reach people in the larger community with a positive message about ourselves as lesbians, our lives and the prejudice that we face. The target group is Women's groups, Community groups, Equality Agencies and Youth groups.

It is also hoped to inform the general public with accurate information about lesbian lives as well as bring information to other women who are questioning their sexuality and who are unable to access our services in a city-centre location.

Staff

This is not an affiliated group but is part of the backbone of LOT. Staff meet on a fortnightly basis to give each other support, discuss related staff issues and any projects that they themselves would like to propose.

Staff take on one or two (depending on the level of activity) of the LOT groups to support, attending that particular group's meetings and offering office support in the form of completing tasks for that group's activities. They have input at group level, but groups are primarily made up of volunteers and decisions are made by consensus.

Ad hoc Groups in LOT

Open Forum

This was a pilot idea in 1994 to hold open discussion-type meetings on any topic of interest to lesbians. It was held once a month for the first six months. The meetings were open to all women and the topics for discussion varied each month. The topics were decided upon by women who wished to organize and see it happen.

Topics that were covered were: bi-sexuality; poetry and prose reading by Mary Dorcey; health issues for lesbians; lesbian mothers and co-parents. The idea behind Open Forum was to generate discussion for more 'out' lesbians and to explore issues for ourselves. Open Forum meetings were very successful, very enjoyable and stimulating. Because of their success and demand more Open Forums are planned for 1995. Some of the topics are: lesbians and the media; lesbian experiences in the 1970s, 1980s and 1990s; an astrological evening.

Public Relations

This group came out of an evaluation that was carried out by LOT early in 1994. The membership felt that there was a need to:

1. improve communication — internally because the organization had grown so much and the level of activity had increased. Also greater communication was needed within the lesbian community so as not to isolate LOT, which is meant to be accessible and available to all lesbians.
2. improve LOT's image through the use of better advertising and positive poster images.

There is a small group of 4–5 women working on this project. Their work ranges from offering support to groups who are carrying out public work to coordinating media requests — interviews and print. Other lesbians help by offering their skills as graphic artists or developing a newsheet which is freely available. It is hoped that the benefits of this project will become much more visible later in 1995.

Alternative LOT

This is a new group and the emphasis is on activities other than discos and group meetings/discussions. It includes alternative forms of entertainment and sporting activities. The type of activities covered are 'Les Cilla' (a night of Blind Date for lesbians), assistance in the setting up of a Ceili night for lesbians to learn this style of Irish dancing, plans to have a lesbian team in the soccer league, some organized activities for lesbians who are interested in the outdoors.

Lesbian and Gay Pride Day

Every year a group of women and men, along with other Lesbian and Gay groups, come together to organize events and the pride march itself. For LOT, this project is a one-off and the women who put much time and energy into making floats and banners for LOT are women who are extremely supportive of LOT but who often prefer not to go to meetings. These women are interested in the arts as a community development medium and support LOT in that way whenever possible.

Networking

Every year LOT has engaged in a weekend trip to another city or town and takes part in workshops/conferences and social activities with another lesbian group. These occasions are tremendous, not least for the bonding and support that takes place. It is also an opportunity to listen and learn from each other. There is always a great sense of solidarity that continues after these weekends. Trips and meetings to Derry, Drogheda, Belfast, Cork have already taken place.

Every year there are always many one-off events. These can be anything from weekends away to other cities, networking and having fun, to hillwalking by an interested group of lesbians. Many lesbians support LOT by offering their professional services to the organization. This can be in the form of carving a plaque for the office, helping with legal documentation, putting up shelving, dropping bus loads of lesbians to other cities for conferences and fun.

All work in LOT is done by lesbians either as a group or as an individual contribution. This includes decision making to support to having fun. The office is run and equipped by lesbians. Everything you see or hear done by LOT has been brought about entirely by lesbian energy and goodwill. Appendix 4 gives examples of work done by LOT women.

Needless to say all of the above bond many women together, build on friendships and there is always a social element to doing any type of work in LOT.

Possible Future of LOT

As yet there is no agreed vision or strategic plan for LOT. It is hoped this will be achieved during 1995. However, in my opinion and in talking to some of the other lesbians in LOT, the following ideas have emerged:

Core Funding

A basic level of Core Funding should be obtained on an annual basis. This would ensure the survival of LOT and having a regular place to meet. At the moment, a minimum of £6,000 annually is required. It is hoped that individual women, lesbian businesses and the Government will provide this minimum resource.

It is essential that we get government backing for the LOT project so that at least one full-time properly paid member of staff is available to support this community-based organization.

Comprehensive Support Services

These, which should be available to all, are: a help line available daily and several evenings during the week; a daily drop-in space; support groups; and counselling that is regularly available. It would include the development of outreach programmes, resource materials and educational information. It would also include the development of effective volunteer programmes, and training to maintain and develop the organization and support its volunteers.

With regard to national links, LOT has, over the last couple of years, networked significantly with Derry, Belfast and Galway, and with Cork and Waterford to a lesser degree. It is important that over the next few years these links are developed and maintained so that we can all support each other no matter where in the country we are situated.

Politics

Politically, the rights of lesbians in Ireland should be clearly identified and protected. This would include:

Employment: Sexual Orientation must be included under any Employment Act.
Partnerships: Partnerships should have legal status with attendant benefits.
Equal Status: This would include equal treatment in places of recreation, entertainment and other social facilities.
Children: Lesbians should have the right to adopt, foster and have custody of children.
Education: Lesbian and Gay contributions to education should be included in all parts of the curriculum.
Public: The media should provide responsible coverage, and equal and appropriate representation should be given to lesbian and gay issues.

We must achieve our rights through lobbying government departments directly. We could launch a nationwide campaign by all lesbians and lesbian groups around the country. We could lobby our local politicians. One step in this process is having the LOT organization recognized by the Government as a legitimate and necessary project for the lesbian community and subsequently providing resources for its development.

Conclusion

By now most of the support services are well under way and each year lesbian activities are becoming more comprehensive and complementary to each other. Though these services reach a large number of women through-out Ireland they are primarily Dublin based.

One of the most interesting aspects of LOT is its diversity. Women in LOT are coming from different social backgrounds, different levels of 'outness', different types of life experience and different awareness of feminism. The other interesting aspect of LOT which complements its diversity is its flexibility. If we can listen and allow for each other's experience then as a lesbian movement we can go far. If we can all contribute in a way that each individual feels is valuable then collectively we will make progress.

What Some Members Say About LOT

Pauline, who is one of the co-founders of LOT: 'Being involved in LOT has been very important for me both personally and politically. On a personal level I have felt supported as a lesbian and as the years have gone on I've become more out through my involvement. On a political level I've found a forum which allows me work on issues which are important to me as a lesbian.'

Margaret, who is a member of the Finance group: 'As a member of LOT I have gained and learned a great deal. As a volunteer with LOT I am happy to be contributing to the development of an organization which creates a positive community and environment for me and other lesbians.'

Antonia, who is team leader of the employment scheme at LOT: 'LOT is my pride and my organization. It is my opportunity to finally speak for myself, to create and follow my own dreams and empower others to do the same. It is learning about differences and acceptance. It is about friendships new and old. LOT hopefully can be Lesbians of Tomorrow.'

Jane, who is a staff member at the LOT office; 'LOT means that I can be part of an exciting and expanding personal and political movement. This gives me the opportunity to express myself as a lesbian in a very vital way. Working for LOT makes it possible for me to feel proud as a lesbian. It is a positive framework for many of us to develop confidence and skills in groupwork.'

References available at LOT

LOT Brochures
Annual Reports 1992–1994
Issues for Irish Lesbians — LEN leaflet 1992
Proposal on Equal Status Legislation — LEN 1994
Leaflet on lesbianism and homophobia — LOT 1994

Speaking for Ourselves — Outreach leaflet 1994

Lesbian pages in GCN — Publishing group
Infopack for Volunteers
LOT bi-monthly newsheet — LOT office

Resource materials for trainers in sexual orientation — 1995
Issues for Lesbian Mothers 1995.

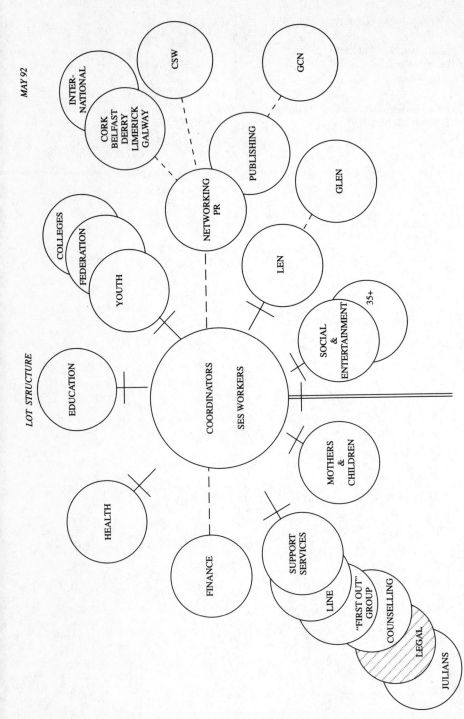

LOT STRUCTURE   *MAY 92*

Appendix 1 Organization Structure 1991

Appendix 2 Organization Structure 1995

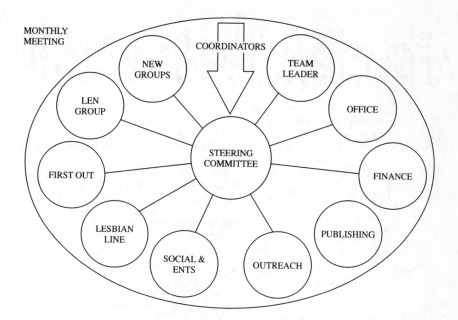

Appendix 3 Decision-making Table

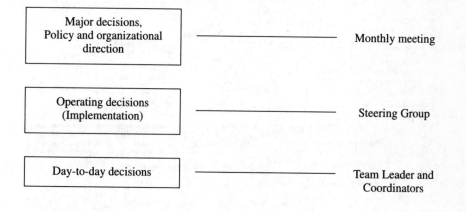

Appendix 4 Examples of Work Done by Women of LOT

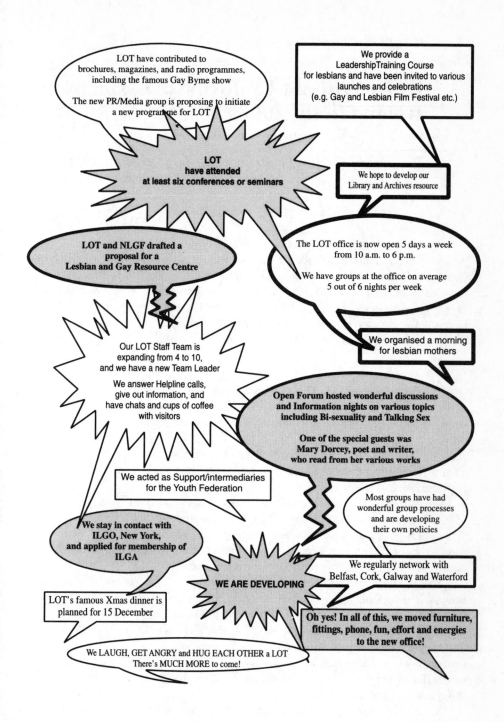

LOT have contributed to brochures, magazines, and radio programmes, including the famous Gay Byme show

The new PR/Media group is proposing to initiate a new programme for LOT

We provide a LeadershipTraining Course for lesbians and have been invited to various launches and celebrations (e.g. Gay and Lesbian Film Festival etc.)

**LOT
have attended
at least six conferences or seminars**

We hope to develop our Library and Archives resource

LOT and NLGF drafted a proposal for a Lesbian and Gay Resource Centre

The LOT office is now open 5 days a week from 10 a.m. to 6 p.m.

We have groups at the office on average 5 out of 6 nights per week

Our LOT Staff Team is expanding from 4 to 10, and we have a new Team Leader

We answer Helpline calls, give out information, and have chats and cups of coffee with visitors

We organised a morning for lesbian mothers

Open Forum hosted wonderful discussions and Information nights on various topics including Bi-sexuality and Talking Sex

One of the special guests was Mary Dorcey, poet and writer, who read from her various works

We acted as Support/intermediaries for the Youth Federation

Most groups have had wonderful group processes and are developing their own policies

We stay in contact with ILGO, New York, and applied for membership of ILGA

WE ARE DEVELOPING

We regularly network with Belfast, Cork, Galway and Waterford

LOT's famous Xmas dinner is planned for 15 December

Oh yes! In all of this, we moved furniture, fittings, phone, fun, effort and energies to the new office!

We LAUGH, GET ANGRY and HUG EACH OTHER a LOT There's MUCH MORE to come!

Chapter 12

Unity Without Uniformity: Lesbians in Ireland in the 1990s

*Rosemary Gibney, Patricia Carey, Izzy Kamikaze
and Kate Frances*

In this chapter, four Irish lesbians look at lesbian activism in the 1990s. Izzy
Kamikaze discusses the 'sex wars' in UK lesbian communities and at the interaction
between lesbianism and feminism; Patricia Carey considers the development of
lesbian activism in Ireland in the 1990s; Rosemary Gibney gives an overview of the
issues and campaigns that are currently engaging Irish lesbian activists, and Kate
Frances looks at the operation of lesbian helplines in Ireland.

Post-Feminism Ha Ha Ha (Izzy Kamikaze)

Issues of definition plague any discussion of feminist activism. Many feminists
dismiss the activism of other feminists (e.g. lesbian and gay movement/socialist/
anarchist feminists) as 'male-identified' or otherwise ideologically 'impure'. So,
what *is* feminist activism? And, as 'post-feminism' trips glibly from many tongues,
is it dead?

Feminist activism survives, but the climate has certainly changed. During the
1990s, resources (women's centres, publications and funding) have been lost.
Without resources, direct action/mass campaigns are almost impossible. Academic
and institutional feminism keep the flag flying, but are inaccessible to many and
cannot, alone, attract or keep a broad-based activist pool.

The right grows constantly stronger, tying many feminists up in rearguard
actions (e.g. defending abortion rights, where they exist). Irish feminists have
struggled against a Constitutional ban on abortion and have been hounded for
providing information about legal abortion elsewhere. Public opinion, however,
moves (gradually) in a more liberal direction — especially since 1992's 'X' case
(Smyth, 1992). The direct action tradition lives on, in an (illegal?) telephone
counselling service for pregnant women. (The current legal status of the Women's
Information Network is unclear.)

Social movements, including feminism, have lost the energies of the unemployed and low-paid to an economic squeeze leaving little room for political activism. In Ireland, even worse, emigration has returned to the levels of the 'bad old days'.

Prevailing winds in the 1990's climate aside, equally devastating storms have rocked the women's movement from within — many fuelled by the craving for ideological purity. Lesbian communities in particular have fragmented, especially in richer countries, where the movement once seemed strongest and the right to direct feminist theory has long been taken for granted. The 'sex wars' of the early 1990s tell a cautionary tale for the movement as a whole.

Ideas generated by political movements can become doctrinaire, and 'feminist fundamentalism' was duly born. Proper concern for the systematic sexual exploitation of women (e.g. in the pornography and sex industries) led to the carving in stone of a 'correct' feminist code of sexual practice (roughly: exclusively lesbian; pro-censorship; anti-sexual 'experimentation' — especially 'femme-butch' or 'SM', both undefined; undecided about monogamy/non-monogamy, but tending towards serial monogamy). Essentially, the feminist '*right* to a self-determined sexuality' was exchanged for an *obligation* on lesbians to adopt a sexuality imposed by a coterie that sought to police the sexual standards of lesbian communities.

The adoption of 'dress codes' (c. 1990) at some British women's events amused occasional visitors like myself, but was soon no laughing matter. In Leeds, the (homophobic, misogynistic) police force was called into a brawl at a women's disco to remove a few women whose clothing 'offended' another few women. Organizers subsequently imposed a dress code and a whole section of the community felt effectively barred from community events (*Leeds Other Paper*, 1991). Purges like this one deeply scarred the communities in which they occurred and the scars have not yet healed. These battles are sometimes represented as struggles between feminist and anti-feminist factions within lesbian communities. More importantly, the disputed rights (to define one's own sexuality and dress as one pleased) had previously been hotly defended by feminists. Unless one accepts the automatic right of one side to define feminism, this must be seen as an internal dispute between feminists.

Thankfully, this is an outsider's account — these wars have not raged in Ireland. It would be nice (and, touch wood, true) to claim superior tolerance but emigration of radicals (including sexual radicals) and confrontation-avoidance within beleaguered communities are other factors. We are not unaffected: Irish emigrants fought both sides of these battles. While many may never return, 'refugees' from fragmented British communities are increasingly settling in Ireland. [Hint: If refused entry to a British women's event, shrug your leather-clad shoulders, sigh and say 'Well, it wouldn't happen in Ireland ...' It won't get you in, but it will offend their sense of innate superiority.]

The 'sex wars' are under-documented, most evidence is anecdotal. However, traditional class divisions were apparent: the fundamentalists were overwhelmingly middle-class, the women they purged were predominantly working class/unemployed. It is also clear that on (as they named it) the 'pro-sex' side (anti-censorship, pro-sexual diversity) were many activists from the AIDS movement, where actual (rather than idealized) sexual practice and the fluidity of sexual identity are confronted daily. Meaningful feminist debate on sexual practice is impossible without input from AIDS movement feminists.

Having worked in the AIDS movement, I resent the charge of 'male-identification'. AIDS is a feminist issue because of the increasing numbers of women who are being infected worldwide; many in circumstances which they cannot control. In 'developed' countries, women most at risk include injecting drug-users, sex workers, prisoners and women who sometimes have sex with (or self-inseminate using the semen of) gay/bisexual man. Lesbian/bisexual women are disproportionately represented in all these groups, so AIDS is a lesbian issue. Similarly, lesbian and gay movement feminists espouse 'a self-defined sexuality' — a feminist aim. 'Some of our best friends' may be men, but feminists participate in both movements because of feminist politics, not just exaggerated sympathy for gay men. Misogynists unfortunately infest both movements and lesbian activists are frequently attacked (Watney, 1992) but solidarity from other lesbians/feminists is not automatic. 'I don't fancy the scenario but . . . (to become HIV+) . . . a penis or penises, semen, infected blood and dirty needles would usually have to come into the picture somewhere . . .' Although lesbians *can* be infected (with syphilis) we do not usually see it as a lesbian issue. 'We know where the responsibility lies' (Hart, nd). This quote is from the mid-1980s, but the sentiments unfortunately survive: *Real* lesbians do not get AIDS, lesbians 'guilty' of unlesbian activities (by fundamentalist standards) do not count. The personal is political? You bet your life (literally) it is! But let us not throw the feminist baby out with the fundamentalist bathwater.

'Post-feminism' is a self-indulgent myth. Feminist activism is irrelevant (or flagging) only from an impossibly ethnocentric viewpoint. The 'Women's Global Network for Reproductive Rights' newsletter (WGNRR, 1994) is a great antidote to 'post-feminism'. It covers feminist struggles worldwide, does not shirk the link between reproductive rights and self-defined sexuality (lesbian struggles are included) and is an excellent source on how AIDS affects women globally. Take four times yearly, until symptoms disappear . . .

Women worldwide are fighting their own battles and defining feminisms appropriate to their own circumstances. A monolithic feminism imposed from above oppresses women and is *anti*-feminist — feminism is the theory of the Women's *Liberation* Movement. Those 'oppressed' by others' difference should pursue happiness on uninhabited islands, the rest of us must co-exist or perish. Remember Sisterhood?

(I am indebted to many women, particularly Liz Willows and Sikaa Hammer for their memories and insights.)

Feminist Activism in Ireland (Patricia Carey)

Irish lesbians' history is characterized not only by working within a repressive Catholic society but also by their influential involvement in the divorce and abortion referenda of the early 1980s. At the outset, however, it needs to be said that lesbians in Ireland have had, and are still developing their own particular brand of activism.

Like most minority groups, lesbians have not found it easy to develop and be active in seeking equality. The problems that exist in Ireland for lesbians are not unique but merit mentioning. The rural/urban divide has made it difficult for activism on a national level to emerge. In recent years, especially since the start of the 1990s, this has changed with many new rural lesbian groups flourishing. These groups, although not beginning as lesbian, often splitting from lesbian and gay groups as issues become gender-focused, are facilitating a new and vibrant lesbian awakening all over Ireland. Cork and Dublin have always been active, with lesbians in Cork leading the way in organizing. They have now been joined by Wexford, Limerick, Galway, Kerry, Drogheda, which gave the city-based lesbian groups more to consider, discuss and fight for. New issues have thus come to light and, in the last five years, lesbians have taken on new agendas such as rural invisibility, lesbian mothers, lesbians and business, and have widened the scope of what is addressed.

With the decriminalization of male homosexuality (including a uniform age of consent) in 1993, the gay movement in Ireland was at one of its peaks. Since then, lesbians have reassessed where they are in relation to law reform. Lesbians are no longer content to be spoken for and written about by gay men. This has caused lesbians to question their needs, which are not always similar to those of gay men. Equal status legislation, employment protection and legal rights to children are now being campaigned for by lesbians with their own groups. The effect of law reform was huge but not as important for lesbians as for gay men. Attitudes have not changed overnight and much needs to be done in terms of education and outreach work, which has been begun by lesbian groups with this specific task in mind.

The gay community as a whole in Ireland has diversified. Lesbian Lines work alongside Gay Switchboards. Lesbian law reform groups such as LEN work in conjunction with, and separate from, gay men's reform groups. The scene has changed, women tend to socialize in women-only venues and organize many events specific to the needs, culture and identity of lesbians. Young lesbians in Ireland have also put a new face and slant on activism. They seem not as interested in feminism as their 'older' sisters would like them to be and a distinct moving away from lesbian separatism is obvious. As a younger lesbian, I see my activism in terms of working within a community to help change for all. However, not all young lesbians want to be active, they are 'out' and they want to enjoy life as much as, if not more than, their heterosexual counterparts. Therefore a 'heavy' political agenda, as they see it, is not appealing. They are involved; they march with Lesbian and Gay Pride all over Ireland (which has seen huge increases in the number of lesbian participants) and they support campaigns and issues within the lesbian movement (see below).

For some lesbians in Ireland, activism is defined by class, i.e. you have to be educated to be an activist or to have a political viewpoint. You have to be a lesbian, separatist mother . . . to be involved. All too often, the perception people have of groups such as LOT (Lesbians Organizing Together) or of Lesbian Lines stops them from getting involved because they feel they would not fit in, be able, be welcome or, more importantly, be needed. This problem needs to be addressed by lesbians in Ireland.

The activism of many is influenced by what has gone before. As a colonized country, this can be dangerous because we take on a victim mentality. Maybe what Irish lesbians need is their own brand of the American (now UK) Lesbian Avengers, to take direct action, reclaim our rights and put a stop to pandering politely to government and other decision-making bodies.

Like all movements, the lesbian community in Ireland has its splits. These factions, real or imaginary, exist on many levels, dinner-party types versus pub and disco dykes; separatists versus new-age inclusive types, etc. Even the names we call ourselves evoke our ethos and beliefs — gay woman; lesbian; femme; dyke; butch bitch. It has often been said of Irish group meetings that the first item on the agenda is the split. Although not totally true, this is the case for some engaged in lesbian activism in Ireland.

We are a diverse community with much to campaign, fight and be active for. Every lesbian in Ireland has a role to play in being active. Our philosophies may differ, yet our cause and rights will remain the same. Lesbian activism in Ireland has changed and will change, but the fact that it has continued, is enough for me to fight on.

Politics in Ireland: Radical and Right (Rosemary Gibney)

In 1992, Irish lesbian activists participated in a highly significant event signalling the beginnings of a new, and more open, understanding of lesbian and gay sexuality: the President, Mary Robinson, invited 34 representatives of the lesbian and gay communities in Ireland to Aras an Uachtarain, the official presidential residence, and thus publicly welcomed lesbians and gays in from the cold.

In 1994, the Irish Lesbian and Gay Pride Programme proudly proclaimed: 'The explosion of lesbian and gay activity in Ireland over the last few years has had to be seen to be believed. There are new groups of lesbian, gay and bisexual people meeting in Belfast, Cork, Derry, Drogheda, Dublin, Galway, Kerry, Limerick, Sligo, Waterford and Wexford ... and maybe some we don't know about yet' (Pride '94, 1994). As Joni Crone said recently: 'What was dreamed of in the seventies is now a reality' (Crone, 1994).

Legislation: Achievements

1993: The Unfair Dismissals Act (1977) is amended to prevent dismissal on grounds of sexual orientation, thus giving employment protection to lesbians and gays; 1994: Decriminalization of homosexuality. In Ireland, as in Britain, lesbianism has never been technically illegal (GLEN, 1994; LEN, 1994a).

Irish lesbian activists are also currently involved in a number of campaigns and projects:

• The present government proposes to introduce equal status legislation 'to make discrimination unlawful not only in the workplace, but also in education, in the provision of goods, facilities and services (including recreational facilities and services, entertainment, accommodation, transport and professional services) and in the disposal of accommodation or other premises' (Department of Equality and Law Reform, 1994). 'Sexual orientation' is included in this legislation. The Lesbian Equality Network (LEN) is currently campaigning to have the provisions of the proposed legislation extended to cover, amongst other things, equal status in partnerships, parenting and in media representation (LEN, 1994b).

• The present government is considering the Refugee Bill, 1994. The Gay and Lesbian Equality Network (GLEN) is campaigning to extend the proposed legislation to cover persecution on grounds of sexual orientation and health status as acceptable grounds for admission of refugees to Ireland.

• A major research project on poverty in the lesbian and gay communities in Ireland (with the Combat Poverty Agency, a government-funded agency).

• A research project (with the Department of Health) on the current work and future needs of the lesbian and gay communities in their collective national and local work on HIV and AIDS (GLEN, 1994).

In discussing lesbianism in Ireland in the 1990s, it is important to put the good news first. And, although I have many questions, there *is* good news. In Ireland, as in most western countries recently, lesbians have been increasingly visible in the media. On chat-shows, on radio phone-in programmes and in weekend colour supplements we have seen more lesbians in the past year or so than ever before. Some are high-profile, successful; some ordinary. Is this increased visibility making life easier for lesbians, is it easier now to come out in Ireland? It is important to remember that the entire population of the Republic of Ireland (the South) is only about half of that of the greater London area. Irish society, even in larger urban areas, is made up of small, close-knit communities. In such a social context coming out can be a highly charged experience, even in the best of circumstances. Coming out, being openly lesbian, can have major consequences for one's family in a small community, and concern for family is one of the biggest factors in virtually all Irish coming-out stories (Dublin Lesbian and Gay Men's Collective, 1986; Byrne and Larkin, 1994). Not all experiences are bad of course. However, Irish parents who may be prepared to accept lesbians on TV may take a very different attitude to having an out lesbian in the family. In speaking of lesbian activism in Ireland, we have to take the broadest possible view: in a situation where only visibility and familiarity can dispel ignorance, prejudice and bigotry, coming out is a highly political act and a great many of the resources of lesbian groups are channelled into supporting women who wish to take this major step (see Maria Power, Chapter 11).

It is important, then, not to overstate 'positive' media attitudes to lesbians. At the National Forum of Lesbian and Gay Groups hosted in October 1994 by Drogheda *OUTCOMERS* group, a Limerick-based activist said that in the previous week, a major regional newspaper in the west of Ireland had refused to carry a display advertisement for a local lesbian and gay helpline. So we must be cautious in assessing improvements in the lives of lesbians in Ireland during the 1990s.

If there has been a perceived increase in visibility or acceptability for lesbians in the Irish media, there has been no corresponding improvement for feminists. The Irish media, as with media elsewhere, have sustained a policy of isolating and ignoring feminist analyses, particularly in relation to sexuality. Has the backlash against feminism affected the lesbian community in Ireland or has there always been a certain tension between lesbianism and feminism in Ireland? Joni Crone, who ran what was for many years Dublin's only lesbian disco, has commented:

> I think the kind of exciting part of the disco was seeing women from so many different walks of live ... I think it did start out more as a ... feminist, maybe middle-class mixture of highly politicised women, and then it changed to being more kind of working-class ... women into, what we'd now call bar dykes, heavy drinking and darts playing and pool playing and stuff ...
>
> (Bradby, 1993)

Class differences in lesbian communities in Ireland are very pronounced. As there is an almost total absence of sociological analysis in Irish lesbian communities, our evidence is entirely anecdotal. Joni Crone's observation seems to me to be still highly pertinent. It supports the idea that for many working-class lesbians, the only lesbian outlet is the disco or the bar and political activism is regarded as patronizing and élitist. Middle-class lesbians are more likely to be college educated, to have the physical and intellectual space to explore sexual politics and ideas and to mix in liberal social circles. Feminism is seen to be for older lesbians who lived through the 1970s and is regarded as almost irrelevant by a lot of younger lesbians. On the other hand, much of the energy that has rejuvenated the lesbian community in Ireland has come from younger lesbians and there is now a wide variety of social activities available to Irish lesbians.

Changes in the political climate in Ireland are inevitably going to affect Irish lesbians. The introduction of divorce will almost certainly mean that more lesbians are going to lose custody of their children and demands for equal rights in parenting and partnerships are growing in the Irish lesbian community. There is a great deal of research underway in Ireland exploring the juridical, constitutional and legislative obstacles to lesbian parenting and partnership rights (LEN, 1994b; WERRC, 1995).

Irish society is changing at a rate that most of us can hardly absorb. The Peace Process in Northern Ireland is, at the time of writing, an unknown quantity but it could be an opportunity for widespread social change, north and south, a chance to push back the constitutional boundaries that have oppressed Irish women for so long. The Church's historical occupation of the high moral ground in matters of sexual morality, privacy and the family has been seriously undermined in recent years by the 'X' case, the Bishop Casey affair and, in 1994, revelations about the cover-up of child sex-abuse cases. The Right in Ireland is a political force but activism around matters of sexuality, including and probably most particularly, the right to choose, will continue to forge a space for lesbian and feminist politics on the island of Ireland.

(Thanks to Deborah Ballard, Editor, Lesbian Pages, *Gay Community News*; Susan Connolly of Outcomers in Drogheda and Eadaoin Ni Chleirigh of the Lesbian Equality Network for their ideas.)

Breaking the Silence: Lesbian Helplines in Ireland (Kate Frances)

> We take it as a given that lesbians have a right to freedom from prejudice and discrimination on the grounds of our sexual orientation and that we have a right to participate as full and equal members in all areas of society.
> (Dublin Lesbian Line, 1991:1)

Sexuality still remains an altogether taboo subject in Irish society. Heterosexuality does not require promotion: it just is, and continues to be, the only legitimate sexual preference. As a result, the existence of lesbians has been effectively silenced, devalorized and ignored.

Lesbians, however, do exist despite a very real lack of role models in visibility which ensures that lesbianism as an identity, a status with equal and fundamental rights, remains fragmented and marginal in a society which scorns 'deviant' behaviour. Consequently, women coming to terms with aspects of their sexuality are forced underground in search of reassurances that they are not alone.

A telephone helpline offers confidential, anonymous information, support and advice to callers. As such, in a socio-political environment of silence rather than acknowledgment, the service provided by lesbian helplines is that of facilitator. Many women contravene social mores every year by calling non-state recognized lesbian helplines. For 'non-out', silenced individuals, their first contact on the point of transition from silence to acknowledgment of their sexual orientation is largely with lesbian helpline services.

The determined silencing of lesbian women in Ireland has been met by an equally determined, but often invisible, element of lesbian activism. Six lesbian helplines have been in operation since the 1970s, four of which are based in the Republic of Ireland (Dublin, Galway, Cork and Limerick) and two in Northern Ireland (Derry and Belfast). More recently, inter-helpline cooperation has assisted in the setting up of Gay and Lesbian Line South-East in May 1994, underpinning the necessity of the services that lesbian lines provide on a national basis (*Gay Community News*, 1994).

It is widely accepted that the services provided by lesbian helplines are essential and in demand. The service of giving advice, support and providing information is common to each helpline. However, on-going difficulties of funding, facilities and status are also common.

Dublin Lesbian Line (DLL) has been in existence for 13 years. Initially, in the 1970s, a service for both lesbian women and gay men was in operation called Tel-a-Friend (TAF). In 1979, Liberation for Irish Lesbians (LIL) moved to Fownes Street (with TAF and DLL). In 1987, DLL (affiliated to Lesbians Organizing Together (LOT) and the Council for the Status of Women (CSW)) moved to a new office from where the service still operates. The office is available to DLL, rent-free, one evening per week. The DLL Collective consists of a number of volunteers who offer their time and energy to the helpline every Thursday evening from 7 to 9pm. A training course is run once or twice a year for new volunteers. Each Thursday two volunteers are on duty to take calls.

The volunteers, however, have other responsibilities: the Collective is represented at CSW and LOT meetings by its members, volunteers reply to letters, organize fund-raising events, answer queries from journalists and researchers, meet callers face to face if requested, accompany callers to social events or venues if requested, assist in running 'First Out' (a twice monthly discussion group for lesbians coming out) and, more recently, have committed themselves to promoting an Outreach Group, in conjunction with LOT, which involves presenting workshops in schools on subjects such as homophobia.

The vigour, perseverence and dedication of volunteers ensure that the voices of the silent are heard. However, the service provided is inadequate. Due to the present circumstances of restricted resources and facilities, an expansion of the service is not possible. It is, however, necessary (DLL, 1991). Similar difficulties are experienced by other lesbian helplines in the Republic of Ireland as a direct result of the non-recognition of such services by the state. Belfast Lesbian Line, as part of the Cara Friend Organization in Northern Ireland, on the other hand, receives donations and grants in conjunction with fund-raising efforts. For example, in 1990, the organization received £5977 from the Department of Health and Social Services in Northern Ireland (Cara Friend, 1990).

The operational difficulties shared by lesbian helplines are addressed by fund-raising efforts. The majority of such events must be confined to within the lesbian and gay community itself as a result of the continued stigmatization of being lesbian or gay in Ireland. Lesbian helpline services however, are crucial to revealing the depth of unmet, unarticulated need in Irish society. Lesbian helplines expose and address this need on a personal level, listening and caring. They are resolute in addressing the difficulties that they encounter. They work together on an on-going basis and are actively working towards the organization of a united group of all lesbian helplines. Meetings are held four times a year to pool energies and forge strategies in search of funding. The formulation of a code of ethics that will lay down requirements for the setting up of future helplines, is being undertaken. Options such as seeking charity status or the foundation of a limited company are also being considered.

Conclusion

Given the environment, socio-cultural, historico-political, in which lesbian women exist in Ireland, the formulation of a sexual identity is often fragmentary, incomplete and involves, to a large extent, self-censure in a society with which such an existence is incompatible. As a direct result of the stigmatization of 'deviant' manifestations of sexual behaviour, coping with one's sexuality can be traumatic. However, the rise in political awareness and the creation of a dedicated lesbian and gay movement presents a reassuring and collective way of providing assistance. Lesbian helplines in Ireland constitute a vital outlet to women who seek information and help. Answering the telephone is only the beginning.

References

BRADBY, BARBARA (1993) 'Lesbians and Popular Music: Does it Matter Who is Singing?', in GRIFFIN, GABRIELE (Ed.) *Outwrite: Lesbianism and Popular Culture*, London: Pluto, pp. 148–71.

BYRNE, SUZY and LARKIN, JUNIOR (1994) *Coming Out*, Dublin: Martello Books.

CARA FRIEND (1990) *'Sixteenth Annual Report'*, Belfast.

CRONE, JONI (1994) 'Lesbian Life in Ireland 1970–1995: A Queer Perspective', lecture presented at Trinity College, Dublin by the Centre for Women's Studies, TCD, 20 October.

DUBLIN LESBIAN AND GAY MEN'S COLLECTIVES (1986) *Out for Ourselves — The Lives of Irish Lesbians and Gay Men*, Dublin: Women's Community Press.

DUBLIN LESBIAN LINE (1991) 'Submission to the Second Commission on the Status of Women', Dublin, Lesbian Line.

DEPARTMENT OF EQUALITY AND LAW REFORM (1994) *Information Leaflet*, Dublin.

Gay Community News (1994) Issue 67, October, Dublin.

GLEN (Gay and Lesbian Equality Network) (1994) *Information Leaflet,* Dublin: GLEN.

HART, VADA (nd) 'Lesbians and AIDS', *Gossip, 2*, London: Onlywomen Press.

LEEDS OTHER PAPER, 1991, Spring. p.4.

LEN (Lesbian Equality Network) (1994a) *Information Leaflet*, Dublin: LEN.

LEN (1994b) *LEN Submission to the Department of Equality and Law Reform*, Dublin: LEN.

PRIDE '94 (1994) 'Programme of Events', Les/Gay/Bi Pride, 43 East Essex Street, Dublin 2.

SMYTH, AILBHE (1992) *The Abortion Papers*, Dublin: Attic Press.

WATNEY, SIMON (1992) 'The Killing Fields of Europe', *Gay Times*, April, London.

WERRC (1995) '"We Are Family" — United Nations International Year of the Family, Lesbian and Gay Responses', Discussion Document, Dublin, Women's Education, Research and Resource Centre, University College.

WGNRR (1994) 'Women's Global Network for Reproductive Rights', NZ Voorburgwal 32, 1012 RZ Amsterdam, Netherlands.

Useful Addresses

Belfast
Cara Friend and Lesbian Line
 PO Box 44, Belfast BT1 1SH, Tel: 238668
LOT Belfast
 29 Donegall Street, Belfast BT1 2FG, Tel: 322 823

Cork
Gay Information and Lesbian Line

The Other Place, 7/8 Augustine Street, Cork, Tel: 317 660

Derry
Gay Line Lesbian Line
 37 Clarendon Street, Derry, Tel: 263120

Drogheda
Outcomers
 7 North Quay, Drogheda, Co. Louth

Dublin
First Out
 c/o LOT, 5 Capel Street, Dublin 1, Tel: 872 7770
Gay Switchboard
 Carmichael House, North Brunswick Street, Dublin 1, Tel: 872 1055
Lesbian Line and Parents Enquiry
 c/o Council for the Status of Women, 32 Upper Fitzwilliam Street, Dublin 2, Tel:
   661 5268
Gay Community News
 The Hirschfeld Centre, 10 Fownes Street, Dublin 2, Tel: 671 0939
Lesbians Organizing Together
 5 Capel Street, Dublin 1, Tel: 872 7770
Lesbian Equality Network
 c/o LOT, 5 Capel Street, Dublin 1, Tel: 872 7770
Women's Education, Research and Resource Centre, Room F104B, Arts Building,
 University College, Belfield, Dublin 4, Tel: 706 8571, Fax: 706 1195

Galway
Gay Helpline Lesbian Line Parents Enquiry
 PO Box 45, Eglinton Street, Galway, Tel: 66134

Limerick
Gay Switchboard Lesbian Line
 PO Box 151, Henry Street, Limerick, Tel: 310101

Waterford
Gay Line Lesbian Line Parents Support
 PO Box 24, GPO, Waterford, Tel: 79907

For information about lesbian groups in other centres around Ireland, contact LOT,
 5 Capel Street, Dublin 1, Tel: 872 7770
Most lesbian helplines operate on a part-time basis, check with LOT for details.

Part VI
Women Working for Change

Chapter 13

Making the Invisible Visible: The Rise of a Professional Women's Network in the 1990s

Frances Moss

Introduction

As women are increasingly active in diverse areas of the labour market, they are organizing themselves as part of their attempt to impact on their working environments. Yet, as recently as 1973, Sheila Rowbotham felt able to state: 'For the woman the public world of work belongs to and is owned by men' (Rowbotham, 1973: 61).

This chapter will examine the formation and behaviour of a particular women's network: Women in Accountancy (WIA). It will consider why women want to enter management or professional jobs, and why they have felt a need to form networks. Do these networks operate in any way that could be considered feminist or at least woman-centred? Are they the spearhead of women gaining access to the hierarchies where most of resource power is currently held in male hands? Do they have an agenda that is likely to change the nature of those hierarchies? Implicitly a possible agenda for the rest of the 1990s will be given.

Women in Top Jobs

Women's occupational aspirations, although often significantly lower than those of men because of existing sex segregation in many high-paying jobs, societal expectations and family pressures, have been growing (Powell, 1993). Management and professional jobs appear, to many women, to provide self-determination, a chance to change things, and substantial material rewards, thereby providing independence.

Of the 3 million jobs in the UK described as management, about 20 per cent were held by women by the late 1980s (Hirsh and Jackson, 1989). The title 'manager' has perhaps increasingly been used as a device to engage people more with their jobs, to extract more effort and dedication from them, rather than to provide genuine autonomy and control. Nevertheless, a growing number of women now have control over both other people and financial and other resources. However, there are still very few women at the top of organizations where major policy decisions are made. The number of women at the top of publicly quoted companies has recently declined. Women Chief Executives/Managing Directors went down from 12 (men 1657) in 1993 to 9 (men 1633) in 1994 (*Crawford's Directory of City Connections*, 1993, 1994). This decline in women's participation at the top of organizations suggests that the glass ceiling, an invisible barrier that somehow prevents women entering the top strategy formulating areas of management, is still very much in place.

For women to be able to effect change they have to be at the top of organizations and hierarchies. As the bulk of resource-based decisions are made in male-dominated managerial hierarchies, without access to them women will not be able to change anything fundamental. Kanter (1977) suggests that until women, or any other underrepresented group, make up at least 20 per cent of a group, they will be discriminated against in a myriad of different ways, being seen as other, and never playing a full part in their organization. Robin Ely (quoted in Nichols, 1993) goes further, emphasizing that the key to changing the way in which women are perceived, both by themselves and by others, is a critical mass of women at senior levels. Otherwise sex role stereotypes persist, and the mainstream is indeed the malestream.

Women have been entering UK professions in increasing numbers. Nearly half of all articled clerks in law are now women, and about 35 per cent of student accountants are women. Women full members of the accountancy professional bodies are on average 14 per cent of the total, and growing fast (Boyer, 1995).

Why would women want to enter such a profession? Accountancy is concerned with the apparently impersonal, rational and objective world of numbers, and with control systems, all stereotypically male concerns. Getting control of the control system is, of course, a good start towards empowerment.

Women who want careers in management often obtain professional qualifications, such as those in accountancy, to provide 'objective' proof that they have the required competence, and should thus be taken seriously. Although this approach to getting accepted through a profession is meeting with some success, it often sidelines women into a technical role, rather than a mainstream general management one. This suits the men in organizations who do not wish to have women involved in the strategic, i.e. important, decisions. When BTR, a major plc, appointed a woman Finance Director, its Chief Executive assured journalists that he did not believe the new appointee should be regarded as the 'deputy managing director or the head of strategy' (*The Economist*, 1992). This is a strange statement to make about a new director whose future potential is unknown. It is a classic example of men undermining women.

Women in Accountancy (WIA)

Women in Accountancy (WIA) was formed in 1992. A woman known through inter-views and journal articles for her sympathetic views on the plight of women in account-ancy was elected to her professional body's ruling council. She was petitioned by many women accountants, asking her what she was going to do about the many perceived bar-riers to women's advancement in their profession. Her response was holistic and perso-nal. She suggested to contacts that she had in the other five accountancy bodies that a group be set up to discuss issues relating to women in the profession.

One of the characteristics of the six professional accountancy bodies under discussion is that they periodically discuss merging, but have so far failed to do so. Joint initiatives tend to disintegrate due to inter-professional rivalry. Thus, a grouping of women from all six bodies, was a significant collaborative act.

WIA is not organized in a hierarchical manner, but is a forum of representatives from the six bodies. Some women are administrative employees of the professional bodies, in the public relations or marketing area, while others are qualified accountants working in a variety of organizations. Hierarchy has been ignored; the only qualification for membership is a sympathetic interest in the group's aims. In this respect WIA is inclusive, not exclusive. The Chair rotates among women from the six bodies, while meetings are held on their various premises. All attempts are made to share and be collaborative, without establishing any ascendancy. This is significant as the size and relative power of the bodies ranges from the Irish Institute with under 8000 members to the usually dominant English and Welsh Chartered Institute with over 90000 members (Boyer, 1995).

WIA's statement of aims maintains:

> Women in Accountancy works to maximise the benefit and economic contribution that can be gained from a balanced workforce. It provides a forum for effective joint activity within the profession on issues of particular concern to women accountants and those responsible for their career development.

This is a typical 'business case' argument for greater equality of treatment for women, similar to that used by Opportunity 2000, the government-supported initiative founded by Business in the Community. Regardless of the private feelings of individuals within WIA, in this respect their public statement speaks to the self-interest of employers. Caroline Langridge, who heads the NHS Women's Unit, has been quoted as saying: 'We're doing what we're doing for sound economic reasons, it's not about social justice' (McKee, 1992).

The underlying argument in all these cases is that the loss of women's contribution to the paid workforce deprives organizations of much needed talent, and also represents a waste of money if already invested in training women. Whether or not this approach represents a betrayal of feminist (and many other) principles, it is the current language of business and government in the UK and thus represents a pragmatic strategy. Are women learning to fight with the enemy's own weapons? Or are they disastrously compromising themselves? This 'business case' approach makes no appeal to rights, justice or morality. It does not address issues of the household and power imbalance within patriarchal family structures. By raising issues previously left ignored, however, its existence may make more women question their own personal power relationships. It starts to make visible what was previously invisible within the workforce, namely that it is not neutral territory where men and women operate on equal terms.

Effecting Change

WIA, which is formally a small group of women who meet only a few times a year, acts as a catalyst for a wide range of activities. It works by encouragement, example and bringing to consciousness, i.e. making visible. It is involved in assisting with conferences (often but not exclusively women only ones), providing role models of successful women, encouraging women to play an active role in the governance of their professional bodies, to make their views known within the formal systems, networking across the whole of the profession to share examples of best practice and explain to employers that some of the most 'successful' employers in the country are also the ones with the most 'family friendly' employment practices. The phrase 'family friendly' can, of course be seen as either liberating for women, or as reinforcing the stereotype of the heterosexual nuclear family where the woman has main responsibility for childcare. WIA also provides a focus for people who wish to carry out research on women in accountancy.

Issues such as sexuality have so far been ignored by WIA in as much as heterosexuality is the assumed norm. Race and class have not been addressed as such, but individual women are becoming more conscious of such previously completely ignored issues.

There is considerable debate about the involvement of men in WIA. Some suggest we need to communicate with them and not be seen as separatist. Others point out that almost everything in accountancy is male dominated (a fact that has, until recently, been invisible). Women need a space in which to share experiences and feel safe. Sharing of personal feelings among women has proved easier without the presence of men; those initially worried about the absence of men may be experiencing the liberating effects of being able to articulate what they truly feel. Although most male accountants remain at best neutral, at worst hostile, a small number of prominent male accountants have been supportive to the group, providing access to funds (albeit at a relatively low level) and advice.

WIA has little access to mainstream resources, sharing what resources it does have in a collaborative way. The Chartered Institute of Public Finance and Accountancy (CIPFA) published a 'Career Break Information Pack' which provided useful information for its (mainly women) members who wanted to take a career break. WIA made it available to all women accountants. This cooperative sharing was achieved without endless amounts of negotiation about charging, which usually happens in such cases.

Included in the Career Break Pack is advice on how to employ a nanny to look after your children while you go back to work. It does not suggest that women in partnerships might try to get their partners to help with childcare (it only suggests 'a member of your family' as one of several possible childcarers). Although it seems like an opportunity missed, the document is distributed through the professional bodies and the authors have striven to be 'neutral and objective'. This denial of the gendered structure of childcare, in the guise of neutrality, again highlights the invisibility of the gender-related power structure of both organizations and households.

Although WIA is starting to question existing structures and ways of working in the world of paid employment, its comments on how non-paid work should be shared is currently confined to issues such as the provision of paternity leave for men. Its role as a forum for sharing experiences of women accountants is more focused on examining, and, by naming them, making visible discriminatory practices and attitudes in the professional workplace. For instance, Human Capital Theory theorists, such as Mincer and Polachek, explain women's relative lack of success in management by suggesting that they do not invest in qualifications and requisite varied experience because they will have career breaks for childbearing. However, there is clear evidence that women are consistently more highly qualified than men in similar positions, do better on average in their professional examinations (Ahmad, 1993) and far more managerial women than men do not have children (Davidson and Cooper, 1992). However, women are often put into 'women's' areas such as personnel or training functions, or they work with charities and financial services companies, which do not provide the conventionally defined 'appropriate experience' needed for later promotion into management. Sex stereotyping leads to insidious sex segregation at an early stage in many women's careers. The apparently neutral 'professional' workplace often puts women into the more relationship-oriented functions, while their male colleagues are involved in what will subsequently be defined as the 'real work'. Later on the women's experience will be viewed as less valid; in answer to the question 'what have you *done*?' they will not have tales of their experience of big projects and adventures, which are, in most cases, seen as necessary prerequisites for further advancement in their careers. The fact that they may have kept a group of staff motivated by helping to provide a shared sense of meaning in their work, which is not easy in the current climate, will not be measurable as an impressive achievement (McKeen and Bukajee, 1994).

Working Against the Grain

WIA can help encourage an awareness of such early ghettoizing, to help women realize that they need a varied range of experience if they wish to gain promotion in their careers. In doing so, however, WIA accepts the existing male-dominated definition of 'real work' being with big manufacturers and not in charities. Women can either fight to achieve the same sets of experiences that are automatically provided to men, or they can work to change perceptions of what is appropriate and necessary work to provide a foundation for further promotion. Until they gain that promotion in sufficient numbers, they will not be in a position of authority that will enable them to change the definitions.

Attitudes of women towards WIA vary. Most seem to welcome it, but there are some who are less supportive. Those few women who have made it to the top often seem to deny their gender and tend to be positively obstructive to other women (the queen bee syndrome as exemplified by Margaret Thatcher's refusal to promote women into her Cabinet), and to have had to make enormous sacrifices in their personal lives. Thus, some prominent women in the accountancy profession are hostile towards WIA. Similarly, many women accountants, especially some of the younger ones who are at an early stage of their careers and do not have children, for example, do not wish to attend women-only meetings. They may feel they do not need any support, as they are apparently succeeding in a patriarchal world, and they often state that they do not want positive discrimination. The pre-existing positive discrimination in favour of men is invisible to them.

Just as feminist scholarship has recovered gender from its invisible status within the 'presumed neutrality of science' (Gilligan, 1982), so women's networks within conservative professions such as accountancy are confronting taken-for-granted assumptions about gender-based power structures (Sheppard, 1989). Thus, the activities of Women in Accountancy cannot help but be perceived as uncomfortable by the mainstream at times. Women members (who have to pay their annual subscriptions like everyone else, so could be entitled to use the fashionable 'customer focus' argument) are asking for equal treatment in the profession. Several of the accountancy bodies have been supporting unemployed members by circulating their details amongst existing members to see if they can be given a job. Women members proposing that places on training courses could be supplied at half price to women taking a career break are suggesting a different use of the organization's funds and can be perceived as both threatening and challenging.

Women are suggesting that branch and district meetings, at which professional updating and general networking occurs, need to be held at times that do not exclude women. It has not occurred to the men organizing them that women might be unable to attend a meeting straight after work because of the necessity of looking after children. Nor does the golf club, with its forbidding 19th hole, reached down a lonely country lane, appeal to women as a place to meet. Women are proposing that times and locations might be changed and are having some success.

Small gestures that may have greater changes on behaviour are happening. At a branch meeting of accountants in a golf club, the woman speaker got everyone to sit in a circle and talk with each other: the norm is for a lead speaker in the front to talk to the relatively passive rest of the group. In the circle the women members, who had not attended such a meeting before, were empowered to explain what they found difficult about men's behaviour in professional settings.

One constant complaint is that men ignore women when organizing social events. One woman told how she plucked up the courage to ask her boss why she was excluded from the annual golf trip. His reply, that he thought she would not like golf, may be true, but by not being included in the group she was excluded from one of the informal networks where many issues are discussed and decided. She has attended every golf meeting since, and other women in the department are now invited. Telling this story in front of male accountants seemed to have the effect of raising their consciousness. Evidence suggests that men who have worked with female managers are much more favourably disposed to them than men who have not had that experience (Powell, 1993). However, the onus is still on the women to prove themselves, to ask for equal treatment, to be included.

The next stage, ludicrous though it may seem, is to suggest that golf is not the only group activity that can be carried out to create informal communications. An even more radical move would be to ensure that the culture of an organization is such that informal good communication occurs as matter of course, and does not need to be confined to special trips, which by their nature will exclude large numbers of the employees in an organization. Here the tension is between trying to get women to be accepted in the male-ordered world, and attempting to change the whole nature of that world. WIA and the many managerial women's networks may have the second aim in the long term, but see the current task to be encouraging women to achieve more positions of power and influence.

The invisible need to make themselves visible. A recurrent position taken by many men is that women have only themselves to blame. 'No women apply' is the reason we are given for the relative shortage of women in top jobs. There is also a growing body of evidence that many senior women are giving up their managerial jobs to do something that they see as more fulfilling, as they take a more holistic view of their lives (Marshall, 1991). The myriad of exclusionary activities that women experience in firms, and the subtle ways in which their confidence is undermined, all contribute to their lack of confidence in applying for senior positions. They know how hostile their reception will be. This phenomenon is now openly discussed in the mainstream *Harvard Business Review* (Schrank, 1977).

One woman at a WIA-organized meeting described how she was recruited at the same time as a fellow male trainee accountant. She passed her examinations more quickly than he did, but he was being recommended for more training and job rotation (to get that significant range of experience and confidence for future promotion). Eventually she had the courage to demand of her male boss why the man was receiving training and opportunities denied to her. He was apparently surprised, asked her what training she wanted and she has been given equal access to training ever since. Somehow, she had been invisible.

The sharing of this story with a group of male and female accountants can help to ensure that they will not marginalize their own staff in a similar way. It shows the WIA group making the personal into a political issue. It can be argued that organizations should not be run in a way that so obviously discriminates against particular groups. However, as biased behaviour occurs, a strategy of exposing it, discussing it, and resolving not to perpetuate it does make changes on the micro level.

WIA has encouraged and helped to sponsor women only accounting con-ferences. In addition to providing essential technical updating, they also offer confidence building, assertiveness and presentation skills. These are areas where women often feel disadvantaged. In an all-female environment it is possible to share experiences and strategies for dealing with them. This is enormously empowering as women realize that they are not alone in their experience, and they are not being paranoid when they feel marginalized.

The timing of conferences has been women-centred. A half day on a Friday and all of Saturday enables many, if not all women to arrange childcare relatively easily, compared with two days during the week, as the assumption is that partners can help at the weekend. This, of course, is still women adapting themselves to suit others' convenience, but it at least established their right to attend such a conference.

The issue of rights of women to attend their own professional or work-related courses and conferences in what might be seen as 'family' time is one that is now being debated. The patriarchal family, where the father's needs are the primary ones so that the whole family adapts itself round his requirements is, in some cases, under review. The functionalist argument (Walby, 1990) that conceives of a household as a unit in which decisions are taken in an egalitarian way in the interests of all members, is seen to be false. Much research on Women in Accountancy ignores this aspect of women's experience. A survey of Irish women accountants, asking them what obstacles they felt they had faced in their careers, mentioned the problem of maternity leave (hostility and marginalization of the pregnant, who are seen as a nuisance, while men who are sick are treated sympathetically), the 'old boy network', difficulties in socializing, lack of female role models, lack of confidence, the structure of work practices, discrimination which can be intangible and subtle, positive action programmes (regarded as token to fulfil quota), being single (seen as gay, and consequently stigmatized) (Barker and Monks, 1994). There is no mention of the sometimes hostile and often unhelpful attitude of male partners to women pursuing an independent career. That aspect of gender power relations remains invisible.

Some women have had to stay at home during a meeting of a WIA group as their male partner has suddenly had something important to do at work. Despite previous negotiations and agreement for the woman to have her own free time for one particular evening, this has been denied at the last minute. Thus, the household seems central to some women's subordination (Walby, 1990), and they cannot rely on reciprocal support from their partners.

Role models seem vitally important to change the perceived norm that management is male. There is evidence that female role models in senior management affect both women's aspirations (Davidson and Cooper, 1992) and men's expectations. A male senior manager joined British Telecom in the early 1980s. He came from an all-male environment at Unilever to one where both his boss and his direct subordinate were women. He was very suspicious of these 'others'. Within six months he swore never to recruit anyone except women as in his experience they were both technically more competent than men, but also more reliable (communication to author). Unfortunately, the women have to prove themselves to be better than men to gain the acceptance that men automatically receive.

A few years ago there were virtually no women on the governing councils of the accountancy bodies. The creation of WIA has coincided with, and perhaps contributed to, the creation of a climate in which women are more willing to apply for office. They have rapidly been elected and in CIMA for instance there are now six women members of the 56-strong Council. Two years ago there was only one woman. However, women are still regarded as 'other' and possibly stigmatized as token women. This makes them feel subject to additional performance pressures that the dominant group, men, do not feel. Primrose McCabe, first woman president of the Institute of Chartered Accountants in Scotland, felt it necessary to comment that her gender 'makes it more important to do the job well' (Anon., 1994). In the accountancy press there have been jokey references to 'Primrose paths' and suchlike; her professional comments have been, at times, trivialized in a way that those of leading men are not.

Kanter describes how tokens (who can be other minorities) experience role encapsulation, whereby they are classified according to the feminine gender stereotype, regardless of their own particular talents. This has been the case at the beginning of the women's presence at CIMA, where all women members of the council were put on to either the public relations or education or membership committees. This is now changing, with women on the 'harder' groups such as the disciplinary committee. As women become more numerous on the governing bodies of their professions they may become more acceptable and accepted. If they start trying to change the constitution, they are likely to find hostility returning. CIMA still has no women on its strategy-formulating Executive Committee where major decisions about allocations of resources are taken.

Networking between different groups of women accountants, across the traditional barriers of the different branches of the profession, is increasing. Encouraging the growing number of researchers into women accountants also helps to make women a more visible constituent of the accountancy profession. If many researchers contact the professional bodies and ask how they are treating their women members, it helps to legitimize the requests that such members might make.

Is the WIA (Future) Feminist?

Is WIA at all feminist? Most of its members would deny this, as most managers 'view feminism and feminists with distaste' (Martin, 1993). This is an example of how male hostility has made a whole political approach unacceptable in the business world. However, if feminism means valuing mutuality and interdependence, participation and self-determination, inclusion and cooperation, empowerment and to improve women's social, economic and symbolic rewards (Martin, 1993), then much of WIA's activities are feminist. They do not, however, claim to be all-inclusive, as members of the so-called second-tier accountancy body — The Association of Accountancy Technicians — have not been invited to participate. This reflects a work and professional hierarchical view, rather than a women-centred one of the group as being concerned with all women involved in the practice of

accountancy. WIA is not currently seeking major reforms of hierarchical organizations, but it is questioning their existing operation and allocation of resources, which
may lead on to further more radical questioning. Patricia Martin, who favours a
feminist reform rather than revolution approach in that she suggests it is possible to
work with existing organizations, nevertheless states:

> I believe that corporations will change only if feminists organise, take
> political action, and force them to. Along with others, I doubt that
> corporations will improve simply because many women work there. I also
> believe that men who benefit from current arrangements will not relinquish
> them without a struggle.

> (Martin, 1993: 279)

WIA may have to become a little more assertive if it is to achieve much more. It can
continue to make women more visible. But we do not want to just play at 'boys'
games'. Ultimately the nature of the games, both how they are played, and the results
that they produce, need changing.

References

AHMAD, N.L. (1993) 'Attitudes of Men and Women in the Accountancy Profession',
    unpublished MSc dissertation, Polytechnic of Central London.
ANON. (1994) 'Changing Places', *Accountancy*, June, p. 22.
BARKER, P. and MONKS, K. (1994) 'Women in Accounting: The Sleeping Partners?' paper
    presented to the Irish Accounting and Finance Association Annual Conference, Queens
    University, Belfast, March.
BOYER, I. (1995) *The Balance on Trial. Women's Careers in Accountancy*, London: Chartered
    Institute of Management Accountants.
Crawford's Directory of City Connections (1993, 1994), 15th edition, 16th edition, Tonbridge:
    Benn Business Information Services Limited. (Quoted in RODGERS, P. (1994) 'Women
    Vanishing from the Top Spots'. *Guardian*, 7 March.)
DAVIDSON, M.J. and COOPER, C.L. (1992) *Shattering the Glass Ceiling: The Woman Manager*,
    London: Paul Chapman.
The Economist (1992) 'Women in Management', The Spare Rib, 28 March, pp. 17–20.
GILLIGAN, C. (1982) *In a Different Voice: Psychological Theory and Women's Development*,
    Cambridge, Mass: Harvard University Press.
HIRSH, W. and JACKSON, C. (1989) 'Women into Management — Issues Influencing the Entry
    of Women into Managerial Jobs', Paper No. 159, University of Sussex: Institute of
    Manpower Studies.
KANTER, R.M. (1977) *Men and Women of the Corporation*, New York: Basic Books.
McKEE, V. (1992) 'A Healthy Operation', *The Times*, 26 February.
McKEEN, C.A. and BUKAJEE, M.L. (1994) 'Taking Women into Account', *CA Magazine*, **127**,
    2, pp. 29–35.
MARSHALL, J. (1991) 'Senior Women Managers Who Leave Employment', *Women in
    Management Review and Abstracts*, **6**, 3, pp. 4–10.
MARTIN, P.Y. (1993) 'Feminist Practice in Organizations: Implications for Management', in
    FANGENSON, E.A. (Ed.) *Women in Management: Trends, Issues and Challenges in*

Managerial Diversity, London: Sage, pp. 274–96.

NICHOLS, N.A. (1993) 'Whatever Happened to Rosie the Riveter?', *Harvard Business Review*, **July–August**, pp. 54–62.

POWELL, G.N. (1993) *Women and Men in Management*, 2nd edition, London: Sage.

ROWBOTHAM, S. (1973) *Woman's Consciousness, Man's World*. Harmondsworth: Penguin.

SCHRANK, R. (1977) 'Two Women, Three Men on a Raft', *Harvard Business Review*, **May–June**, pp. 100–108; reprinted **May–June**, 1994, pp. 68–76.

SHEPPARD, D.L. (1989) 'Organisations, Power and Sexuality: The Image and Self-Image of Women Managers', in HEARN, J., SHEPPARD, D.L., TANCRED-SHERIFF, P. and BURRELL, G. (Eds) *The Sexuality of Organisation*, London: Sage.

WALBY, S. (1990) *Theorizing Patriarchy*, Oxford: Blackwell.

Chapter 14

Women's Studies as Feminist Activism

Alex Warwick and Rosemary Auchmuty

Women's Studies as Feminist Activism

In her pioneering study *Black Feminist Thought* Patricia Hill Collins points out that White masculine definitions of words such as power, activism and resistance 'fail to capture the meaning of these concepts in Black women's lives' (Collins, 1990:140). Activism for Black women in western societies, she argues, has taken the form of a struggle for group survival and a struggle for institutional transformation. 'Education has long served as a powerful symbol for the important connections among self, change, and empowerment in African-American communities', especially for women (Collins, 1990:141–2, 147ff).

While not ignoring the particular meanings that activism and education must have for Black people in a White supremacist society, these observations can nevertheless be used to illuminate the position of *all* women in western societies. Women's activism, too, has included a struggle for survival and a struggle for institutional transformation. The acquisition of knowledge and critical tools has been empowering for all groups, such as women and Black people, historically denied access to education and still denied access to information about our own position and past. 'If there is a single thing which empowers women of all kinds it is education', declared Tessa Blackstone, Master of Birkbeck College, London (Neustatter, 1989:173). But more than this, Collins's words remind us of the dangers of accepting traditional definitions (that is, those which support a masculine agenda) of words like activism. Access to conventional education will reveal to us what we are up against and what we have to master [*sic*] in order to challenge and transform it, but it will not necessarily teach us how to question and decode the meanings of words that describe and perpetuate a masculine world view. But access to a *feminist* education may do this. Women's Studies embodies the goal of feminist education, the analysis of society from *women's* perspectives with a view to changing it.

Activism ('Policy of vigorous action in politics, etc.', according to the *Concise Oxford Dictionary*) tends to connote activity in party politics, trade unions, and other lobbying and campaigning groups. The Women's Liberation Movement extended the word to encompass those activities which focused on working with women and for women's causes directly; for example, campaigning against pornography, setting up and running rape crisis centres and women's refuges, the peace camps at Greenham Common. A well-founded suspicion of institutions organized around patriarchal structures and ideas led many feminists to believe that the way forward lay in organizing separately, in empowering women rather than struggling to change male-dominated institutions, and men themselves, from within those institutions. Those women who did choose to work within the patriarchal structures and, especially, those who succeeded within them, were often seen as un-feminist or anti-feminist, more concerned with personal power than transforming society to benefit all women. And, indeed, this was a fair description of women like Margaret Thatcher. Feminist activism came to be seen, therefore, as lying not in male-dominated institutions like the universities but in smaller, community-based, grassroots activities under the control of women.

The Development of Women's Studies: From Feminist Activism to Academic Feminism

In Britain, the Women's Liberation Movement and Women's Studies have the same roots, and for many years were inextricably linked. The women who called the first National Women's Liberation Conference in Oxford in 1970 were the women who taught the first Women's Studies classes in the 1970s: disaffected left-wing intellectuals, tired of labour men's refusal to take the study of women, and women themselves, seriously.[1] The consciousness-raising groups that proliferated in the 1970s shared personal experiences and understandings to develop an analysis of women's position and strategies for change, but in pursuit of this goal they also read and discussed the significant texts on women — starting with Firestone, Millett, Greer, and a great deal of home-grown material cheaply printed and disseminated — in ways which came to characterize Women's Studies classes. Women sought to find out more about women's history, particularly the history of the 'First Wave' of feminism, in a desire to claim our heritage, to grasp the workings of patriarchal oppression, and to celebrate former resistance and heroines. The more grassroots educational agencies, which were often staffed by feminists, were quick to respond to a perceived need. Women's Studies classes were mounted by the Workers' Educational Association, local Adult Education Institutes and, in London, the University of London's Extra-Mural Department and the Polytechnic of Central London. During the 1970s and 1980s, these were among the most successful Adult Education classes in the country, reaching thousands of women.

As long as Women's Studies stayed at community level, Women's Studies teachers could be defined as activists. Indeed, that was how we saw ourselves. Adult Education provision at this time was cheap, plentiful (in urban areas at least), non-threatening (no assessed work was required), and user-friendly, often offering creches and other facilities to make study easier for women students. As teachers we believed we were not only bringing much-wanted knowledge and skills to ordinary women, but facilitating the sharing of knowledge and experience, support and friendship: empowering women, and even changing lives. And it wasn't only students' lives which were being changed.

> For the most part today, except for isolated phenomena like the Greenham Common occupation, women do not experience active participation in public life. Most of us haven't a public life at all, by which I mean a place in which our various selves can be exchanged, given, taken up and recognised. But for me the South London Women's Studies Group has provided a measure of participation in public life. Along with other members of our group I am interested in helping mount and teach women's studies courses for women that higher or conventional adult education would not reach.
>
> (Quoted in Hughes and Kennedy, 1985:130)

So wrote a woman in the mid-1980s. By the late 1980s, however, Women's Studies had become established not only within Adult Education but in a number of institutions of higher education. It was feminists who had battled to find a place for it there: we wanted Women's Studies to be recognized as a subject worthy of academic study; we wanted to offer women more advanced Women's Studies classes, and courses for which they might gain credit and qualifications; we wanted to challenge the patriarchal curriculum and provide the current generation of students with less alienating courses than we ourselves had experienced as undergraduates and postgraduates. But our victory — and it *was* a victory, with practically all universities in Britain offering Women's Studies by the mid-1990s — was won at a cost. In entering the patriarchal structures of higher education, we lost some of our control over what, how and whom we taught. In particular, we were forced to accept that Women's Studies courses must be assessed like any other academic studies in order to attract credit.

In a chapter entitled 'Worming into Women's Studies' the Taking Liberties Collective, a group of mostly working-class women's studies students from Southampton, pointed out the problems of siting Women's Studies within the universities:

> If we take the view that 'anything is better than nothing', then courses influenced by an understanding of feminism and intended to make women the focus of study, have to be applauded. We know that very often a lot of fierce debate has gone into getting them funded and properly recognised. We don't underestimate the persistence and commitment of many of those who have worked from within the corridors of power to see them established. But if we take the view that 'anything' is not actually good enough, we can see that Women's Studies still has a long way to go in providing the proper kind of political challenge to men's education that would begin to make real changes for women.
>
> (Taking Liberties Collective, 1989:127)

Among the threats to feminist learning presented by the university environment, they list the presence of male students in Women's Studies classes, and even male teachers of Women's Studies; the use of non-feminist teaching and assessment practices; a White, middle-class bias, because of the sorts of students (and staff) that the universities attract; unchanged and unsympathetic institutional structures (for instance, many universities have no creches).

As a result, teachers of Women's Studies within universities, and increasingly within Adult Education too where courses are now more expensive and credit-driven, have come to be seen as cut off from the wider community of women, dedicated to their own personal advancement within patriarchal institutions rather than presenting a challenge to those institutions, and to teaching students whose primary concern is the acquisition of a qualification rather than the understanding of women's oppression and desire to overcome it.

At the same time, feminist theorizing — once seen as a vital step in the processing of knowledge and experience into forms useful for planning and conducting political campaigns — has become increasingly arcane and independent of politics. Indeed, the two developments were interlinked, the increasing sophistication and difficulty of the concepts and language of feminist theory being seen by many as essential to its acceptance by the academic community. When the texts became actually unintelligible to the great majority of women whose lives they purported to theorize, the lines of demarcation between feminist thinkers and feminist activists were drawn. Academic feminists were accused of losing touch with activism, of ignoring the vital connexion between ideas and political movements — the notion that the one should emerge out of, and feed back into, the other.

There is some truth in these accusations. Compromises have had to be made when Women's Studies is imported into the academy. Some students, by their own admission, are not feminists; some teachers have no interest in the women's movement as such. Nevertheless, we would argue, Women's Studies retains its potential for being a form of feminist activism — a powerful, perhaps *the* most powerful, agent for change in an increasingly anti-feminist society. We would also argue that this potential has not remained unrealized and that a great deal has been, and is still being achieved through academic feminism.

The Student Body

The changes are visible on an everyday basis in universities, as well as being supported by research analysis, and experienced by students, staff and the institutions themselves. The composition of the student community has changed considerably, particularly in the last 15 years, through revisions of admissions policies and the introduction of access and certificate courses as a possible means of entry to degrees. During the 1980s, the number of part-time students in higher education rose by 50 per cent and the number of female students tripled. New universities (the former polytechnics and colleges of higher education) have led the way and are now being followed to a large extent by the old universities. While it is true that these policy changes have not solely been the result of feminist action, clearly the presence of women students and teachers has been instrumental in changing attitudes about admissions. One of the major arguments of early feminist educators was that only formal, male-biased knowledge was regarded as being of value, consequently devaluing women's informal, and very different, knowledge and experience. The principle of recognition of experience and the valuation of informal learning are now enshrined in educational practice, with very obvious benefits to women wishing to enter or re-enter university. On the MA, which we teach, for example, we accept students without first degrees who have other professional qualifications or experience. Apart from widening the student community, it also means that there are women from organizations more usually perceived as activist, such as women's housing projects or advice centres, on the course, providing a tangible example of feminist activism in alliance with academic feminism and of the loop of feedback that theorizing should provide.

The range of women now studying in higher education belies the notion that Women's Studies courses are the province of White middle-class women, and the challenges offered to the women's movement by women of diverse national, racial, ethnic and class backgrounds have also been experienced in education, producing changes in the types of courses available. Modules in subjects like Black feminist thought and Lesbian Studies are beginning to be placed alongside the more familiar courses in literature and history and attract students who might previously have felt excluded from Women's Studies because their own experience was not recognized in the courses.

The Student Experience

Clearly, the increased admission of women to degree and higher degree courses, while an important advance, is not inevitably linked to changes being made in the lives of those women, and if change is the goal of activism, then this must be available within Women's Studies. Once inside the institution, are students offered, or able to take the opportunity for change? One of the arguments against Women's Studies in higher education is that women's energy is neutralized or diverted away from activism, yet if we define activism as activity towards change, this would certainly seem to be the most significant aspect of student expectation; students believe that the courses they are following will make an important difference to their lives. Each year on our own MA course we begin with a discussion which includes asking women why they have chosen to do Women's Studies, and the overwhelming answer is 'to enable me to make changes in my life'. Other supplementary responses usually include developing the ability to recognize and counter individual and institutional sexism, to meet and learn from the experience of other women, and to revise male-centred learning encountered in earlier academic careers, all goals shared by feminist educators. These are not unusual justifications, but reflect the kinds of answers offered by most women on such courses (Robinson, 1993:9). Obtaining a higher degree or validation through an institution never features prominently, if at all, in their list of reasons. The process, rather than the outcome is what is anticipated and we would argue that process is an important concept in both feminism and Women's Studies, as in Nancy Hartsock's definition of feminism: 'a mode of analysis, a method of approaching life and politics' (Hartsock, 1981:35) rather than simply a set of political conclusions.

The expectations of students, and the effects of the accomplishment of them, can be difficult to manage within the academic environment. As Jalna Hanmer observes:

> On Women's Studies courses, women students can behave in new ways. They often feel able to demand, discharge and disclose in ways unthinkable on traditional discipline, or interdisciplinary, or professional courses.
>
> (Hanmer, 1991:113)

This process is often a painful one, both for students and staff, as women analyse and question the roles and relationships they occupy and undertake the task of modifying or rejecting those roles. It is sometimes assumed that women able to enter higher education are in privileged positions and thus do not need support towards change; this is clearly not always the case. Along with the real pleasures of working and learning with other women, the consciousness-raising aspect of the course often produces pain, anger and resentment, the repercussions of which go beyond the classroom, and teachers become involved in pastoral as well as academic counselling. As many staff and students in Women's Studies are active in or in contact with women's groups of different kinds, information is available enabling women to form groups outside the course, or join the work of other non-academic organizations in order to continue what has been started in Women's Studies. If Women's Studies really is a safe retreat from the hard issues that activism is thought to engage in, would it produce these effects? Academic feminism does not aim to replace all other forms of activism, or pretend to be entirely sufficient in itself, but it has a place within what should be recognized as a range of feminist activity.

The Teacher's Role

Teachers involved in Women's Studies classes in Adult Education during the 1970s and 1980s wrote about how it was not only the students who underwent changes as a result of their experience in Women's Studies, but also the teachers themselves. This still holds true for Women's Studies teachers working within the universities. Women academics are also involved in the continuing process of examining and changing their own lives. The role of teachers within Women's Studies can be a difficult one. We are frequently seen, and indeed see ourselves, as the interface between students and the institutions that are still male dominated, and thus as having conflicting loyalties. This interface, however, can be most productive of activism for staff, who are not only involved in pedagogical matters, but in fighting for issues such as ensuring the safety of women on campuses, combating sexual and racial harassment through the implementation of anti-discrimination policies and pressing for child-care provision for students. As Jill Radford observes:

> From my perspective at the interface of activism and academia I seek support from the academy in challenging political and institutional separations, re-working the connections to help with the building of an including women's anti-racist anti-homophobic liberatory resistance movement. Women's Studies has an important potential in this project.
>
> (Radford, 1994:56)

In many ways too, our expectations are similar to those of women students: that our lives as teachers will be changed, that we will meet and learn from other women, and that we too will be able to develop our ability to distinguish and to challenge anti-feminist practices. Catherine Stimpson's description of the feminist project within the academy as composed of deconstruction, reconstruction and construction (Stimpson, 1984) is a useful one, and these elements can be applied to all areas of our work. The re-negotiation of teacher – student relationships, for example, is a common feature of Women's Studies, in which the traditional patriarchal nature of pedagogy is continually re- examined, broken down and reconstituted in non-hierarchical ways (see Friedman, 1985). For many of us who are also involved in teaching other disciplines as well as Women's Studies, this has had profound effects on the kind of teaching we do elsewhere, in ways that can redress the gender imbalance in classes in the traditional disciplines. Just as the composition of the student community has changed, so has that of the teachers. There are now many more women teachers from diverse backgrounds providing significant role models for students. This can be observed informally, but it is also apparent in written student feedback: 'The presence of lesbian tutors on the module has been a source of great strength and pride' (University of Westminster Student feedback, June 1994).

Language

One of the most visible means of measuring changes through feminism in the institution has been change in the use of language. Though the debate about so-called political correctness still continues in many arenas, with anti-feminists using our attention to language as evidence of our obvious irrationality, the movement towards inclusive language seems inexorable. The public documentation and other written material of universities now exists in inclusive language, and while this may seem inconsiderable as an achievement, it is genuinely empowering for women students and staff not to notice constantly that the official discourse excludes them.

The possibilities for collective activity by women within masculine structures are sometimes questioned by those critical of Women's Studies teachers, though the operation of group processes, sharing of skills and responsibilities, collective decision making and so on have often only been negotiated with difficulty, even in autonomous women's groups (Bunch and Pollack, 1983). Collective activism can work in a number of different ways in universities. Women's Studies courses are usually staffed by self-selected, voluntary groupings of women from different disciplines and different parts of the university. This cross-faculty grouping in itself challenges the separating of women by subject and by position, but also allows the transmission of knowledge and experience in ways that force change in the university's practice.

The development of more student-centred teaching practices, for example, is characteristic of Women's Studies, and feminist teachers are found on many of the bodies dedicated to innovative learning strategies throughout the university. The hierarchical structure is challenged by incorporating collective working methods such as joint essays, projects and presentations, women's autobiography and reflective experiential accounts, team teaching and assessment. It is not only how subjects are taught, but the content of courses that is affected. Many fields such as the social sciences and the humanities have been transformed by feminist scholarship, which has an effect on male teachers and students as well as empowering women students in the classroom. There has also been the recognition that other fields such as technology, business and the physical sciences have not yet been sufficiently affected by feminist scholarship. It is often the case that feminists working in these fields are isolated and the support of other women from within the university is vital for them.

There are many advantages for activism in the nature of Women's Studies, in that it is both inter-disciplinary and a field of study in itself. One of the most striking of these in our experience is the way in which working with other women from other fields, other faculties and other sites has allowed us to gain knowledge of other areas and subjects, but also knowledge of the working practices of the institution itself. This would seem to accord with one of the first principles of feminist activism which is the breaking down of large and divisive structures through the connexion of women working together. We can support each other in initiatives that we may be making by gathering and sharing of information and by giving support in resisting oppression. Feminist academics are usually to be found on union bodies, equal opportunities groups and as trainers on equal opportunities courses, in which all staff are now expected to participate. If we are role models for students, then we are also role models for one another as we work at different levels of seniority and are able to provide informal mentoring systems, countering the 'glass ceiling' effect. Arguably too, as more women who have lived through the Women's Movement come to occupy higher positions, more change may be possible. As Dale Spender comments:

> If it is the case that young women do need the example and support of more experienced and successful women to see themselves attaining comparable achievements, then it could be quite an efficacious form of male resistance to obstruct women's entry to positions of role model and mentor for the next generation.

> (Spender, 1993:235)

Alex Warwick's experience in a department headed by a woman, located in a school also headed by a woman, bears this out. Both have been extremely supportive in releasing her from teaching in her other subjects in order to set up and teach on the

MA Women's Studies. In turn, she has tried to ensure that women post-graduates and other part-time tutors are given as much opportunity as possible to gain teaching experience. The presence of women at all levels in the university serves to combat the forms of male resistance outlined by Spender.

Women's Studies is both a product and a producer of feminist knowledge. It is political in that it raises questions about academic and political goals in classroom teaching, Women's Studies and the women's movement itself. It has serious implications for organizational structures, and has an impact on the university system as a whole. Yet suspicion and criticism of Women's Studies in higher education remains and even seems to increase. We are squeezed between reactionary anti-feminist critics within the institution and by criticism, often by other feminists, from outside. The latter may be due to the perception that the rise of Women's Studies and the apparent fragmentation of the women's movement appear to coincide. Women's Studies is accused of drawing off the energies of women into at worst, patriarchal structures and at best, the fruitless pursuit of reading words on paper. The constant opposition of theory and activism has become an entrenched and increasingly sterile debate, which is in danger of driving the two further apart. Surely the development of the women's movement in many different directions is evidence of its flexibility and the recognition of the different needs, desires and abilities of those who would call themselves feminist, rather than its fragmentation and the dissolution of its energies. The interests of those involved in Women's Studies are *not* always identical with those of activists in other areas, but it must be acknowledged that even organizations more usually recognized as activist do not necessarily share interests beyond that of dealing with and opposing the effects and causes of women's oppression. To reject Women's Studies as 'academic' in its narrow sense ignores the diversity, range and political commitment of feminist teachers and students. It also ignores the fact that teachers and students of Women's Studies are frequently involved in work outside the academy and outside formal education of any kind, which is often informed by their academic lives. Even within the institution we see and are often involved in the struggles of single parents, the difficulties of non-British women in a white-dominated society, the surfacing of the traumas of rape and child abuse, and the real effects of poverty. The university is no longer the ivory tower of popular mythology, cut off from the issues, concerns and practicalities of 'real life'.

To decry Women's Studies as non-activist is to succumb to a narrow definition of the word and to a narrow definition of politics and political activity. If the personal is still political, does Women's Studies not do part of the work of bringing the two together in a theorized form, continuing the work of identification, naming and exploration of the structures of oppression that still exist? It actively works to change and to break down the structures of those institutions in which it is found, and gives its students access to and support through the processes of change. If power is a network that exists everywhere, then it is also something which can be resisted everywhere.

Notes

1   The first Women's Studies class in Britain is believed to have been taught by Juliet Mitchell at the anti-university in 1968–1969. Other women who were both prominent in the Women's Liberation Movement and taught Women's Studies in the early years were Sheila Rowbotham, Sally Alexander, Anna Davin and Barbara Taylor. See Hughes and Kennedy, 1985:34; Coote and Campbell, 1987; Neustatter, 1989.

References

BUNCH, CHARLOTTE and POLLACK, SUSAN (1983) *Learning Our Way: Essays in Feminist Education*, New York: Crossing Press.

COLLINS, PATRICIA HILL (1990) *Black Feminist Thought*, London: Routledge.

COOTE, ANNA AND CAMPBELL, BEATRIX (1987) *Sweet Freedom. The Struggle for Women's Liberation*, 2nd edition, Oxford: Blackwell.

FRIEDMAN, SUSAN (1985) 'Authority in the Feminist Classroom: A Contradiction in Terms?', in CULLEY, MARGOT and PORTUGES, CATHERINE (Eds) *Gendered Subjects: The Dynamics of Feminist Teaching*, London: Routledge and Kegan Paul.

HANMER, JALNA (1991) 'Women's Studies – A Transitional Programme', in AARON, JANE and WALBY, SYLVIA (Eds) *Out of the Margins: Women's Studies in the Nineties*, pp. 60–80, London: Falmer Press.

HARTSOCK, NANCY (1981) 'Fundamental Feminism: Process and Perspective', in BUNCH, CHARLOTTE (Ed.) *Building Feminist Theory; Essays from Quest*, London: Longman.

HUGHES, MARY and KENNEDY, MARY (1985) *New Futures. Changing Women's Education*, London: Routledge and Kegan Paul.

NEUSTATTER, ANGELA (1989) *Hyenas in Petticoats. A Look at Twenty Years of Feminism*, London: Harrap.

RADFORD, JILL (1994) 'History of Women's Liberation Movements in Britain: A Reflective Personal History', in GRIFFIN, GABRIELE, HESTER, MARIANNE, RAI, SHIRIN and ROSENEIL, SASHA (Eds) *Stirring It: Challenges for Feminism*, London: Taylor & Francis, pp. 40–58.

ROBINSON, VICTORIA (1993) 'Introducing Women's Studies', in RICHARDSON, DIANE and ROBINSON, VICTORIA (Eds) *Introducing Women's Studies*, London: Macmillan.

SPENDER, DALE (1993) 'The Entry of Women to the Education of Men', in KRAMARAE, CHERIS and SPENDER, DALE (Eds) *The Knowledge Explosion*, London: Harvester.

STIMPSON, CATHERINE (1984) *Feminist Visions*, Alabama: University of Alabama Press.

TAKING LIBERTIES COLLECTIVE (1989) *Learning the Hard Way. Women's Oppression in Men's Education*, London: Macmillan.

Chapter 15

Haystacks in my Mind or How to Stay SAFE (Sane, Angry and Feminist) in the 1990s

---

Ailbhe Smyth

To be taken irregularly in (very) small mouthfuls, with extremely large pinches of salt. Must not, on any account, be rubbed into the wound.[1]

Part I: Random Micro-Messages

November 1992

The 'Abortion Referendum' means I put my politics where my mouth is and say where I stand. But to be vociferously 'pro-abortion' in Ireland, even in 1992, is not a wise route to the brownie points of power, privilege, voice and credibility. A 'pro-abortion' academic politicizes what is 'outside politics', and thus becomes a displaced person in the academic world. (It is OK to be anti-abortion: that's 'natural', not political).[2] Of course, feminism has *never* been acceptable — only a little light women's studies (gender studies is preferable), nothing too serious or extensive. My home is in the Women's Liberation Movement — but my job (yes, I know, at least I have one) is in academia, seriously and extensively in women's studies. Will I ever get to work from home? (See April 1993, below.)

January 1993

Burnt-out (burn-out is not a myth) after the referendum, and despite our victory (that's not a myth either), I take a break and return to find my computer and address book have been stolen from my house (yes, I know, I have one of those too — they go together: to those that have, more shall be given — and sometimes taken away, in punishment). The facts of my current life, most of it, were on that computer — personal, political, professional, whatever. Now in someone else's hands. A sinister intrusion.

March 1993

I am on a radio newspaper review programme, with others. Among various things, I talk about violent crimes against women in Ireland and in ex-Yugoslavia, about media hype of 'Political Correctness', and about severe discrimination against lesbians in the workplace, issues all headlined (or sidelined) in our national press. A (male) listener phones in to know if 'Ailbhe Smyth is a lesbian or does she just hate all men?'. To which there is no satisfactory answer — damned if I do *and* if I do not. My mother is very upset. And so am I, although for different reasons. More times than I can count over the past year I have been called 'man-hating' — by men, yes, but also by women. It is always a code word for lesbian.

April 1993

I apply in the normal way of things for promotion in my job. I do not get it although it is (over)due. No reasons are given — *are* there valid professional reasons? I cannot find them. I remain a junior lecturer at this advanced stage of my 'career' (I jest, I jest) because I am perceived as political, radical, feminist and man-hating, and therefore neither a 'real' academic nor, of course, a 'real' woman. And you cannot promote someone who has no 'real' existence.

May 1993

Within the space of a week, I hear it said that women's studies is 'just advocacy' and that 'women's studies should be moved into a department' (where, presumably, it could be immobilized). Women's studies students are worried (and worse) by the increasing number of homophobic attacks, verbal and even physical, within the university. And so am I.

June 1993

Entirely unprovoked, a woman journalist whom I have never met represents me as 'wearisome and PC sloganizing' with 'self-righteous' views that are 'abhorrent and objectionable' (among other slurs). She presents no evidence for her claims and her piece is illogical, but the paper has a wide circulation.

September 1993

During the year, I have had nuisance telephone calls and had to have my number changed and unlisted. Now I get a spate of unspeakable (and unanswerable) obscene 'messages' on my answering machine. And an unanswerable message on my car: 'You are a bloody shithead'.

October 1993

Two public debates are organized — by a trade union and a students' union — in which I am asked to participate. One proposes that 'Feminism is a Vital Challenge, not a Trumped Up Grievance', the other that 'Feminism has had its Day'. My 16-year-old daughter also participates in two debates: 'Behind Every Great Man is an Even Greater Woman', and 'A Woman's Place is in the Home'. Five years ago, two years ago, even last year, I would have thought (and probably said quite loudly), 'Give me a break'. But not now. It feels crucial to go out there and *defend* the idea and the reality of feminism as a vital politics and practice — after 20 years of the women's liberation movement. What will young women like and unlike my daughter be doing in another 20 years time? Still defending?

> 'Why have we failed? / Feminism has failed women'.
> *Mea culpa, mea culpa.*
> No — I will not assume classic guilt.
> Feminism has not failed — it is being pushed.

> It's dead
> If it's not dead,
> It's dying,
> So to be on the safe side
> let's kill it anyway,
> In case there's any life left in it.[3]

Straws in the Wind

These are micro-messages, not exemplars; stories, really, a (selective) personal (recent) history. Taken separately, as they occurred, they just seem like unconnected experiences, incidents, features, facts; unimportant portents, straws in the wind. But I do not live my life separately, and nothing is ever 'just' as it seems, is it? Behind every sign, great or small, lie even greater, or smaller, circuits of signification simply begging to be dis/connected (depending on your politics) to/from the macro-messages. My politics being what they are, when I find a lot of straws all being blown in roughly the same direction by an increasingly chill wind, I do eventually begin to wonder if they might not add up to a haystack, which is a pretty massively connected sort of thing altogether.

Who am I to wonder that or anything at all? What credence can you give the straws I bring you, light-weight as they are? I say, I am a feminist academic, living contradiction in word and act/activism. What proofs can I offer you of my bona fides? None, unless your politics and mine blow more or less together. My word — no more than yours — is neither proof nor truth, or so they say, thus all we (may) have in common is a sense of the wind and the way it blows. And who are you to say otherwise?

Actually, I avoided making the connections for as long as I could, for two (interconnected) reasons: (1) because I might be thought 'paranoid', which academics are never allowed to be and feminists are accused of being all the time; and (2) because I might be thought stupid, since making connections is not at all a fashionable academic (feminist) pursuit just now. For a self-identifying feminist (academic) to spend/waste (depending on your politics) time connecting stories instead of disconnecting theories, or to think (aloud) in terms of a great global (or even a small local) patriarchal plot is a guarantee of damnation and dismissal.

Don't be so ridiculous / over-sensitive / Where's your (common) sense of proportion / humour? / You don't *seriously* think they're out to get you?

Well, yes, in the privacy and simplicity of my own mind, I do think seriously about these matters (NB simple academics only have to think seriously, while *feminist* academics have to think seriously with humour). But I think about them, these straws, entirely unhumorously, because they have a habit of staying at the front of my mind, no matter how smartly and separately I despatch each as far to the back as I can reach. I do not talk much about them or about my increasing edginess at their decreasingly random occurrence — or only in the most offhand manner, designed (of course, and like this paper) to test audience response.[4]

Nothing in my academic life (if that's the correct term) has prepared me for dealing with a haystack at the front of my mind. Because (1) it is not supposed to be there: academic life is not about the personal or the political (so what is it about?); and (2) life (including feminist academic) is 'erratic and disconnected ... a series of [discursive] arenas' (Pringle and Watson, 1992) (I quote from a currently popular handbook). Academic workers should not tell stories at all ('anecdotage' is an unacademic activity) and most certainly not about themselves; feminist academic workers *may* tell personal stories, *provided* they do so modestly and do not use them to make sense of anything. The problem is that straws in the wind and haystacks in the mind tend to make life (any kind) exceedingly difficult. I mean, it is hard to think with a haystack in your mind, even harder if it gets out and spreads to where you live or work or play.

There are days when you wake up believing all you read in the papers and doubting your own straws: 'Academia is being infested by an outbreak of dubious scholarship and worthless courses. From peace studies to women's studies, from literature courses which take as their primary concern the political stance of the writers — rather than their skill with language, history courses which aim to rewrite the past rather than objectively scrutinise it' (O'Hanlon, 1993a). Euphoria — tinged with sadness (as the cliche has it): The revolution has come and I was sleeping. I rush to check — but no, all is as it was the day before, no overnight outbreaks of doubt or questioning or change or infestations of women's studies. Just the usual objectivities and certainties, although some now circulate cunningly cross-dressed as 'heterogeneity, discontinuity, displacement, destabilization' (Bordo, 1992:161). How strange. A destabilized and displaced world, yet which looks identical to the old one in all its systems and structures. Who is the dreamer?

Not that my waking moments all centre on the academic — although centring us on the notion of the decentred world is as good a trick as any for keeping us off the streets and out of the revolution. Certainly, some things are changing. In Ireland, the promise of new Equal Status legislation, and even D.I.V.O.R.C.E.; homosexuality no longer a criminal offence;[5] sexual harassment on the political and trade union agendas, and being written about, thoughtfully, in the press; more media coverage of rape, sexual abuse and incest; government ministers (well, one, a woman) publicly exposing the 'frank prejudice' against women politicians; budding acknowledgement of Irish women's achievements in sport: 'Sonia Boom — Sonia O'Sullivan confirms her status as Ireland's top track athlete' (Humphries, 1993) — and so on (I am playing fair — it is as random a selection as the others).

All there, in the papers, everywhere, everyday, word for word. Women, and 'women's issues', are making it, at last, across the print barriers and into the sound bites and news values, in politics, in sport, in the workforce. 'Women' have clearly never had it more or better. So I am paranoid, OK? I am clutching at straws. Then why will the edginess not just edge right out of my mind? But it is not at the edge — it is at the front, centred, however I turn it, micro or macro.

Part II: Random Macro-Messages

Economy

Growing poverty and unemployment rates for women are not 'stories' but facts, like the fact of the increasing casualization of women's paid work, its continuing sectorization and the disparities between male and female wages.[6] I have seen virtually no coverage of these facts in our media over the past six months. Since the Hill/Thomas hearings, sexual harassment has a 'positive' news value; it is a 'sexy' story. Poverty is not. Women's rising unemployment is not (it is a secret).[7] The exploitation of women workers is not. Because women are 'really' unpaid homeworkers, still, whatever they are *actually* doing. That's their 'natural' role and 'nature' is not 'news'.

The message is silent. Women do not count economically.

Spring–Summer 1993

A spate of articles in *The Irish Times* 'objectively' exploring the current state of (and need for) feminism: 'Backlash against Feminism?'; 'Do We Really Want a Women's Day?'; 'Is there Room for Doubts About Feminism?' And a barrage of specifically anti-feminism/anti-specific-feminists articles in *The Sunday Independent*, the country's biggest circulation Sunday paper, conservative, populist and increasingly misogynist.[8]

Law

The incidence of reported violent crime against women is spiralling — sexual harassment, assault, incest, rape, [9] but women who challenge or speak out against the judicial system get short shrift. In July 1993, Lavinia Kerwick appealed against the judge's suspended one-year sentence on the man who had raped her. The Central Criminal Court, hearing the appeal, gave the rapist a nine-year suspended sentence on the basis that he had shown 'clear and convincing remorse' (*The Irish Times*, 1993). Rape means (sometimes) having to say sorry; that is all — unless you happen to be Lavinia Kerwick or any other raped woman.[10]

The message is loud and clear. Women do not count sexually, socially, or legally.

May 1993

'Why Didn't Her Mother Do More?' Thus ran the full-page headline to a commentary on the official government report on a particularly horrendous and complex incest case (O'Morain, 1993). The report of the Commission of Inquiry into the case had scrupulously avoided holding the victim's mother solely responsible for the appalling brutality to which the young woman was subjected by her father, as the small print of the newspaper commentary made clear. Why did her father do it at all?

Politics

The 20 women elected to Dail Eireann (Parliament) in November 1992 (a record 12 per cent of representatives) were subjected to a sustained barrage of double-speak. Having hailed their election as a 'breakthrough' in Irish politics (which it is, although not a bolt from the blue, following on as it did from the election of Mary Robinson as President in 1990), the media then proceeded to invite our women politicians to explain how they could be looking after their children and the needs of the nation at one and the same time, and to proffer unsolicited observations on their youth, or appearance.

The message is confused. Women *do* count (12 per cent), but they should not.

Ailbhe Smyth

April–September 1993

Two major feature series, in Ireland's only 'liberal' quality daily paper, focus on 'parenting in crisis' and the declining birth rate, along with several one-off features on motherhood as women's primary role, pregnancy in middle-age, breast-feeding in the 'board- room', and alcoholism and its effects on 'mothers'. The features page in question is in effect the 'women's page' of the newspaper — 'women' apparently being significantly construed and constrained within the parameters of motherhood and mothering — as 'good' mothers, victims (and incompetents) or 'witches'.[11]

Academia

Since 1990, women's studies has been officially established in most of Ireland's universities, north and south. It has gone from strength to strength, generating dynamic research programmes and with thousands of women following graduate, under-graduate and pre-graduate courses. In her first year of office, President Robinson launched no less than four programmes, giving them status, credibility and unimpeach-able *profile*. The powers-that-be (powerful) cannot publicly say something's unim-portant if the President clearly thinks otherwise. But even our ubiquitous President cannot keep opening and reopening women's studies centres every year. Although lipservice is paid to the importance of such initiatives, no resources are given for their consolidation or development and none of the women running such programmes has professorial status. The pressure to osmose into 'gender studies' is a constant temptation for those who know that while 'women' — *a fortiori* 'feminism' — is a sure-fire career killer, boy-including 'gender' keeps you on the ladder.

The message is coded, but clear: The University is an Equal Opportunities employer. Gendered People are strongly encouraged to apply. Feminists go home. (But where is home?)

November 1993

A woman journalist takes an almighty and lengthy swipe at 'Second-rate Sister Studies' in a national Sunday newspaper. Women's Studies, she argues (no, that cannot be the right words) is 'intellectually redundant bunkum', that is, 'partial ... unscholarly ... woolly ... bland ... undemanding ... comforting'. Who needs enemies with such a well-informed, sympathetic, first-rate sister? (O'Hanlon, 1993b).

Culture

The *Field Day Anthology of Irish Writing* was published in 1992, a gigantic three-volume enterprise, auto-hyped as 'comprehensive' and 'defining the range and quality of one of the most distinctive literatures of the world'. There was, however, a small matter the 20-odd Field Day editors had overlooked, i.e. the quasi-entirety of writing by Irish women. When (some) women writers and critics loudly critiqued this monument to Irishness, the editors pleaded ignorance ('We didn't know there were so many Irish women writers'), said they were sorry (see 'Law' above), and invited (other) women to edit a fourth volume.

The message is insulting: if women figure in 'Irish culture' it is as an addendum, an erratum slip, an afterthought.

Chill Wind Blowing

At no time in human history has change occurred more rapidly and earth-shatteringly than during the twentieth century.[12] The ways in which we relate to the physical, material world have altered as dramatically and as profoundly as the ways in which people relate to one another, collectively and individually, across geographical horizons and the vast and complicated spectrums of the social organizing systems of class, race, sexuality and gender. The difficulties and the challenges of change affect *everyone*, women and men. But not *alike*. Women and men are differently positioned within and in relation to the social world, and therefore to the process of change, so that we not only react, negotiate and seek to initiate change in significantly different ways, but we also experience and live it differently.

In a very real sense, women's lives in this last decade of the century are a far more visible and tangible barometer of the extent of the changes we are hurtling through at breakneck speed. Changes in women's lives send shock waves throughout the entire socio-economic and cultural system as historically determined, administered and enjoyed by men.

Demography

The reverberations, for example, on family formations of women deciding (throughout the west) to remain single longer, to have fewer children, to divorce more readily.

Labour

Women remaining in the labour force after marriage and the birth of children; demanding equal access and treatment in training and paid work; and, most notably, women's *de facto* denial of the *de facto* division of labour into private (women's) and public (men's) spheres.

Public Life

Women seeking 'voice' and 'space' in public life; demanding changes in policy agendas and forcing change, by their very presence, in the style and practice and public politics.[13]

Sexuality

Women bringing sexuality out of the hidden 'private' world, and profoundly questioning the role of sexuality, of heterosexuality and of gender in the production of *unequal, and unjust*, power relations. Women asking the simple watershed questions: *WHY* is this class of persons (men) invariably more powerful than that class of persons (women)? Is this *just*? Is it *immutable*?

I am categorically *not* saying that all women act and react, question and decide in the same ways.[14] As a social tracking system, gender is one of the most powerful factors in determining who will have power over whom, but it functions interactively with other systems such as socio-economic class, race, ability/disability, sexual orientation, nationality, ethnicity and so on. Women as a social class are internally diverse and also unequally placed in relation to one another. But the crucial point articulated by feminism is that female gender is invariably defined as subordinate to male gender, for reasons which have nothing to do with reason, and no basis in justice.

The Backlash Haystack

Blowing in the right direction, change can be exhilarating, although perhaps uniquely for those who decide on its direction. For too many and for too much of the time, it's exhausting, bewildering. And bewilderment nurtures fear of change itself, happy breeding ground of the consensus makers and the *status quo*. The sense of perplexity and fear increases as certainties, safeguards, 'survival kits', disappear before you can say 'Mary Robinson'.

'Gender discomfort' which, I assume, means men's oppression of women, is alive and growing daily, as thinking about the past year in Irish society and politics (micro and macro) makes very plain. The major problem with shifting (gendered) power relations is that it is women who do most of the shifting, while men hold on to most of the power. Thus, rapid changes in women's aspirations and expectations, and in the meanings and values women ascribe to gender roles, have not been paralleled by changes in the material conditions of women's lives, and confusion flourishes — and is fostered — in the straining gap between the two. Women want to live *more* and differently than the hegemonically male socio-economic and political system is prepared to 'allow', ever mindful of its own (gender) comfort. Thus, quite clearly feminism is not the 'problem', but rather the power system in place that is profoundly threatened by the *challenge* of feminism.

Change generates inevitable tension and conflict between the forces of conservatism ('where we were') and progress ('where we are — and where we are going'). One step forwards, two to the side and, in the 1990s, three steps back. The backlash quick-step. Too many women are doing it. And sometimes in (at least) two directions at once.

The backlash is a reaction to change — and specifically to *specific* changes. It is not at all paradoxical to say that I *know* feminism is successful precisely because the hostility towards it is so strong: you know you are on the way to somewhere important when they start putting up road blocks to stop you getting there. But 'success', in the sense of transforming the system in place, may be *partial*: because feminism has put the system under pressure, it does not automatically follow that positive change, benefitting all women, necessarily occurs. In the 1990s, it is crystal clear that direct, life-enhancing benefits have principally accrued to relatively small numbers of (White, educated, 'first world') women. Without a significant feminist *counter-offensive* history may well repeat 'itself' and the backlash succeed in eventually turning the tables and quashing the ground-swell of women-propelled momentum for change.[15] The unequally enjoyed and always threatened gains of feminism make it all the more important, in my view, for feminists (whoever and wherever) to constantly reassess both our objectives and our strategies.

I think, then, that it is worth trying to identify at least minimal principles and practices of a backlash against feminism. What I discern, of course, emerges out of my experience and understanding of the current backlash in Ireland, which is not exactly the centre of the world.[16] But located and specific antifeminist micro-straws, wherever and however they blow, do seem to have a habit of becoming redoutably 'macro' (and disturbingly global) haystacks. This is another way of saying that it is hard to keep someone else's straws out of your own backyard — and vice versa.

Powerful groups react to defend their power base when they perceive it to be seriously under pressure. A backlash is fundamentally defensive, for all its aggressive stance and strategies. However, 'defensive' does not mean less dangerous or vicious. Rather the reverse. Powerful interest groups deal with those who challenge their power in a number of different and often concurrent ways, not all of them 'consensually' acceptable (which does not necessarily mean they are not practised) in democratic regimes: challengers can be (1) zeroed, (2) neutralized, or (3) recuperated.[17]

In my backyard, women are systematically reduced to non-existence — 'zeroed'. Countless women have been (are being) *beaten* into silence, through physical and sexual violence, through poverty and deprivation, through the legal, moral and psychological denial of rights and personhood. Resistant women are not allowed to speak 'out' or to act 'up' in public. If they find a way of doing so (not easy), they are ignored, or dismissed as mad, bad or stupid — neutralized. Countless women have left jobs, marriages, politics, the country, because they cannot or will not put up with being kept down and out. These are not 'choices' (i.e. freely made decisions), they are necessary survival strategies. The price paid by resistant women is literally incalculable, (that is, I know of no currency in which its cost can be counted). It is thus not at all surprising that the temptation to 'dilute' the challenge is not always resistible, or resisted. Recuperative tactics come wrapped in very attractive packages that seem to promise real power. It is only when you undo the layers of 'power-speak' that the extent of the compromise is revealed. Sometimes, we compromise ourselves out of existence, and end up 'zeroed'.

> What is most surprising to me, is the number, the determination, the bravery of resistant women who go on fighting, despite the logical odds and against the grain.

I have been using militaristic terminology deliberately, because in a backlash scenario, polarization and confrontation are inevitable. *Any* challenge, protest or even questioning is automatically construed by powerful groups as an assault on their (hegemonic) authority, moral, political and/or economic, and a counter-assault is swiftly mounted. Accommodation is not an acceptable position, nor is negotiation a preferred strategy for those who are seeking to defend what they perceive as their 'legitimate' position of superiority. There is no evidence whatsoever to suggest that those who hold power (anywhere, in any sphere) are interested in voluntary 'power-sharing'. For the challengers (and I mean feminists) to believe that it is possible to negotiate with groups to whom the very notion is anathema, in that it would necessarily signify their defeat, seems to me to be naïve in the extreme.[18]

The aim of the backlash against feminism is to reverse societal changes in the direction of equality between women and men and to re-appropriate the terrain 'occupied' by feminists/women. The major backlash strategy itself revolves around reversal, i.e. turning feminist aims (constructing a just world, ending male domination and socio-economic exploitation, achieving freedom and autonomy, and so on) against feminists, and turning women against feminism.

The backlash tactical arsenal includes:

1. *Polarization*, or classic 'divide and rule' tactics: 'women' are set against feminists; feminists against 'mothers'; 'radical' feminists against liberal reformists; and so on. 'Women' and 'feminists' are (mis)represented as sharply differentiated groups, with feminism specifically characterized as antagonistic to the group interests of 'women'.

2. *Denigration and de-naturalization*: feminists are represented as 'unnatural', monsters, deviants, not 'real' women. Paradoxically, this involves *de-individualizing* feminists (not representing feminists as diverse, with nuanced views, politics, life-styles, etc), and *personalizing* attacks against feminism, which effectively hides the systemic and structural nature of oppression, and *depoliticizes* protest and resistance.

3. *Falsification*: the goals, ideas, values and practices of feminism, and of feminists, are generalized, exaggerated or distorted beyond reason or recognition. Falsification serves as much to undermine feminist solidarity as it does to alienate 'women' from the Women's Movement. Labelling, stereotyping, mockery and caricature all play a crucial role in the process of falsification. What backlash proponents perceive as the most extreme or frightening elements

are a particular target: not only 'feminists' in the group women, but lesbians in the group 'feminists', for example.

4. *Accusation*: feminists are charged with responsibility for the 'collapse' of The Family, of the entire social value system, and anything (everything) else that is wrong in the west (at least); they are blamed for 'creating' women's (supposed) unhappiness and dissatisfaction (with The Family, the west, whatever, wherever). Such a tactic is designed to guilt-trip 'women' back into the bosom of The Family, and (not least) to turn 'feminists' in dangerously defensive and backtracking directions.[19]

5. *(Re-)appropriation* of feminist language and values: for example, the self-representation of anti-abortionists as 'pro-life' and the accusations levelled against feminists of rigidity, dogmatism, absolutism and 'political correctness' are especially potent.

6. *Provocation*: predicting apocalyptically nightmarish scenarios as a consequence of 'unbridled' feminist activism (the end of civilization / the family as 'we' know it / the disintegration of law and order and so on), with the aim of alienating people (men as well as women) from feminist goals.

Powerful interest groups recruit popular support, or work to construct consensus, by seeking to marginalize and discredit those who challenge the prevailing order, an aim they achieve by persistently and deliberately mis-representing them. A backlash functions in terms of the simple but a-moral principle that 'the end justifies the means'.

In Ireland, the backlash 'markers' are certainly 'content-specific', focusing primarily on 'family values', abortion and — often more subtly — on homosexuality and lesbianism.[20] The straws in the wind do indeed add up to a mighty haystack. Still, as a friend of mine is fond of remarking, it takes two to tango — or to do the backlash quickstep.

Part III: Remaining SAFe in the 1990s

There is no magic password to a SAFe future. Although it does seem to me that beating the backlash is precisely about remaining sane and angry and resolutely committed to feminism (and feminists, and women). The temptation to simply jump off the top of the haystack, or, worse, to burrow into its warm dark (but, I should think, rather prickly) interior is strong. The temptations are not new, although they now come in guises that were undreamed of in the 1970s. It is one of the classic ironies of a successful movement that, as it pushes the powerful harder and further, the powerful learn to become more subtle, insidious — and vicious. This is not a matter of 'blaming' feminism, but rather of thinking that it is useful to recognize *why* we are encountering such resistance, and to take some heart from that understanding.

Perhaps the single most important, if paradoxical, thing to realize about the backlash is that actually women are not lying down and giving up the struggle. When you look at the facts and the figures (and if our backlashers do, they never admit it), the backlash emerges as the biggest failure of the century. Women who do not call themselves feminist (why not? what is shameful about being up for justice? for freedom? for dignity?), these very women none the less are making the kinds of choices that have become possible *because* feminists, for a long time, have been protesting the injustice of the gendered power system.

Women are not only barometers or indicators of change: women are also sculptors, agents, initiators, making decisions about how we live our lives and about the kind of society in which we want to live.

Feminism is not about name-calling or person-bashing or pointing the finger or guilt-tripping (backlashers, please note). Feminism is for change, yes, and that is not easy (no-one ever said it was.) It is not about just any old change: feminism is a vision of the world in which women would *enjoy* (and not constantly have to struggle for) the same freedoms as men, a world where gender — neither maleness nor femaleness — would *no longer* be a qualification for the exercise of power. A vision, a body of ideas, a politics that seeks to (re)create the world in terms of justice and equality is not a problem — it is an aspiration, a hope, the promise of optimism. Which is why, despite their materiality, I do not care too much about the haystacks, most of the time.

Notes

1. An earlier version of this paper was given at the WISE Conference in Paris, October 1993.
2. For a range of feminist perspectives on the Irish abortion situation, including the repercussions of pro-abortion activism, see Smyth (1992).
3. Susan Faludi (1991) analyses the role of 'pop psychology' in so constructing women's self-perceptions that we interpret the effects and pressures of the backlash as primarily 'our own' problem, which perpetuates the guilt and dependency syndrome.
4. Although we tend to behave as if it is either more *or* less instrumental, thought is always, at some level, therapeutic: enabling us to achieve distance from the 'world', to strengthen ourselves to face it, to negotiate and survive it, to shape and control it.
5. The Minister for Equality has circulated a draft outline of a new 'Equal Status Bill' which will address a range of 'social exclusions', including sexual orientation, disability and ethnicity, as well as gender. The Government is currently 'tidying up' legislation relating to marital home ownership, and other matters, prior to holding another referendum on divorce in 1995. A referendum proposal to delete the article in the Irish Constitution which prohibits divorce was defeated in 1986. Following protracted battles in the Irish and European Courts, the Sexual Offences Act (1993) legalizes homosexual relations between men over the age of 17.
6. See Blackwell (1989). Also Second Commission on the Status of Women (1993).
7. Twenty-three per cent of registered unemployed in Ireland are women. However, Pauline Conroy Jackson suggests that only 48 per cent of unemployed women are registered as compared with 85 per cent of unemployed men (1991).
8. A considerable number of the anti-feminist articles I have assembled over the six-month April–September period in 1993 were written by just *two* women journalists, one of whom (a freelance writer) seems to be commissioned indiscriminately by both the

progressive 'quality' *Irish Times* and the conservative 'trash' *Sunday Independent*. Which demonstrates that it is not absolute numbers, but context, location and prominence which determines the force of the backlash. One 'well-placed' article is worth ten sidelines. But in Ireland at least, the backlashers are neither moral nor a majority. What they are is hegemonically powerful, with media access effectively denied to feminists. See Emily O'Reilly (1992) for discussion of the power channels of the extreme Right in Ireland.

9. See Annual Reports of Rape Crisis Centres throughout Ireland, and of Women's Aid, and Shanahan (1992).

10. A disturbing sidelight was thrown up by an opposition spokesman for Justice in an article on the treatment of jailed sex offenders: 'Though it appears there are some who do not want this made public, a diet of increasingly violent and explicitly pornographic videos is used as a method of subduing certain prisoners [in Irish prisons]; these films are openly shown and are available to sex offenders. That these videos are available in the community is not the point, that they are used to subdue some prisoners is'. (Gay Mitchell, TD, *The Irish Times*, 11 August 1993).

11. The media are to some extent self-contradicting, or rather they 'allow' a certain dose of counter-hegemonic representation (Roland Barthes' famous 'inoculation' theory). However, it is remarkable how, in Ireland at present, a backlash orientation has become a clear 'features value', with journalists being commissioned (or 'allowed') to write stories (the correct term, I believe) that are far more about the 'gender-crisis' than about the parenting-or-anything-else crisis.

12. Truisms can also be true.

13. See for example Jo Freeman's discussion, for the USA, of the extent to which 'women's issues' have permeated the Republican and Democrat agendas (1993); for Ireland, see Smyth (1992).

14. There seems to be an automatic assumption that feminists are 'universalizing' and 'essentializing', unless (1) one is clearly postmodernist, or (2) one says one is not. It irritates me that postmodernists should adopt a 'holier than thou' position. Protests of 'non-essentialism' are absurd in any case, because saying one is not something proves remarkably little. Good intentions have never been a safeguard against bad politics — or faulty reasoning. But I fall into the defensive trap, every time.

15. I am grateful to Christine Delphy for raising this point in a discussion following presentation of an earlier draft of this chapter. The 'wavelike quality' of feminist activism, and specifically the dialectical response of organized antifeminism towards it, is discussed by Janet Saltzman Chafetz (1989).

16. Although a pertinent Irish riddle springs to my mind: 'Q: Where is the centre of the world? A: Here'.

17. This triple formulation of strategies was prompted, ironically, by Gisela Kaplan's discussion of revolutionary movements: 'Put bluntly, in a revolution there are basically only three things one can do with those individuals or groups who are identified as the oppressors: kill them, force them to leave, or force them to undergo ideological re-education' (Kaplan, 1992:273). However, such strategies are not the sole property of 'revolutionaries' — and the oppressors are typically in a stronger position to execute them.

18. For example, Beatrix Campbell, in her complex, nuanced analysis of late-twentieth-century Britain, *Goliath: Britain's Dangerous Places*, comments: 'Since the hidden agenda of the underclass theory is an attack on mothers as practitioners of parenting and feminism as a theory of male domination, its exponents are paralysed by the problem of

marauding masculinities in the cities. Like the men they criticise, however, they cannot imagine a political and cultural coalition with women' (Campbell, 1993:313).

19. See Judith Stacey's critique of Germaine Greer, Jean Bethke Elshtain and Betty Friedan (Stacey, 1986). Or, from a contrary perspective, the defensive emphasis Yvonne Roberts places on 'men and women [continuing] to make serious attempts at stable family life' (Roberts, 1993).

20. Is the content markedly different in North America, Australia, New Zealand, EC countries? I think not.

References

BLACKWELL, JOHN (1989) *Women in the Labour Force*, Dublin: Employment Equality Agency.

BORDO, SUSAN (1992) 'Postmodern Subjects, Postmodern Bodies', *Feminist Studies*, **18** 1, pp. 159–75.

CAMPBELL, BEATRIX (1993) *Goliath: Britain's Dangerous Places*, London: Methuen.

CHAFETZ, JANET SALTZMAN (1989) 'Gender Equality: Towards a Theory of Change', in WALLACE, RUTH A. (Ed.) *Feminism and Sociological Theory*, London: Sage, pp. 135–60.

FALUDI, SUSAN (1991) *Backlash: The Undeclared War Against American Women*, New York: Crown Books.

HUMPHRIES, TOM (1993) 'Sonia Boom', *The Irish Times*, 17 July, Weekend Section, p. 1.

JACKSON, PAULINE CONROY (1991) Unpublished Discussion Paper, prepared for the Combat Poverty Agency, Dublin.

KAPLAN, GISELA (1992) *Contemporary Western European Feminism*, London: Allen and Unwin.

O'HANLON, EILIS (1993a) 'Corrective Measures Doomed to Fail', *Sunday Independent*, 1 August, People Section, p. 10.

O'HANLON, EILIS (1993b) 'Second-rate Sister Studies', The *Sunday Independent*, 14 November, People Section, p. 11.

O'MORAIN, PADRAIG (1993) 'Why didn't the Mother do More?', *The Irish Times*, 22 May, p. 6.

O'REILLY, EMILY (1992) *Masterminds of the Right*, Dublin: Attic Press.

PRINGLE, ROSEMARY and WATSON, SOPHIE (1992) ' "Women's Interests" and the Post-structuralist State', in BARRETT, MICHELE and PHILLIPS, ANNE (Eds) *Destabilising Theory: Contemporary Feminist Debates*, London: Polity.

ROBERTS, YVONNE (1993) 'We are Becoming Divorced from Reality', *New Statesman and Society*, 24 September, pp. 16–19.

SECOND COMMISSION ON THE STATUS OF WOMEN (1993) *Report to Government, Dublin: Stationary Office.*

SHANAHAN, KATE (1992) *Crimes Worse than Death*, Dublin: Attic Press.

SMYTH, AILBHE (1992) ' "A Great Day for the Women of Ireland": The Meaning of Mary Robinson's Presidency for Irish Women', *Canadian Journal of Irish Studies*, **18**, 1, pp. 61–75.

SMYTH, AILBHE (Ed.) (1992) *The Abortion Papers: Ireland*, Dublin: Attic Press.

STACEY, JUDITH (1986) 'Are Feminists Afraid to Leave Home? The Challenge of Conservative Pro-Family Feminism', in MITCHELL, JULIET and OAKLEY, ANN (Eds) *What is Feminism?*, Oxford: Basil Blackwell, pp. 219–42.

THE IRISH TIMES (1993) 'Kilkenny Rape Case', 15 July, p. 4.

Contributors

Rosemary Auchmuty teaches law and Women's Studies at the University of Westminster. She is author of *A World of Girls* (Women's Press, 1992), and is currently working on a book about women and home ownership in the mid-twentieth century.

Julie Bindel has been involved in feminist activism since 1979. She has worked almost exclusively around issues of male violence against women. She co-founded Justice for Women in 1991 and continues to be actively involved in the campaigns to free women who kill violent men in self-defence.

Lou Brown is committed to an understanding of health in social and political contexts. She has been a volunteer with her local HIV/AIDS agency for the last three years. She studied librarianship at North London Polytechnic and is currently working as Information and Resources Officer for Leicestershire Health Promotion Centre.

Patricia Carey is a graduate in theology and sociology from Maynooth University. She is a teacher and founder member of Lesbians Organizing Together (LOT).

Debjani Chatterjee is a versatile writer, editor and storyteller whose first poetry collection was *I Was That Woman* (Hippopotamus Press, 1989). Her poetry has won numerous prizes. She has also written children's books. She has worked as Director of the Racial Equality Council in Sheffield and Oxford, and is a founder member of the Bengali Women's Support Group in Sheffield.

Kate Cook used to be a radical feminist bank manager. She is still a radical feminist, but is now studying law and is a member of Manchester Justice for Women and Manchester Rape Crisis.

Kate Frances is a teacher of English and a graduate of the MA programme in Women's Studies at WERRC, University College Dublin. She has extensively researched the operation of lesbian helplines in Ireland.

Rosemary Gibney is a graduate of the MA programme in Women's Studies at the Women's Education, Research and Resource Centre (WERRC), University College Dublin. She is currently preparing her doctoral thesis on sexuality in Ireland.

Gabriele Griffin is Professor of Women's Studies at Nene College, Northampton. She has co-edited *Stirring It: Challenges for Feminism* (Taylor & Francis, 1994), edited *Difference in View: Women and Modernism* (Taylor & Francis, 1994), *Changing Our Lives: Doing Women's Studies* (Pluto Press, 1994), *Outwrite: Lesbianism and Popular Culture* (Pluto Press, 1993), and wrote *Heavenly Love? Lesbian Images in 20th Century Women's Writing* (Manchester UP, 1993).

Nicki Hastie was a Research Assistant in the area of English/Women's studies at Nene College, Northampton. She is interested in representations of women, and particularly lesbians, in literature and the media. She has taken an active involvement in feminist politics since the late 1980s, and has published on lesbian cultural production.

Anja Hohmeyer studied anthropology at London University. She has been involved with reproductive rights issues since 1989. From September 1990 to December 1991 she worked as a secretary for the European Network for Women's Rights to Abortion and Contraception (ENWRAC). She has been a member of the NAC Management Committee since December 1993.

Izzy Kamikaze is a lesbian non-conformist, pagan, feminist, anti-authoritarian kamikaze gender bandit and an activist of quare nation and quare notions. She is presenter of 'Kamikaze Queer' on Radio Active, an anti-censorship radio station.

Liz Kelly has done feminist work on violence against women for (too) many years, including direct support, research and activism. She is a member of Manchester Justice for Women.

Terri MacDermott is completing her PhD in the Crime Reduction Research Unit at Nottingham Trent University. Her work explores the relationship between the experience of residential child care, the impact this has on female adolescent self-identity, and the relationship that exists between self-identity and offending behaviour.

Debi Morgan is a Youth and Community Worker. She is currently working for Milton Keynes Youth Council, supporting and encouraging young people to become involved in decision making locally, nationally and internationally. Her particular areas of interest are young women, disability and sexuality.

Frances Moss is Principal Lecturer in Finance and Strategy at the University of Westminster, which she joined in 1987. Prior to that she had an extensive career as an accountant in business. She teaches a variety of mostly critical approaches to accounting and business, as well as a course on women in management. In 1993, she chaired Women in Accountancy (WIA). Her research focuses on social and environmental aspects of accounting.

Sarah Porch has been actively involved in campaigning around women's health and women's rights since the 'Fight the Alton Bill Campaign', 1987–1988. She studied social policy and sociology at Sheffield University, and at the same time became an HIV/AIDS Peer Education Trainer. She is currently working as a Health Promotion Officer in Leicestershire with a remit for Sexual Health and Young People.

Maria Power lives in Dublin with her partner Margaret. She has been active in LOT and related lesbian activities since the formation of LOT in 1991. She works as a Financial Management Consultant in the community and voluntary sector.

Jill Radford is a feminist activist, campaigner and researcher, currently working at Rights of Women, a feminist legal project. She has published widely in the area of sexual violence and was co-editor, with Diana Russell, of *Femicide: The Politics of Woman-Killing* (1992). She was a founding member of the British Sociological Association women's caucus Violence Against Women Study Group, and has remained an active member.

Anjona Roy is completing an MA in Women's Studies at Nene College, Northampton. She has been an activist on women's and Black community issues for 13 years and works in the voluntary sector across Northamptonshire. Her research interests are in Asian women's identities, social and community care.

Ailbhe Smyth is joint Irish/UK Editor of *Women's Studies International Forum* and Director of the Women's Education, Research and Resource Centre (WERRC) at University College, Dublin. She writes on Irish feminism. Her publications (as editor) include: *Wildish Things: An Anthology of New Irish Women's Writing* (Attic Press, 1989), *The Abortion Papers: Ireland* (Attic Press, 1992), and *The Irish Women's Studies Reader* (Attic Press, 1993).

Alex Warwick teaches in the English Department at the University of Westminster, where she is also Course Leader of the MA in Women's Studies. Her interests are in culture, politics and women's writing of the late-nineteenth century, and her most recent publication is 'Vampires and the Empire' in *Cultural Politics in the Fin de Siecle*, edited by S. Ledger and S. McCracken (CUP, 1995).

Debbie Weekes is completing a PhD in the Department of Applied Social Studies at Nottingham Trent University. Her research focuses on the racialized gendered identity of Black female adolescents.

Tamsin Wilton is Senior Lecturer in Health and Social Policy at the University of the West of England, Bristol, where she also teaches Women's Studies and Lesbian Studies. She has written widely on HIV/AIDS and on Lesbian Studies, and is now working on a book on the politics of lesbian sexuality, *Fingerlicking Good*, for Cassell.

Index